A Life in the 'Burg
By John C. Goolrick

Things That Happened After
George Washington Left Town

Growing Up In Fredericksburg, Virginia

© Copyright 2003 John C. Goolrick. All rights reserved.

No part of this publication may be reproduced, stored in a retrieval system, or transmitted, in any form or by any means, electronic, mechanical, photocopying, recording, or otherwise, without the written prior permission of the author.

Printed in Victoria, Canada

```
National Library of Canada Cataloguing in Publication

Goolrick, John C.
     A life in the 'burg' / John C. Goolrick.
ISBN 1-4120-0699-6
     I. Title.
F234.F8G66 2003        975.5'366'092          C2003-904062-3
```

TRAFFORD

This book was published *on-demand* in cooperation with Trafford Publishing.
On-demand publishing is a unique process and service of making a book available for retail sale to the public taking advantage of on-demand manufacturing and Internet marketing.
On-demand publishing includes promotions, retail sales, manufacturing, order fulfilment, accounting and collecting royalties on behalf of the author.

Suite 6E, 2333 Government St., Victoria, B.C. V8T 4P4, CANADA
Phone   250-383-6864   Toll-free 1-888-232-4444 (Canada & US)
Fax   250-383-6804   E-mail   sales@trafford.com
Web site www.trafford.com   TRAFFORD PUBLISHING IS A DIVISION OF TRAFFORD HOLDINGS LTD.
Trafford Catalogue #03-1069   www.trafford.com/robots/03-1069.html

10   9   8   7   6   5   4   3   2   1

A LIFE IN THE 'BURG

DEDICATION

TO MY MOTHER AND FATHER, DAUGHTER AND GRANDSONS, BROTHER AND FAMILY, THE JONES AND GOOLRICK KIN, AND THE MEMORY OF LORI ROACH, BELOVED DAUGHTER OF MY COUSIN SHELDA

WITH SPECIAL THANKS TO HEATHER AND MATY YOUNG, JENNY AND GINGER STEIN, AND JOHN EDWARDS AND BILL GARNETT,
AND TO SILVER COMPANIES FOR PROVIDING COPIES TO LIBRARIES AND OTHER ORGANIZATIONS,
AND TO SANDY, SAMMY AND SANDRA, THE CORGIS, AND FOSTER GRANT, THE SHEEPDOG, AND ALSO FOR MY PRESENT DAY EVER- FAITHFUL COMPANION, SAMUEL (BriarFoxSamuelAdams),THE CORGI WHO LOVES EVERYONE. AND TO DINO AND PEBBLES, MY DAUGHTER'S ST. BERNARDS' WHO ARE BIG BUT LOVABLE.

1ST EDITION 2003
UNIVERSITY OF PASSAPATANZY PRESS
ALL RIGHTS RESERVED

FOREWORD

Though my grandfather, Judge John T. Goolrick Sr., and my father, John T. Goolrick, Jr., both wrote several histories of Fredericksburg and the surrounding area, this work is not an attempt to duplicate their efforts.

It is merely a collection of scattered memories, anecdotal and otherwise, of one who has lived all his life in these parts, has seen a sea change in the character of the area and had an opportunity to meet a variety of people along the way.

It is also not an autobiography for few would care about my thoughts during a life that has spanned more than 68 years. It is essentially a tale of growing up in what once was a rural community, working with politicians both as a journalist and an aide and consultant, and somehow managing to muddle through.

Someday I hope my two grandsons, Corey John and Cody Scott Martin, will use the book to have some references as to what their grandfather did and the nature of the times in which he lived.

When several years ago I gave Cody a copy of a book I had written about another individual, he took it, but added, "Granddaddy, I'd rather read a book about you."

This book is about me to the extent that the life described in the 'Burg has been mine. But it is really more about people and events I've observed in a number of capacities. Because many of the things I've participated in over the years were connected by no common thread, the book is not strictly chronological and if it seems disjointed at times, accept my apology. But life is often disjointed and prone to veer off in many directions.

Sometimes I think that I remember more vividly life in a small town and rural area than I do things that happened just a few weeks ago. I still recall as a child of four or five looking up at the sky and marveling as a small yellow biplane flew over on its way to a local airport. Seeing a plane was relatively rare in those days of the late 1930s and I thought how thrilling it must be to get a bird's-eye view of earth. Now many years later I have flown across the Atlantic and Pacific oceans dozens of times on big jumbo jets a hundred or more times bigger than that small yellow plane.

The first car in which I rode belonged to a friend of the family who took his son to school one day and let us ride in the rumble seat of his Model A Ford. It was a profound experience. Then there was an uncle who lived in Quantico, where he was postmaster, who took my brother and me to Westmoreland State Park in his Pontiac automobile. He was the only family member in those days who had a car.

Some years ago I took my grandsons and daughter to New York City. In the space of just one day my grandsons rode in a truck, a chauffeured limousine, a bus, a jet airplane, a taxi, a subway train, an elevator, an escalator and, to top it off, a boat that took us to the Statue of Liberty. They took it completely in stride. But when I start thinking that kids today are too blasé, I conclude that with advancing age I am probably exaggerating my own reaction as a child to such pleasures as riding in a car or spotting a plane in the sky.

I have done more and been more places than I could possibly have imagined as a boy dressed in faded (but clean) J.C. Penney overalls (called dungarees now, I believe), but my life has been far from extraordinary. All those books I meant to write later remain unwritten and I have learned how soon 'later' comes.

I have made my living largely by writing, nevertheless, and I'm sure that any small talent I possess in that regard was inherited from my father who was a prolific writer. I wish I had inherited more of my mother's temperament because she invariably looked charitably on others and never said unkind things about anyone. My parents are both buried at Oak Hill Cemetery. My father died in 1949 when I was not quite 14 and he was 69. My mother was 83 when she died in 1990. With the passage of time I have come to realize ever more the great sacrifices she made on our behalf.

There is probably no better environment I could have grown up in than the sleepy town of Fredericksburg. Along the streets of this small city have walked such giants as George Washington, his mother, Mary, his sister, Betty, her husband, the patriot Fielding Lewis, and Jefferson, Henry, Mercer, Monroe, Madison, Lee, Lincoln, Clara Barton and many more. It is a place that knew the terrible ravages of war far greater than most other towns of America and its people, tested by fire in a terrible conflict, not only survived but eventually prospered.

When I grew up there was a saying that if you drank the waters of the Gunnery Spring you would always return to Fredericksburg. As a boy,

I cupped my hands together and drank from the old spring many times and no matter where I have gone, I have always been destined to return.

A question I suppose comes into the mind of all who reach a certain age is how the time went so fast. I am no different in that respect for it seems only yesterday that I was racing with childhood pals to the Colonial Theater downtown (now the Fredericksburg Galleria) to spend Saturday afternoons thrilling to my larger than life cowboy western heroes such as Whip Wilson, Lash LaRue, Roy Rogers, Gene Autry, Tex Ritter and all the rest.

Finally, I believe to the best of my memory that the various incidents and events described herein happened as I tell them. Yet I must issue the disclaimer that I saved no notes and kept no diaries and all that follows is drawn strictly from recollection and recollection is sometimes imperfect.

CHAPTER ONE

The Desert Fox

When I came into the world on July 7, 1935, at the old Mary Washington Hospital on Fauquier Street (now high priced condominiums) the seeds of a great war had already been planted with the rise to power in Germany two years earlier of Adolph Hitler.

But Americans in the mid-1930s had much more on their minds than war for The Great Depression was still raging and millions were out of work.

I'm fortunate to be here at all since, though I weighed in at a hefty eleven pounds, I quickly developed pneumonia and Dr. John Eugene Cole, who delivered me, had doubts that I would make it through my second night.

Thanks to him and others I survived and my grateful parents changed my name from John T. Goolrick III to John Cole Goolrick.

Leaving that aside, I suppose my birth could be considered a longshot. My grandfather, Judge John T. Goolrick, had as a very young man joined the Fredericksburg Artillery, was wounded in the left thigh on Oct. 17, 1864 and spent time in Chimborazo Hospital, Richmond before returning to duty in February, 1865. He was at Appomattox when General Robert E. Lee surrendered the Army of Northern Virginia to General Grant. My grandfather then walked home, stopping along the way to beg food from some of his fellow defeated Virginians.

Three of his brothers also served with the Army of Northern Virginia, Charles. Peter Jr. and Robert Emmett Goolrick. The latter was a Lieutenant who was wounded on July 6, 1863 at Gettysburg and was undable to return to duty until the following May. Charles Goolrick was wounded in the Battle of Chancellorsville. He became a Captain. Peter Goolrick was assistant surgeon with the 49th Virginia Regiment and was also at Appomattox when the surrender took place. My grandfather used to say after the war that he must have been the only Private in the Confederate Army since all the others were saying they had been officers.

Judge Goolrick was the son of Peter Goolrick and Jane Tackett Goolrick. Peter Goolrick was referred to by The Free Lance-Star as "a political immigrant" who was born in Ireland (no doubt that it was somewhere near Sligo in the northern part of southern Ireland) but there have been so many Goolricks in that region of Ireland, nearly all of them Roman Catholic, that I have been unable to discover who his parents were. And apparently he had a brother named John Goolrick who may have come over before him. There was a John C. Goolrick who served as clerk of the Alabama House of Delegates in 1818.

My grandfather served first as judge of courts in Fredericksburg and Spotsylvania, then as commonwealth's attorney in Fredericksburg and subsequently as judge of the Fredericksburg Corporation Court. In later years, Judge Goolrick often spoke at Confederate reunions and was one of the principal organizers shortly after the turn of the century of the first reunion of the Army of the Potomac held below the Mason-Dixon line.

The former northern enemies were treated so well at the Fredericksburg reunion that one of the Yankee generals, the somewhat notorious Dan Sickles (he had once killed a man in a brawl but lost a leg in the war while bravely fighting) wrote back to say that this time the southerners had nearly killed them with kindness.

Fifteen years earlier he had become the first Confederate veteran invited to speak to a reunion of the Grand Army of the Potomac. That reunion was held in Pittsburgh.

My paternal grandfather died in 1925, ten years before I was born and is buried along with my grandmother in the Confederate Cemetery. He wrote several histories of Fredericksburg and a biography of Hugh Mercer. He also wrote a book called, 'Irishmen In The Civil War' but I have never been able to locate a copy of it. I would have loved to have listened to his war experiences.

At his death in 1868 at age 68 The Petersburg Times noted that Peter Goolrick, who served as Fredericksburg Mayor in the 1850s, was the largest landowner in Fredericksburg and also owned a number of slaves. A Peter Goolrick also served as assistant surgeon in the Confederacy during the Civil War and it was probably one of the sons since Peter and Jane Goolrick had a number of children and there is a Peter Goolrick listed as a physician practicing in Washington, D.C. in 1870. The Civil War apparently greatly diminished the fortune Peter Goolrick had amassed in land and goods. He and his wife had five sons and four daughters who survived, among them my grandfather.

My daughter's research first finds Peter Goolrick in Virginia in the 1820s and he was elected a member of the Town Council in 1831. By 1860

He was apparently worth at least $150,000, a vast fortune in those times. His brother, John, bought a house on Caroline Street in 1804 and was called Professor Goolrick by the newspaper-and the house became known as the Goolrick-Caldwell house. He apparently opened a school in 1808. So far as can be ascertained, he had just one child, James, who became a lawyer, married a woman from Middlesex County and practiced law there.

Jane Tackett was the daughter of John Tackett, the owner of Tackett's Mill of Stafford and later the Washington Manufacturing company. (See copy of letter contained herein from R.E. Lee of Lexington to John Tackett dated Nov. 30, 1868.) She and Peter Goolrick were married by the Rev.S.B. Wilson on August 29, 1832 in Stafford County.

My daughter's family research has been locating Goolricks that I did not know existed. My father, born in 1880, had three brothers, C. O'Conor Goolrick (born 1876) who as a member of the House of Delegates introduced the legislation that founded Mary Washington College and as a member of the State Senate in the early 1920s argued the case for bond issues for roads against Harry Byrd Sr. who favored pay as you go. Byrd won that argument.

Chester Goolrick Sr., (born 1883) was commissioner of the revenue in Fredericksburg for years. His son, Chester Jr., was a professor of history at VMI and wrote a humor column that got widespread attention. A young brother, Col. Robert Emmett Mason Goolrick, (born 1887) who joined the Army Air Corps, was commander of Keesler Air Field in Mississippi at the time of his death in 1946.

My grandfather and grandmother also had two other children who died in infancy. The first, John Bernard Goolrick, lived just four months after his birth in 1873 and Fannie Chester Goolrick lived about two and a half years after her birth in 1874.

One of the last Goolricks in Fredericksburg, Frances Goolrick Ashby, now deceased ,was the widow of James Ashby Sr., a highly respected lawyer and prince of a man who had practiced with her father. One of their sons, O'Conor Goolrick Ashby, practices law in Fredericksburg, another, James Jr., who was an attorney, died of cancer several years ago. There are also daughters Turner and Nancy.

Kinloch Goolrick, my father's cousin, was a son of William K. Goolrick, an attorney everyone called Willie. Kinloch, a prominent author, is now in his 80s and lives in New York City. He was on Patton's staff during World War II and was seriously injured during the Battle of the Bulge. His daughter, Page, is an architect in New York and son Robbie is a consultant. I have heard recently from Faye Goolrick in Atlanta, a writer who was unknown to me until I found her name on the internet. She is a daughter of the late Chester Goolrick, Jr. Lindlay Goolrick Hinkle, sister of Chester Jr., still lives in the area.

My paternal grandmother, Frances Bernard White, did write about Union shells falling near her home during the Battle of Fredericksburg when she was a teenager, and a subsequent evacuation of the town on orders of General Lee. A number of her letters are on file at the Virginia Historical Society and also available at the Central Rappahannock Regional Library headquarters Virginia section. Her mother Frances "Fannie" Seymour White was a granddaughter of George Mason of Gunston Hall.

My father, John T. Goolrick Jr., spent most of his adult life roaming around this country and other parts of the world. Along the way he found work for himself as a writer for a number of newspapers to keep himself going. In an appendix to this book there appears a paper he did on his life while working for the National Park Service during Depression days. While practicing shallow diving in Hawaii, he broke his neck and was laid up in a hospital nearly five years.

Why he returned to Fredericksburg, the place of his birth, I don't know. But he returned, wrote a biography of General George Meade, a Union General while with the Park Service and met and married my mother. He was 53 at the time and she was 25. I was born about a year and four months after my brother, Robert Mason Goolrick, whose birth was on March 25, 1934.

The Goolricks have been around Fredericksburg a long time. Some day I may attempt a Goolrick family history. As I mentioned Goolrick is are fairly common name in and around Sligo, a beautiful town. Its people are overwhelmingly Catholic, but there were apparently Goolricks of both the Catholic and Protestant faiths.

Various descendants of Peter and Jane Goolrick became merchants, journalists, lawyers, teachers and even a drug store owner. I have no record on any children James Goolrick may have had. So far as I know all Goolricks in America are related.

On my mother's side, her parents, Ross and Elizabeth Sisson Jones, came from families in the Quantico area. Mr. Jones, 'Papa' as I called him, was a carpenter for the Richmond, Fredericksburg and Potomac Railroad and managed to get a family of 10 children safely through the Depression years (four of their children died in infancy, not at all uncommon in ads reminding people to 'Save Fats,' 'Buy Liberty Bonds,' 'Don't Drive Needlessly,' 'Plant Victory Gardens,' and for a long time I thought it improbable that we would ever again achieve such a sense of national unity of purpose. And the truth is we have not despite 9/11.

I had uncles in the Army and Navy who came home in their uniforms from time to time and with all the soldiers and Marines (from Quantico) milling around town, there were constant reminders of the war. Once a General at A.P. Hill let loose nearly his whole division on liberty at one time and within an hour every beer, candy bar and pack of cigarettes in every store in town were sold. The local police force consisted of just a few cops and occasional fights broke out between servicemen. As I recall, one of the police officers was Hugh 'Tootsie' Rose, a tough brawny man suitably equipped to break off an eruption of fisticuffs in public places.

Though I was just seven or eight, I tried to keep up with news of the war. I had a difficult time in the fall of 1942 trying to comprehend why our soldiers were fighting German and Italian troops in Africa since Africa to me meant the lush, snake-infested jungles where Johnny Weissmueller playing Tarzan used vines as his chief means of transportation. Now suddenly somewhere in Africa a German General (Erwin Rommel) called, 'The Desert Fox' was fighting British and American troops in tank warfare. I do recall that I was increasingly enamored by the exploits of a general named George S. Patton Jr. and remain so to this day. Much later I learned that Patton's ancestors had come from Fredericksburg (his grandfather, also George Patton, had been a Confederate soldier fatally wounded at the Battle of Winchester) and that he was a direct descendant of General Hugh Mercer, who was killed at the Battle of Princeton during the Revolutionary War. Mercer, who had been exiled from his native Scotland, made his home in Fredericksburg for years and operated an apothecary shop that today is a notable tourist attraction.

Even with a war on, people sought entertainment and diversion. In summer months it was great fun to go to one of the carnivals sponsored by such groups as the Elks, Odd Fellows, Knights of Pythias or American Legion on the big vacant lot at Jackson and Wolfe streets. A memorable experience, and one I used to tell my grandchildren about, was the night my friend, Douglas Pulliam (known to all as 'Baby Dumpling') and I got on the Ferris wheel and were at the top when it stalled and a hard storm ensued. We were scared and drenched to the skin by the time we finally got down (it seemed an hour but was probably only a few minutes). I think telling that story is probably the reason neither of my grandsons would go near a Ferris wheel when they were much younger.

But movies were the prime source of entertainment. There were two theaters in town owned by Benjamin T. Pitts—The Victoria and The Colonial. Pitts also owned much real estate and theaters in other places and was, by all accounts, the richest man in town. And when we passed the Elks Lodge building at 525 Caroline Street with its B.P.O.E. sign we sometimes joked that it meant, 'Benny Pitts Owns Everything.'

Pitts a self-made man, was extremely generous in supporting charitable causes. The so-called best movies such as 'Gone With The Wind' were shown at The Victoria (a property now owned by Fredericksburg Baptist Church) though in retrospect I realize that such movies did not find their way to backwater movie theaters such as those in Fredericksburg until they had first played in major markets for a number of months.

The favorite theater of all of us boys who palled around was The Colonial, also affectionately known as 'The Rat Hole', where you could see a double feature western starring Gene Autry and Johnny Mack Brown, plus a Bugs Bunny cartoon, a Three Stooges comedy, a newsreel and maybe even a Pete Smith Special for a dime. For another nickel you could get a huge candy bar, a Baby Ruth or a Hershey with almonds. I will never live long enough to find any more pleasure than I did in the hours I spent in the darkness of 'The Rat Hole' on a Saturday afternoon. In those days the guys in the white hats always won.

But as time passes there is no escaping reality. One of the highlights of my young life was meeting Al 'Lash' LaRue a cowboy movie star who showed up one night at The Colonial Theater and signed autographs. After his death, I learned that he had made only a few movies and practically no money and later lived in the Southwest in a trailer park where he managed to exist off odd jobs. It was disillusioning to learn that this man who seemed larger than life had been paid peanuts for those westerns ground out in a few days and had lived thereafter in poverty.

After the movies ended, if you had some change leftover, you could treat yourself to a hotdog with mustard, onions and relish, a Coca Cola or RC and an ice-cream cone at Scotty's on Lafayette Boulevard (owned by Warren Nash) for a total cost of about a quarter. Or you could walk across the street to Mac McGhee's place for a fifteen-cent barbecue that to this day remains in my memory as the best barbecue I ever tasted. Although Alman's, a fixture in town since the 1950s runs a close second.

In those simpler times parents weren't afraid to let their children wander about without adult supervision. Many people didn't bother to lock their doors and serious crimes were practically non-existent. Nobody was fearful when wandering hoboes who traveled on freight train boxcars came around and asked for handouts. My maternal grandmother, who all her adult life cooked three full meals a day, was always a soft touch and would give such unfortunates a heaping plate of food in exchange for a bit of work such as cutting the grass.

Growing up, I lived only a few blocks from the train station and it was not unusual to see hoboes, as these poor wandering hungry men were called, sneaking off freight trains when they stopped to put water in the steam engines. It's amazing that many thousands of such men were roaming the country and begging food and work, but that the overwhelming majority did not resort to thievery or brutality, but simply sought handouts. This would be impossible in an age when our society has become increasingly corrupt and lawless and not only must we keep doors locked to protect ourselves, but have guns we are prepared to use. Of course the ACLU (American Criminal Liberties Union) is always ready to jump to the defense of murderers, rapists, pedophiles and assorted other human monsters.

In those days, ticket sellers were on duty at the train station around the clock and train service was frequent. Most of the passenger trains were owned by the Richmond, Fredericksburg and Potomac Railroad whose initials RF&P some of us said stood for, 'Run Fast and Push.' Notwithstanding such youthful tomfoolery, it was a very good railroad and provided gainful employment to many people, including my maternal grandfather.

As its name implied, its service was limited to the distance between the old Broad Street Station in Richmond and Union Station in Washington with lots of stops in-between.

The RF&P trains were local ones and I can recall riding northward from Fredericksburg to Washington with stops at Brooke, Arkendale, Widewater, Aquia, Quantico, Occoquan, Woodbridge, Alexandria and other stations whose names I have long forgotten. It cost only a couple of bucks for a round-trip ticket to Washington and people frequently took trains both to Washington and Richmond. During the height of World War II as many as a hundred trains a day came through, many of them passenger trains filled with soldiers going both north and south to duty stations. The passage of time has given it an aura of romance and there was also something awe inspiring about the loud earsplitting screech of metal against metal as one of those monstrous steam locomotives brought the rest of the train to a grinding halt.

As a youngster, I found it thrilling to stand on the platform as the 'Iron Horse' thundered into the station and we eagerly climbed aboard for a trip to Washington to see the Ringling Brothers & Barnum and Bailey Circus, The Greatest Show on Earth so it proclaimed. It was fascinating to listen to the conductor coming through and announcing the next stop in a loud voice . . . 'Wiiiiiiiide . . .waaaaaater next station is Wiiiiiide . . . waaaaaater.' Amtrak has taken all the glamour out of riding the train with its awful service and dispirited employees. If you still want to get any pleasure from passenger trains, you have to go to Britain or the Continent.

CHAPTER TWO

Acute Indigestion

Apparently medical science knew little about heart disease in those days since when sudden chest pains struck and people died, their sudden expiration was often attributed to something called 'acute indigestion.' The word diet never came up in any conversation. Food was fried in heavy fats and folks ate fatty foods from sunup to sundown. Real butter, lots of eggs, bacon, scrapple, pork, steak, strawberry shortcake with lots of whipped cream-whatever your heart desired.

Being thin was not considered any great virtue and people in that condition were often told they ought 'to put a little meat on your bones.' 'Papa', my grandfather, ate three big meals a day and would have scoffed at some of the things that are popular today. I doubt if he would have considered pizza of any kind edible.

Medical care was rather primitive, too, and lots of people died from diseases such as typhoid fever caused by unsanitary conditions.

There were just a few physicians who practiced in the community. Doctors Cole and Frank Pratt come to mind as well as Dr. Philip Cox and Dr. Earle Ware. Cole made house calls, as did some of the others, in his old Ford and treated nearly every medical condition with the exception of those requiring advanced surgery. He never sent a bill and his favorite remedy for childhood diseases seemed to be steady doses of castor oil which is not something one is ever likely to acquire a taste for. Cole, like other physicians of that time, wrote out prescriptions in Latin, a practice I never understood except it was apparently a medical tradition that is no longer used.

A lifelong bachelor, Dr. Cole dined out practically every night with his bachelor brother, W.B.F. 'Billy' Cole who was Commonwealth's Attorney in Fredericksburg for many years. Dr. Cole was a courtly southern gentleman who invariably tipped his hat in the presence of women. He was one of the most unselfish and caring men who ever graced the city with his presence. When my daughter was born, we named her Lisa Cole in his honor.

There is another man to whom I owe gratitude. When I was quite young I fell on a rusty shovel and cut a huge chunk in my left leg. The man, who was working at a sawmill across the street, took me in his arms and rushed me to Doctor Cole's office where the leg was sewn up. Without his presence, the consequences might have been much worse.

The man's name was Dudley Pendleton and he died a few years ago. He was a black gentleman whose company I thoroughly enjoyed in later years. Dudley spent his growing up years in a society in Fredericksburg that was strictly segregated as that of South Africa when apartheid reigned. It seems remote and unnatural now, but it was true enough that state-sanctioned barriers existed between whites and blacks. But more about that later.

FREDERICKSBURG BC

When anyone asks who can be considered someone who came from 'old time' Fredericksburg, I answer that it is someone who lived in Fredericksburg BC.

Before Carl's, that is.

That means before Carl D. Silver's Used Car Lot, 1947, and Carl's Frozen Custard, also 1947, came along.

The era of Silverized cars has long since passed, but the custard stand is still there with long lines waiting for the frozen treats first dispensed by Carl Sponsella. It was one of the favorite places in bygone days for Al Gore, later Vice President of the United States, whose uncle owned the General Washington Inn hotel and restaurant across the street. As a young man, Al often visited Carl's for a multi-layered cone of chocolate custard. The hotel is now an office building owned by my close friend Tommy Mitchell who used to wait tables there.

Though today we have Old Town Fredericksburg with all its charm, a lot of the old time Frederickburg I knew is gone except the historic shrines such as Kenmore, The Rising Sun Tavern, the Hugh Mercer Apothecary Shop, the James Monroe Museum, the Mary Washington House and others. And many of the same churches still remain, including Fredericksburg Baptist, St. George's Episcopal Fredericksburg Presbyterian (the Rev. Peter Fisher is a great guy and the kind of minister who can relate to people well), Shiloh Old Site, Shiloh New Site and Mt. Zion Baptist. St. Mary's Catholic Church outgrew its Princess Anne Street location and moved to the College Heights area.

Among commercial enterprises we still have Goolrick's Drug Store,

The Burgess Barber Shop, the recreational pool hall with its wonderful chili dogs, Ulman's Jewelry, Ann's Grill, Dinty Moore's, Crismond's Shoes, Crown Jewelry, National Bank of Fredericksburg (no longer locally owned), Bazzanella Fur Shop, the First Virginia Bank (formerly Farmers and Merchants Bank) and Fredericksburg Hardware (although the business was located in the 300 block William Street then and operated by D. Letcher Stoner and then by Mac Janney. Stoner also had a tourist attraction called Stoner's Store that was full of fascinating and nostalgic items but that, too, is gone).

The Fredericksburg Elks Lodge 875 was a fixture at 525 Street from 1903 until it moved to Spotsylvania County in 1997 thanks in large measure to the leadership of Judge William Cox, attorney Ron Hicks who both served as heads of the Lodge, and Elks stalwarts such as Richard G. Smith and Steve Ravinsky who played leading roles). It has been beautifully restored as the Fredericksburg Square reception complex by its new owners Mrs.and Mrs. Van Peroy.

The Bradford Building and Mayflower Restaurant are history. The Princess Anne Hotel, where both Lloyd George and Winston Churchill were entertained, is now an office building. The Maury Hotel is a restaurant and apartment complex. The Athens Hotel a rooming house. Dugan's Restaurant is Sammy T's. The Stratford Hotel, later the General Washington Inn, is an office building. The Young Men's Shop operated for many years by John Herndon and his son Kendrick (a friend of long standing through our Elks association) is gone and so are Goldsmith's, once the oldest store in town, and Washington Woolen Mills (owned by Frank Levinson and then Tommy Rattican). Buckner's Seafood, with its delicious oyster stew, is a mere memory as are the Colonial and Victoria Theaters, Baylor's Barber Shop, Scott's Hardware, E.C. Ninde Furniture, Beck Furniture, Colonial Office Supply, Western Auto, Thrift Auto, Ferrara's, Morton's Drug Store, Cotton Lewis' Drug Store and Mag Lewis' Drug Store (both on William Street) Sunshine Laundry (on Caroline Street) Newberry's, Woolworth, Carley's, The Fashion Plate, Trussell's Jewelry, Boston Variety, Gulla's, The Blue Mirror, Lum's Den and Joe's Snack Bar, Spotless, Jones Grocery, Hirsh's clothing store,The Southern Diner, The Palms Restaurant, Slyman's Grocery, Elkins Funeral Home, Belman's Grocery, the Fredericksburg Fish Market, Roger Clarke Insurance, Allison and Young Realty, The Wakefield Hotel (now the Colonial Inn complex), Goodwin Brothers Furniture, Beck Furniture (operated for years by solid citizen WiInfrey Wright, Scotty's Bakery,

Jones Grocery Store on William Street, Slyman's and Johnson's Groceries in Darbytown and Kishpaugh's Stationery (its owner Bob Kishpaugh was the first person in Fredericksburg to own a car).

There were also a number of feed stores in days when the area was largely agricultural, including Hirsh's, Young-Sweetser and Roxbury Mills.

Also distant memories are the tourist homes dotting U.S. 1. There were a number along Princess Anne Street and Lafayette Boulevard. One popular place was Haydon Hall near the present Main Post Office.

The City Hall where I used to cover City Council meetings presided over by C.M. Cowan (the Mayor had no vote then) now houses the Fredericksburg Museum and Cultural Center where executive director Ed Watson does an excellent job, and the former Main Post Office is now the City Hall. Both are located on Princess Anne Street.

I suppose all of these are just simple reminders of the impermanency of life. When I ride along Kenmore Avenue and cross its intersection with Hanover Street I am reminded of Proctor's Store which once stood there near what is now called Maury Stadium where I played little league baseball.

One of the best parts of being on a ball club was that after the game you were treated to soft drinks and candy at Proctor's. It was an old time store with big containers filled with ice-cold water holding bottles of soft drinks. The drinks were super cold and my favorite was True Ade Orange accompanied by a Big Town, a confection that was akin to what we now call a Moon Pie. My friend Tony Bradley, who is younger but grew up just around the block from me, thinks the French fries served by Mrs. Proctor were the best he ever had.

Yet Fredericksburg today is still a neat place. I get that feeling every time I drive up Caroline Street (Main Street always to me) and see all the tourists and townsfolk browsing in the antique shops and, perhaps, on a nice day having lunch on the sidewalk in front of Sammy T's.

I have walked and driven along Main Street for nearly seven decades and although much about it has changed, in some respects it has remained much the same.

It still has that small town 'It's a Wonderful Life' atmosphere and particularly during the Yule season when all the lights are turned on. It possessed that even in the days when it was the area's major shopping center since while going from store to store, you knew many of the fellow shoppers who passed by amid the decorations.

The demise of downtown as the central shopping district was probably inevitable, but some of the impact might have been avoided if the city had followed the examples of such places as Charlottesville and Winchester where traffic was eliminated on key downtown streets and pedestrian malls created. There was talk for years of turning downtown Fredericksburg into a mall arrangement but procrastination won the day and major downtown businesses started moving to Spotsylvania County.

And yet the gradual comeback of downtown led by a number of individuals and groups has created a district that is probably more attractive to tourists since it has a history that is unequaled by any other city of its size in America. My father called it, 'America's Most Historic City,' and while that might have been an exaggeration, I don't think it was very far off the mark.

River City

Fredericksburg has always been a river town whose fate has depended on the whims of the beautiful Rappahannock. When I was four years old in 1939 rising waters washed out a bridge across the river from the city to Falmouth and also caused a spectacular fire at Standard Oil tanks near what is now called the City Dock (some folks used to call it the Steamboat Wharf harkening back to Colonial days).

My memory of that flood is dim, yet I remember vividly the great flood of October, 1942, the largest ever recorded in the area.

Rains, presumably from some unnamed tropical storm that came up the southeast coast, drenched the ground for days as the river started to rise dramatically. It finally reached Main (Caroline) Street. We had to abandon our house on Princess Elizabeth Street and went to stay with friends. I have never forgotten the sight of men paddling boats along the downtown shopping district. We have had more floods since, most notably in 1972, but fortunately nothing yet to equal the 1942 flood which was the great one hundred year flood and more. Two days after the waters reached their crest, I found myself along with hundreds of other citizens in a school gymnasium where typhoid shots were being administered by the health department.

The floods of 1939 and 1942 coming so close touched off talk of a huge dam on the upper Rappahannock in Spotsylvania County that would protect the region from future flooding as well as generate electrical power, provide recreation benefits and possibly help economic development. The Army Corps of Engineers wanted to build the dam and at first it seemed it would come inevitably, but over the years environmental opposition built.

I suppose I wrote a few hundred thousand words about what came to be known as the Salem Church Dam. I attended several congressional hearings on the subject and countless other local hearings. I listened as politicians alternated at favoring and opposing the dam. I met people who had bought river front property thinking the dam was certain to come and then realizing that it probably wouldn't come and that their land, located in flood zones, was no longer worth nearly the money they had paid for it. The dam was finally authorized by Congress at a cost of more than one hundred million dollars but the actual money to build it was never appropriated for a variety of reasons, some fiscal, some political.

My feelings about the dam were always mixed, but I think it was best that the river was left unspoiled for it is one of the most scenic rivers on the east coast and some of its whitewater areas would have been obliterated. Those who argued that the dam was needed to spur growth in the area were wrong for plenty of growth came and continues without it-some think far too much growth. And we have found ways to provide an adequate water supply by other means. The flooding danger remains and sooner or later another huge flood will inevitably come. The one thing that remains constant is that the lovely and unpredictable waters of the Rappahannock are our lifeblood and will remain so. And while it is lovely to live or have a business place within the river's flood plain, it poses dangers too as many have learned to their great sorrow.

But flood or not, the river, as indispensable as it is, has claimed drowning victims year after year from time immemorial and still does. I have never been able to understand why people, most of them young, don't realize novices can't canoe the rapid waters of the river or swim in it while it is at flood tide. I remember as a youngster playing on a vacant lot that is now a Virginia Railway Express Parking lot and seeing a rescue squad vehicle pass heading for the river. The victim, as I recall, was a young son of Margolas 'Goldie' Lowery, one of the best athletes ever to come from this area and the son of a barber who had a shop in the 100 block of Lafayette Boulevard. I talked with Goldie at the Elks many times in subsequent years but that was one subject that never came up.

Walking the Battlefields

I regret that I never had a chance to get to know my father, John T. Goolrick Jr., who died when I was in my early teens. In time I came to realize what an adventurous life he had lived which is summed up somewhat in an appendix to this book. He had been a pageboy in the U.S. House of Representatives and ran errands for such notables as William Jennings Bryan. He had gone west to become a pseudo-cowboy, wandered around the west coast working for periods of times as a newsman, lived in Africa and then in Hawaii. The book he wrote about Union General George Meade was never published, but is now in possession of the General Meade Society of Philadelphia. I belong to the society honoring the General whose victory at Gettysburg insured victory for the Union forces.

After he died and I grew up, I had many town residents tell me they had often seen him walking the Civil War Battlefields of the area, retracing the fateful steps of Union and Confederate armies. Since he did not drive, he usually took a cab to the battlefields, always driven by the somewhat legendary cabbie Socks Richardson, a black man who knew everybody in town. If you measure someone by their financial status, he was not a success. Yet he left behind a good name and reputation. An editorial said upon his death that he was the kind of person who could walk with kings or commoners and treat them just the same. I share the belief of Rudyard Kipling, whose poetry I greatly admire, that this is a fine measure of the worth of a man.

The Rotten Smell of Success

As I grew up sometimes when the wind was blowing in a particular direction my nostrils were met with the smell of what might be imagined as rotten eggs.

It was the smell of sulfuric acid emanating from the smokestacks of the Sylvania Plant off State Route 2 in Spotsylvania. And if you lived in the Fredericksburg area, that bad smell was actually the sweet smell of success.

It was the smell of money. In the 1950s there were about 2,500 people who worked at the place that was the largest cellophane manufacturing plant in the world. The plant was by far the biggest employer in the region from the time of its opening in the late 1920s and kept the Great Depression from inflicting much more severe pain on the area.

Practically everybody had a relative who worked at the plant. It was a 24-hour a day operation and most of the employees were shift workers. The plant was then owned by the American Viscose Corporation but was later purchased by the FMC Corporation. It had been originally built in 1927 by the Sylvania Corporation and thus the name Sylvania Plant stuck until its demise in the 1970s.

In my boyhood years it was inconceivable that the plant would not always be around. The area's economy largely revolved around it and for it to shut down would have been like ripping the heart out of the region, leaving it to die. Fortunately, when Interstate 95 opened in the mid-1960s new businesses and industries were attracted to the area so when the plant closed, as it did in the 1970s, the region was better able to absorb the shock.

Most young people these days probably don't know what cellophane is. It is a transparent film product made from wood and was in widespread use until a number of petroleum based substitutes came along to replace it. Though by the time it closed the plant was just a shadow of its former self, even so it caused a disruption in the lives of many who would never fully recover. Skilled workers such as my good friend Dick Limerick, now deceased, who had been making $16 or $17 an hour were forced to take jobs that paid only $5 or $6 an hour. I still occasionally run into people who were working there at the time of its closure and who tell me what a devastating effect it had on them.

The plant will never again be what it once was, but one of the businesses operating in part at the old plant these days is the A. Smith Bowman distillery, the makers of Virginia Gentleman bourbon and distributors of other products, both alcoholic and non-alcoholic. Jay Adams, who runs the family business, is someone I greatly admire because of his service to the state and what he has done for others.

CHAPTER THREE

Separate Ways

When I heard that the South African system of apartheid had at last collapsed, I could not help but think that less than a half-century had passed since racial segregation was an everyday fact of life in America's South.

I never went to school with a black, not in grade school, high school or college. State law forbid mixing of the races in public places and the law was vigorously enforced.

In Fredericksburg, there was the Lafayette Elementary School and a middle school and high school for white children, and the Walker-Grant elementary and high schools for black children. In theory they were separate but equal. But that was far from the case. The white schools were much better equipped and teachers more qualified in terms of educational backgrounds.

There were separate drinking fountains marked 'White' and 'Colored' at area courthouses and other places; separate waiting rooms for the races at the RF&P Train station and the Greyhound bus station. Blacks were not allowed to eat at lunch counters of downtown stores or drug stores and at most of what then passed for fast food establishments blacks could only get carry out orders. One notable exception, according to barber Jack Sullivan a contemporary who has cut my hair for years, was the Busy Bee Restaurant on William Street where blacks and whites freely mingled socially and bought beer, wine and food. Sullivan recalls that his father, Earl, sold cigarettes singly for a nickel each in an age when a pack of cigarettes cost only about 20 cents.

Since Negroes could not use white facilities, there were hotels for their use, such as the McGuire Hotel, on lower Princess Anne Street. I recall on that same block Brown's Funeral Home for blacks operated by a lady known as, for some reason, Madam Queen. Also on the block were Dr. Tate's drugstore and The Paris Inn. Dr. Tate, whose last name I cannot recall, was a courtly black man who served both black and white customers.

As a very young child I observed that when my mother took me to the movies the white people would be in one line and the blacks in another. It was explained to me that blacks had to go upstairs and sit in a section reserved for them in the balcony. I accepted the explanation unquestioningly. This was simply the way things were and I presumed the way they were meant to be.

Every year, one of the civic clubs, possibly the Lions, sponsored a Minstrel Show featuring white men in blackface. Such shows were a standard in communities north and south and had a format, as I recall, that included Mr. Bones, an Endman and others who attempted to speak in Negro dialect. It was a time when blacks as well as other ethnic groups were the butt of demeaning jokes, behavior that was socially acceptable. In movies, for instances, black actors such as Stephen Fetchit or Birmingham, Charlie Chan's sidekick, were shown petrified when confronted with dead bodies or what they regarded as the presence of ghosts.

There were colored barbershops in the city that white men patronized. But it was tacitly understood that such barbers could never cut, at least in public, the hair of another colored man for that would cost them the business of their white customers. Every barber shop had its shoe shine 'boy', often an adult black male, who would shine shoes for a dime and whatever tip might be offered. A haircut was around fifty cents then. Jack Sullivan, who was the son in law of the late Dr. Lloyd Bush, has his shop in the Professional Building at Caroline and Amelia streets owned by Jack and his wife. On the Amelia side of the building is a barbershop I always think of as Scott's since black barber John Scott ran that business for a long time.

Henry Gillis

Little socializing occurred among adult whites and blacks. On Sundays, the races would go to their own churches as they had done since the first blacks came into the community as slaves. Men of the cloth, both black and white, were among the most respected members of the community. Dr. Robert Caverlee, pastor of Fredericksburg Baptist Church where my mother was a member, was a recognizable figure wherever he went. 'Dr. Bob', as he was affectionately known, had a warm caring outgoing personality and a radio voice that was golden in tone.

Whereas Baptists had often been vilified, even tarred and feathered, in Colonial times, they had taken over majority status in Virginia and the Baptist Church in nearly any Virginia town usually had the largest congregation.

Fredericksburg then and now was notable for the spires of the Fredericksburg Baptist Church and St. George's Episcopal Church. In photos taken of the city from across the Rappahannock, the steeples of these churches always dominate.

Despite the rigid segregation, I probably had more black playmates growing up than did most northern kids. We would get together after school for games of pickup baseball, football or basketball or during summer months go to the old swimming hole on Hazel Run. I still recall black friends with nicknames such as 'Guitar', 'Red Dog', 'Bullhead','Cottongin', and others though I have no idea what their last names were or whatever happened to them. We talked and played and then went our separate ways because it was understood that we could not invite each other to our houses.

Walker-Grant High School always had a superb football team and even better cheerleaders and marching band. It seemed to me that their games played at James Monroe field (now Maury Field) were considerably more colorful and exciting than the James Monroe games. One of the stars of the football team was Henry Gillis, a running back who could break through the opposing line like greased lightening.

Maybe I'm wrong, but my recollection is that Henry stayed in school only through football season than returned to his job at the icehouse. I have been told that Henry played considerably more football seasons than should have been allowed.

Unfortunately, Henry, like so many other gifted black athletes, lived in an age where opportunities were very limited. I have no doubt if he were playing today he would be ardently recruited by many college football coaches and could even be a future professional making big dollars. But Henry remained a laborer all his life. His is just one example of all the black men and women of that time who were deprived of the opportunities open to whites from any social strata. It is remarkable, when I think about, that the era of total segregation was not that long ago. And fortunate, too, that as generations pass, it may become a distant, though unpleasant, memory.

Sleepy Hollow

Fredericksburg was a very small place—still is-with only about 12,000 citizens. It was sleepy and had a certain undeniable southern charm that it still possesses. Most of the people who lived in the town were descendants of others who had been residents and newcomers, particularly those who might have come from up north, were looked upon with suspicion. It seemed to me that folks in the community, particularly the blue-bloods, lived in perpetual fear that people from north of the Mason-Dixon line would arrive in droves again as they had in 1862 and infect the insular town with some sort of Yankee virus (more later on that subject).

Exceptions were made for some northerners. They were the young men who had come down during the Depression as part of the CCC camps in the area. Included among their ranks were such people as Conrad 'Jiggs' Brennan, Al Campbell, Tommy Mayhugh and others who married local women and established residence here the rest of their lives. They were not only accepted in the community, but had many friends.

Because the town was so small, everybody knew everybody else's business. Even in the 1950s and 60s the area was still a pretty provincial place and the local newspaper ran so-called 'country letters' from outlying area of Stafford and Spotsylvania. A typical entry might be something like, 'Jimmy and Edith Smith and their four children recently motored from Paytes to Richmond,' or 'Bessie Hockday of Wildcat Corner received a phone call last Sunday from her sister, Flossie, who lives in California.'

It has long since gone out of business, but once there was a place at Wolfe and Jackson streets called The Farmers Creamery in Fredericksburg that was a large employer. Dairy farmers from the region—and there were many of them—sold their milk to the creamery where it was bottled. There was door-to-door delivery early each morning of milk in bottles, not plastic containers. My grandmother had two bottles of fresh milk delivered every weekday. I thought of this when I was back in Brecon, Wales a few years ago and saw the milkmen making their rounds in the early morning hours. In those days practically everybody drank a glass or two of milk a day and the creamery flourished for many years until changing times and supermarkets drove it out of business.

Calling Captain Video

By the late 1940s television was arriving in our area, though not many folks yet owned sets. We did have a phone with a number something like 126, a radio and a phonograph player but no TV. Incredible as it may sound to my grandchildren, when you wanted to make a phone call there was no dial or push button mechanism but you had to pick up the phone and an operator on the other end would say, 'Number Please' and you would say, perhaps, 149 and be connected with somebody a couple of miles across town. Trying to get someone long distance was more complicated.

But though we had no television, thanks to a kind-hearted man named Charlie Estes who ran Estes Bar and Grill on lower Princess Anne Street, I was able, along with some of my young friends, to venture into his establishment, buy a Royal Crown Cola and sit fascinated while watching such pioneer programs as Frontier Theater, Captain Video or even a Washington Senators baseball game on the seven-inch Dumont set with a huge cabinet around it. I can still name many of the players on those awful Senator teams as well as those who played for the equally inept Washington Capitols basketball team.

Charles Estes was a prince of a man, big and burly but decent to the bone. He insisted on order in his place and those who violated the rules were soon shown the door. When I became older and Charlie had long since given up his businesses, I got great pleasure from talking with him some evenings at the Elks Lodge when he would visit. He was never what you would call a community leader, but he quietly paid his taxes and was a good citizen.

Another outstanding citizen was a colored barber named Chester Baylor who lived just around the block from where we lived and operated Baylor's Barber Shop. He was the epitome of a gentleman, always neatly dressed with tie and always soft-spoken and courteous. He was an intelligent man and I have wondered since what he thought of the demeaning system of segregation that existed here and throughout Virginia and the South. Since his income came from white customers, he was in no position to lead any crusades, but surely he realized that the black children sent to Walker-Grant had little chance of receiving the same quality education as the white children who attended James Monroe. This is no reflection on the dedication of those who taught at Walker-Grant for they were good people, but were not given the facilities or tools to properly do the job.

When I got older, I would see Chester Baylor occasionally and greet him, but we never really spoke seriously about anything and I suppose it would have been awkward for the both of us. Yet looking back through a lens shaped by the transformation of society that occurred in my young adulthood and beyond, I wish I had asked some of the questions of people like Chester Baylor that were on my mind. That is merely wishful thinking now that so many have taken their great stores of knowledge and thought to their graves with only scant record left for posterity.

John Scott, a black barber, and Dr. Philip Wyatt, a black dentist, were both active in the NAACP locally and on the state level. Scott's son, John, is now a widely admired Circuit Judge in the Fredericksburg area and I'm sure his father, who often cut my hair would be proud of him. Along with Alvin Gray, a deacon of his church who shined shoes at Scott's Barber Shop, we generally talked baseball. They and others like them finally broke down the walls that had put up barriers to opportunities for southern blacks for generations.

The Great War

Since my grandfather served in the Civil War and my father was a historian who specialized in the Civil War, one might think I grew up learning all I could about that epic struggle, particularly since a significant part of it occurred in my own backyard.

But that wasn't the case. While I was aware of the rich history that permeated our entire area, I was too busy with youthful pursuits to pay much attention. Thus when people say nowadays they are discouraged that young people don't care for history, I discount that in the belief that as they get older their experience will be the same as mine and others. They will realize with increasing maturity history is something that applies mightily to their own lives and has shaped the small part of the world in which they live.

When I was a teenager, many of the same buildings and structures stood in Fredericksburg that still stand, yet I see them in a different light. The Hugh Mercer Statue conjures up a vision of an extraordinarily brave man who willingly gave his life so that a new nation conceived in liberty could be born. The Rising Sun Tavern (built by George Washington's brother) comes alive as a gathering place for those who drank glasses of ale as Americans after the Revolution. Kenmore was the plantation of the patriot Fielding Lewis. And a walk in any battlefield in the area, or any cemetery that holds the remains of men who fought in the Civil War, makes one aware that the United States were never truly united until that war essentially ended at Appomattox.

There is an ongoing dispute between landowners and preservationists about property rights. I hope that ways can be found to preserve the area's history without a Big Brother approach that will, in the long run, prove counterproductive.

CHAPTER FOUR

BASEBALL AND APPLE PIE

Like nearly every young American boy, I grew up with a passion for baseball, the national pastime as it was called. As kids, we played pickup games on a corner lot, sometimes knocking out windows of nearby homes and scattering before we could be chased down by irate occupants.

I joined the Little League and played for the Optimist Club team coached by Lucien F. Jones, a fine man who was a student of the game. I wasn't a bad player and made the All-Star team, but I have to admit there were lots of better players around than me.

The highlight of the 1945 season was a trip to my first major league baseball game at Griffith Stadium in Washington. It was a double header between the Washington Senators and the New York Yankees and watching such Yankee greats as Joe DiMaggio, Charlie Keller, Tommy Heinrich and others I immediately became a life long Yankee fan.

As a teenager, I often went to games at Griffith Stadium and hung around outside the visiting team locker rooms seeking autographs, something possible in those times. In that fashion I collected hundreds of autographs from such all time great players as Bob Feller, Ted Williams, Joe and Dom DiMaggio, Allie Reynolds, Mickey Mantle and many others. I estimate if I have saved all the comic books I had collected as a child (early editions of Batman, Superman, etc. and the autographs of all the baseball stars, I would be able to cash in on a small fortune today. But unfortunately when I went off to college, I told my mother those weren't important and somehow they disappeared when she moved. I can only think of what Satchel Paige (whose autograph I got several times when he played with the Cleveland Indians) said: 'Don't look back, something may be gaining on you.'

A group of us that included Bill Bullock and John Perry Jr.(whose career as a street cop ended when he decided to become a minister) saved money from part-time summer jobs and traveled by train several summers to New York City. Once there we saw major league baseball games at Yankee Stadium (New York Yankees), Polo Grounds (New York Giants) and Ebbetts Field (Brooklyn Dodgers) all week and then stopped off at Shibe

Park in Philadelphia (Philadelphia Athletics and Philadelphia Phillies) to see another game or two.

Ebbetts Field was like no other ballpark in the world. It was small and the seats were practically on top of the players. The fences were short and cheap home runs abounded. But the most impressive thing about the park was its fans. They were the most rabid anywhere and though I did not particularly care for the Dodgers, I dared not root against them while in Ebbetts Field. It is hard to believe that at one time there were in New York City three center fielders playing at the same time who belong among the immortals of the game — Mickey Mantle, Willie Mays, Duke Snider. I saw them all many times. If they were playing today what with the era of high-powered agents and free agency and the millions doled out to mediocre players, they would have to own the teams on which they played.

There were a number of semi-pro baseball teams in the area over the years and some played at what was called Powell Stadium at Five Mile Fork but could be most accurately described as a bumpy farm field marked with baseball lines. The most prominent team among them was the Fredericksburg All Stars formed in the late 1940s by Watson Finney, a cattle broker and restaurant owner. I saw about every home game the All Stars played. They were a mixture of local and out of town talent. Among the top local players were Cotton Billingsley, Gilly Sullivan, Bob Stephens, Marion Timberlake, Graham Morris, Bill Finney and Ralph Ramer. Bill Rittner who later became a great friend of mine assisted with team management Any one of the players noted above would have a good shot at the major leagues today, particularly Billingsley, Stephens and Timberlake (Cotton Billingsley, a native of Fredericksburg, now lives in Richmond. As a Marine, he saw intense combat at Iwo Jima. His brother, Ralph, served with the Navy in the South Pacific and another brother, Sydnor, was a successful businessman with Billingsley Printing and Engraving. The Billingsley family has deep roots in the city).

For a short period the All Stars were a Brooklyn Dodgers farm team and wore similar uniforms. They were part of the first night baseball game in Fredericksburg when the House of David brought their portable lights to Maury Stadium around 1947. Permanent lights were installed at the stadium not longer thereafter.

The House of David lights were very limited in scope. They were passable so long as you were playing in fair territory but anyone who chased a ball over the foul line found himself in semi-darkness. And if you were a spectator, you practically viewed the game from darkness as if you were in a darkened theater with the lights shining only on stage. I believe the All Stars beat the barnstorming bearded members of the House of David who were supposedly all Jewish players, but were professionals of all ethnic groups who toured the country and got paid reasonably well for it.

The All Stars drew large crowds whenever they played for in that postwar era people were starved for entertainment, particularly in a small town such as Fredericksburg. The downfall of such baseball teams began when television started to take hold and people stayed home to watch Milton Berle instead of taking in a ball game. And it must also be mentioned that now we could watch the Washington Senators for free on television and did so although they were a terrible team with a miserly owner named Clark Griffith.

One of those who played occasionally with the All Stars was Russell 'Rabbit' Sullivan of White Oak. He went on to the minor leagues where he was a consistent .300 plus hitter and sometimes led his leagues in batting. He played briefly in the majors with the Detroit Tigers.

I was there when Sullivan hit a gigantic home run at what is now called Maury Stadium. A left handed hitter, he connected with the ball and it went all the way on the fly to where a building now stands that is used as a sports locker room.

In the 1950s a group of us went to Griffith Stadium at Florida and Georgia avenues and saw the Tigers play the Senators a double header. Batting against a right handed pitcher in the first game, Sullivan doubled to left field the first time up and then the next at bat hit a ball over the tall right field fence that resembled Fenway Park's 'Green Monster.'

When the ball cleared the fence, several dozen Sullivan fans from the area cheered long and loud and a guy sitting next to me asked if I'd ever heard of him. I told him that where I came from everybody had heard of him. Sullivan returned to Fredericksburg, became a highly successful builder and has contributed many thousands of dollars to worthwhile causes.

D-Day, June 6, 1944

I was an assistant carrier on a paper route in 1944 when the D-Day invasion occurred on June 6 and the local paper carried the story in big bold headlines.

I think I realized even then that the outcome of the war might depend on whether the invasion was a success. General Eisenhower had risen from obscurity in just a few years to become a national hero affectionately known as Ike. But while I felt he deserved the adulation, I was most intrigued by General George Patton who had the colorful nickname 'Old Blood and Guts.' Not until later did I learn that many of his ancestors had come from Fredericksburg and some had fought on the side of the South in the American Civil War.

It's hard to describe adequately the military fervor of those days to present generations, not even after the events of September 11, 2001. Life revolved almost totally around the war effort and it was part of most every daily activity. And nearly every family had some member wearing the uniform.

In 1945 first came VE day and then VJ day and suddenly the war was over and most of the young men who had left the area to join the Army, Navy or Marines were coming home, though there were a few dozen from the region who were killed in action.

My mother had four brothers. One was in the Navy, two in the Army and one in the Army Air Corps. The eldest son, Ross Jones, had been stationed at Schofield Barracks at the time of the attack on Pearl Harbor and told me later he had helped man machine gun positions when Schofield was attacked by Jap planes. They all came back safely, though the brother in the Air Corps decided to make a career of it.

The returning veterans were anxious to get their disrupted civilian lives jump-started. Many took advantage of the new GI bill of rights to learn trades and to go into business. Others used special government programs to secure loans for business ventures. Bill Hicks opened his Vets Market at Princess Anne and Frederick Streets. Navy veteran Ranny Mills and others went back to James Monroe High School and played football. They had changed from boys to men during the war and were often competing against kids much younger. As one who went to all the high school athletic events possible, I was intrigued by those few years when a much older generation dominated the teams.

It did not take long for the familiar wartime rumble of military convoys through town to vanish. No longer were hundreds of uniformed men seen on streets over weekends. The war was over and people were anxious to get it behind them, though membership in local American Legion and VFW posts swelled. National Guard units were re-established in the city as well as Marine and Navy reserve units, but nobody really felt that we would be involved in another war in their lifetimes. Little did they realize that the Korean War was just a few years down the road and that some of them, including Marine officer Lem Houston, who had served in the Pacific during World War II and was appointed Fredericksburg postmaster in 1949, would be among those called back to duty. Lem was postmaster until 1972 when he retired and became marketing officer of The National Bank of Fredericksburg.

With the end of the war, gasoline rationing ended and people were able to buy cars again so traffic greatly increased. It is difficult to believe now but in those days all traffic on U.S. 1 from Maine to Florida had to come through the city along Princess Anne Street and Dead Man's Curve on Lafayette Boulevard got its colorful name because of the frequency of automobile accidents there, many of them resulting in fatalities. Every time I round that curve with the National Cemetery just across the street, I remember that era. When the U.S. Bypass was built, many Fredericksburg businesses, hotels and tourist homes loudly protested since it would be greatly detrimental to their businesses. Indeed such service stations (filling stations as they were called) as Sidney Armstrong's, Cowan's and Pat Passagulppi's saw an almost overnight decline in gasoline sales. Sidney Armstrong recalls that coping with the change had been very traumatic.

The Foxhole-Best Dogs in Town

One of my fond memories of the immediate postwar years is that of a small hut at Princess Anne Street and Lafayette Boulevard called 'The Foxhole' and operated by a veteran named Shelton. It served the best hot dogs in town, topped with mustard, finely chopped onions and relish for just a nickel. For some reason it was there just a couple of years and was suddenly gone.

Not far from The Foxhole was the tall brick building at 525 Caroline Street owned by the Fredericksburg Elks Lodge. There was a lighted sign in front of the building with an Elk likeness on it and the letters B.P.O.E. Elks.

I didn't know what Elks did, but was given to understand they raised considerable amounts of money for worthwhile charities. Every summer the Elks would sponsor a carnival and members of the Lodge would work the various games. They also raffled off an automobile in connection with the fair.

I was in my late 20s when I finally joined the Elks, little realizing the organization would become a major part of my life. Obviously I won't name names, but I was surprised upon joining to see some men who were very prominent in the community playing cards for money and rolling dice in the basement of the building where the bar was located. I found it fascinating that such prominent people used the Lodge as a means of getting away from the pressures of everyday life and letting their hair down a bit, among them a superintendent of schools and a banker from whom I eventually bought three white Cadillac convertibles after he had used each a year or two.

Two people I saw playing pool often at the Elks were Warren Forbush and Linwood 'Pigeon' Jones, both car salesmen. Pigeon coached American Legion baseball teams for years and I still see Warren and his wife, Jinxie, occasionally. (Pigeon would occasionally take a shot of a bourbon he called 'Old Forrestal' but whose real name was Old Forrester).

On a hot day Buck Cox and Jim Byram, both good citizens and friends, could drink a pitcher of beer in no time flat. By contrast, Carlton Heflin and Garland Atkins, also friends, could make a bottle of beer last for hours.

Over the years I became greatly involved in the Elks and was elected four times as the head of Lodge 875. I have attended as of this writing some 14 national Elks conventions in such cities as Chicago, Las Vegas, Seattle, Atlanta, Denver, New Orleans, Hawaii and other. And I have gone to countless state and regional meetings.

I have enjoyed membership in the Elks, an organization with about a million and a half members, as well as participating in the various Elks programs that contribute time and money to worthwhile local charities and organizations and national programs designed to benefit veterans, provide scholarships for young people and promote Americanism.

The old downtown building, now known as Fredericksburg Square, was a great place and when I pass it, memories come flooding back. Our Lodge has long since relocated to a place on State Route 2 in Spotsylvania County and we have prospered there. I was the chairman of the committee that purchased from Jimmy Carver, Harry Franklin and other partners the 30.5 acres where we are located. On the remaining part of the land where the old Massaponax Sand and Gravel Company was located (and where troops undoubtedly marched in the Civil War) was placed the elegant North Club subdivision.

Among the most memorable characters I encountered in the Elks was the late Brewer Beckwith. A retired city fireman, Brewer had a story for every occasion and must have known everyone who ever set foot in Fredericksburg. He had a friendly manner and people were forever buying him drinks. One day Brewer allowed that he had a couple of turkeys in his freezer at home and suggested we cook them and a have a little get together.

The little get together turned into something more as everybody started to invite others to the point a hundred or more people would be coming. When Brewer brought in the so-called turkeys, they looked more like pigeons. But I dreamed up a quick fund raising project and we had a great dinner, highlighted by Brewer making a hilarious talk that I wish we had taped. I felt that he missed his calling as a stand up comedian.

In those days we had constant activities at the Elks. Pool tournaments, card tournaments, crap shooting for high score, crab feasts, dinner dances, horseshoe tournaments, and so on. Every day a couple of dozen men—in that time only men could be members-would gather in the afternoon and sit around what we called 'the round table'. It was a table designed to accommodate only about six or seven, but somehow we managed to fit in everyone and beverages flowed freely.

Wilmer 'Bouncer' Heflin, another local legend, and I would bet a buck or two on whether the next member coming through the door would have false teeth or be wearing socks or have a tattoo or be wearing an undershirt. I loved to be around such people as Brewer and Bouncer and Billy Goldsmith, Hunk Anderson (the great enock rummy player), Willie Mills, Dick Limerick, Stanley Snellings, Robert James, Bob Heflin and many others. The late Earl Hollibaugh Sr., a great cook, did a lot of cooking for the Elks and other organizations. His son, Earl Jr. is also an excellent cook, though at least one of his dishes at every meal is likely to be very spicy. A good friend and great patriot was the late Ed Greater who had made the Navy a career.

The Elks Lodge has played a major role in the Fredericksburg community for the past 100 years. The fraternal part of it is certainly very important, but the Lodge has donated countless thousands to various charities and programs and continues to do so. When the order amended its constitution to allow women to join, I sponsored the first female to join the Fredericksburg Lodge. Some of the men were at first opposed to the notion of women members, but now I find that those who were once the chief opponents are now the biggest proponents. Just as I expected, the women have turned out to be the hardest working members in the Lodge. The head of the Lodge in 2003 is Judy Brevik, the first woman ever accorded the honor.

I mentioned earlier my friend Willie Mills. He and I traveled to a number of national conventions together and to Europe on three or four occasions. A more modest and unassuming guy never lived than Willie. He had been in the Marines during World War II and was twice wounded in combat in the Pacific. Yet though he was a true hero, he would never talk about his experiences though I was interested in hearing his story. When I tried to bring up the subject, he just said it was just something that happened and was over and not worth discussion. Willie had grown up on Wolfe Street in the height of the Great Depression and knew was it was like to go to bed hungry. So he always appreciated whatever he got in life and could not understand people who were always griping or complaining as if someone owed them a living. There was nothing Willie enjoyed more than watching an old movie on television. I recall our being in a nice hotel room on Wakkiki Beach in Hawaii near the ocean and Willie laughing uproariously at some ancient Laurel and Hardy movie. He died of cancer in the late 1980s and I have missed him very much.

The Banker

Arthur Smith was a man to whom I shall always be grateful. When after my college days were nearly over I wanted to buy my first automobile, I was turned down by one local banker who said no collateral, no loan. I went to Arthur who was vice president of the Farmers & Merchants Bank and asked for the loan. He gave me the hundred bucks I needed to buy the 1949 Chrysler which sold for about ninety-five dollars.

In later years after joining the Elks where Arthur was treasurer, I saw him practically every night and enjoyed his company. Arthur was a man of great integrity who invariably was dressed in suit and tie. He was a lifelong bachelor and his trademark was the cigar stuck in his mouth all day long. He was a member of numerous organizations in the area, served on City Council for a long time, and was a pillar of the community. He helped people constantly in a quiet manner and sought absolutely no credit for doing so. It is a shame that people who are blatant self promoters often get the credit and remembrance while men like Arthur Smith are too often forgotten and not fully appreciated.

What I enjoyed about talking with Arthur- Mr. Smith as I called him- was his recollection of bygone days in the city. He had organized a baseball team that played at what was called Gouldman Park located somewhere near the old Pratt Clinic on Fall Hill Avenue. Arthur recollected that the games drew large crowds since no admission was charged. In talking to people such as Arthur and Grover Gouldman, it became clear to me that Fredericksburg's small town atmosphere had really changed little since the Civil War. I think it was for the best that the downtown section, once the regional shopping hub, has now become a series of antique shops, restaurants and small stores. The shopping area near the Interstate 95 corridor is exactly where it belongs with the historic district intact and even more impressive than in former times. (Another banker I admired was Carl Hill of Farmers & Merchants who sold me three of his white Cadillac convertibles over a period of years).

CHAPTER FIVE

Christmas Shopping

The first barber I went to was a man who had a little shop just below the railroad tracks. He used hand clippers during part of the haircut process and I never cared much for them since he did not always use them skillfully.

Just to give an example of how things that happen when you are very young stick with you all your life, I saw not long ago a set of hand clippers used by barbers in the past and it sent chills up my spine as I thought of the old barber, maybe with a nip or two of alcohol in him, clipping my hair and inflicting pain at the same time.

In those days holidays were a bigger deal than today, or at least observed more to the point of their true intent. Nobody started shopping for Christmas in early November. The Christmas decorations weren't put up in stores until around the first week of December and there weren't people dressed up as Santa on every corner. There was one Santa who arrived and he came in a parade and practically every kid in town was there to greet him as he tossed candy to those scattered along the parade route. My brother and I would get a couple of toys for Christmas and maybe a sack of fruit and candy. It is hackneyed to say that kids nowadays get too much in the way of material things all year to the point that Christmas isn't awaited with the same eager anticipation. Yet it's true.

In those simpler times when downtown was the area shopping center, folks from the counties flocked to town on Friday night, when the stores stayed open until nine, and on Saturday. Before a stoplight was put at William and Caroline Streets, police officer Shortstop Smith used a wooden sign with STOP on one side and GO on the other. At the end of the evening he would put the sign on a street corner and nobody ever stole it. Just try that today. The device would not last five minutes before someone took it.

Trick or Trick

I shudder to think of some of the reckless things we did when Halloween rolled around and I'm glad that this has now been turned into a more civilized event. Undoubtedly, some of our pranks were not only downright mischievous but almost malicious, such as setting fire to piles of leaves in someone's backyard or putting big firecrackers in mailboxes and exploding them. It's amazing that more kids, including myself, didn't lose fingers or hands while playing with firecrackers since in those days it was perfectly legal to acquire fireworks with a good deal of explosive force. Come to think of it, it was even possible to order such dangerous stuff by mail which I did. God only knows why the Post Office allowed that.

You could mail a letter for three cents and have perfect confidence it would reach its destination. In the city mail was delivered to homes twice a day on weekdays and once on Saturdays. I was a mail order freak and loved nothing better than to send off for some offer or another to acquire a special code breaker ring advertised in a comic book or some novelty or joke being peddled in a catalog from the Johnson Novelty Company. Or magic tricks, which I loved. Like other boys, I tried to sell Cloverine Salve and Christmas cards to make extra money, but ended up selling most of the stuff to relatives just as is the case with kids today (my grandsons have sold me all sorts of magazines I never read and popcorn I never popped).

I can recall when I got older walking to Shannon Airport and watching planes take off and land. I was fascinated by planes even then and dreamed of someday having the opportunity of flying in one. My first flight came when a guy I met in college arranged for me a brief trip in a small plane piloted by his father. Since then I have been in many kinds of planes, including several flights to Europe in military cargo planes.

Free Rides for Politicians

Whenever you hear of a plane crashing and killing some politician — particularly a small plane — bear in mind that politicians seeking office will often take whatever is free without worrying too much about potential consequences.

Over the years while following politicians across Virginia during various statewide campaigns I climbed into a lot of small planes that carried the press along with the candidates and I had no idea whether the planes were in safe condition or whether the pilot or pilots knew what they were doing. I assumed that politicians would not get into any plane they figured wasn't safe but I was disabused of this notion by a young man named John Marshall Coleman who by then was Attorney General of Virginia.

That occurred when Richard Obenshain, nominated by Republicans for U.S. Senate in the summer of 1978, got into a small plane one night in Winchester, Virginia following a campaign appearance. The plane crashed into trees short of a runway in Chesterfield County, killing Obenshain and two men who were pilots. It turned out that those flying the plane had limited night flying experience.

As Coleman told me, 'Beggars can't be choosers. When you're running for statewide office all out and it's important to get from one place to another fast, you don't ask whoever loans you the plane or flies it to show their credentials. You just hop in and hope you'll land safely.'

Other politicians told me the same thing and the practice is still going on. I was on one flight in a small plane when Henry Howell ran for governor. As we suddenly went thorough a very violent storm that tossed the small plane around like a straw in the wind, Henry, a very great and personable man, acted as if everything were normal but it was white-knuckle time for the rest of us.

I flew several times with John Chichester when he was the Republican candidate for lieutenant governor in 1985 and he was an excellent pilot. I flew with him once over the West Virginia mountains down to Fort Knox, Kentucky where we had both spent six months training, although mine preceded his. As we were given a VIP tour of the place by jeep going up what they called Agony and Misery Hills, I wondered aloud how I had ever managed in younger days to climb up them loaded with field pack and rifle. But more later on military experiences.

Cars and Custard

A true Fredericksburger, as I mentioned previously, is one who was here before Carl's Frozen Custard and Carl D. Silver's used cars, both starting in 1947. They were just a block or so apart and both quickly became local institutions.

At war's end, Carl Sponsella had worked for relatives at a similar place in Northern Virginia and decided to export the idea to Fredericksburg. Seldom has such genius been exhibited since I think if all the people who have ever lined up at Carl's small place for custard and other delights were counted, it would be more than enough to reach the moon. The place has provided temporary employment for countless young people, including Richard Garnett who went on to become Superintendent of City Schools and later a member of the City Council. Garnett married Ann Schwartz, the daughter of Arthur Schwartz, a teacher at James Monroe and a close friend of mine in later life. We were both ardent New York Yankee fans and he did much for the community and deserves a place on its Wall of Fame.

If I could cast my ballot for the all time Fredericksburg meal it would be a barbecue with coleslaw and special sauce from Mac McGhee's, a hotdog with mustard, onion and relish from Scotty's, a cheeseburger from Eddie Mack's, fresh roasted peanuts from Ferrara's, oyster stew from Buckner's near the Chatham Bridge and a thick milkshake from Carl's. And also throw in a tuna sandwich on toasted bread from Goolrick's and eggs and home fries from Ann's Grill. Of course, in modern times the places I never tire of are the upscale La Petite Auberge owned by my friend Christian Renault and Renato's just up the street.

CHAPER SIX

Blowing Smoke

Smoking cigarettes these days is so politically incorrect that Mary Washington Hospital in Fredericksburg has gone to the extreme measure of banning smoking on any part of its property.

I am not condoning smoking since it undoubtedly is a health hazard. But it puzzles me that when I go overseas to places such as England or Ireland or Germany everybody seems to be smoking American made cigarettes (usually Marlboro) and there are no warnings on the packages. So I guess it is okay in the name of commerce to export cancer to the rest of the world so long as the anti-smoking elements here in the homeland have their own way.

My mother smoked Camel cigarettes from the time she was a teenager to a couple of years before her death at age 83. My grandfather Jones, her father, did not smoke but used up a couple of packages of Apple chewing tobacco each day.

Smoking was not only socially acceptable in my growing up years but portrayed as glamorous. Many of the leading men and ladies in Hollywood movies puffed on weeds. Tobacco companies sponsored various radio and television programs and commercials showed actors contentedly puffing away. I will never forget that huge sign in Times Square with the open mouth that blew out very large smoke rings once or twice a minute (If you're old enough to recall such cigarette brands as Wings, Marvels and Piedmont or when lots of people rolled their own or what the slogan LSMFT stood for then you have to be about my age or older).

When I went to work for the local newspaper back in the 1950s just about everybody in the newsroom smoked, and the same was true of the composing room, front office and advertising department. Nobody raised any fuss about smoking in those days.

Not long ago I was down in the Danville area in the heart of Virginia's tobacco country and saw no 'No smoking' signs in eating establishments. The folks in those places were puffing away on unfiltered cigarettes. The tobacco they have stored in their barns is like pure gold to them.

The Fredericksburg area once had a major connection with the tobacco industry since cigarette packages were wrapped in cellophane and the world's largest cellophane factory was located in Spotsylvania County. I suppose cellophane still has its uses, although you hear little about it anymore.

I have found that the hottest properties in life, the things that are considered almost indispensable, in time have a habit of becoming either obsolete or near obsolete. One such formerly hot commodity might be the American worker. We once had in Fredericksburg and surroundings not only a cellophane factory but places where they made shoes, shirts and pants. Those factories are long gone and I suppose what used to be made here is now being made in Taiwan, Formosa or Korea.

But I have drifted away from the subject of tobacco. One of my best friends, Willie Mills, died as a result of long years of tobacco smoking so I know the tragedy this seemingly pleasurable habit can cause. Yet John Dalton, former Governor of Virginia, a man I knew and admired, died of lung cancer and he had never smoked in his life.

So what do we do about tobacco, the golden crop that hearkens back to the first settlers on our Virginia shores? Is it to be eliminated as a cash crop in this state and others? Is it possible to convince all those who smoke to quit and those who don't never to start? Can we reopen some of those abandoned factories in the Fredericksburg area to manufacture nicotine patches? (I have just learned that most Virginia tobacco farmers are planting less these days because of the fear of continuing costly litigation against tobacco and those who produce and sell it).

The anti-tobacco voices are getting louder and more strident all the time. Certainly everything should be done to discourage people from smoking, but I don't think selling cigarettes ought to be declared illegal. (Incidentally LSMFT meant 'Lucky Strike Means Fine Tobacco').

Quality of Life

Is life better today in Fredericksburg and the area than it was when I was born?

I suppose the answer has to be yes. I into the world in the middle of a depression when millions of people could not find work and many went hungry. There was no social safety net in those days. My father was lucky enough to sign on with a government funded Work Projects Administration (WPA) program. I still have an unpublished biography of General George Gordon Meade he wrote as a result of that employment. My mother was also able to find work at a pants factory, though the hours were long and the pay small.

Life has to be better does it not now since in those days there was no television, it was difficult enough to make phone calls across town never mind to California or overseas, there were no computers, no cars with automatic transmissions, no jumbo jets to whisk you anywhere in the world you wanted to go, no frozen foods that let you eat anything you wanted winter, summer, spring and fall, no microwave ovens, no shopping malls, no six lane roads, no disposable razors. There were many homes in Fredericksburg with no indoor plumbing and it was a common sight to see chickens in backyard coops. When a housewife wanted to cook chicken for supper many did not go to the supermarket but to the backyard where she chopped off a chicken's neck, plucked the feathers and cut the chicken up into parts.

Lots of people worked at the Sylvania plant, the area's principal employer. Today two of the chief employers physically located in the region are Mary Washington Hospital, a far cry from the small little hospital where I was born, and Mary Washington College, an even farther cry from the little single sex cow college of my younger days. Occasionally as a college student I would date MWC girls but it was almost an ordeal since you had to wear coat and tie to meet Miss Bushnell's approval and you absolutely had to have the girl back safely to her dorm by the eleven o'clock weekend curfew. All that has changed dramatically since men and women now attend the college and there not only is not a curfew, but there seemed to be few rules governing the conduct of students outside of school hours.

There was no air-conditioning when I was a boy except in movie houses. Imagine that if you can. No air-conditioning. I can remember lying in bed on stifling summer nights with the window open but no breeze stirring outside and being drenched in sweat. As one who relies on air-conditioning to get through the oppressive summer months of Virginia, for that reason alone I would not want to go back to boyhood days.

There is no way I can expect my young grandsons, or any child in 21st Century America, to even remotely imagine life in the Fredericksburg of the 1930s, 40s and 50s. Even I find it hard to imagine those simpler times when life was not nearly so complicated or nearly so convenient. Listening to the radio programs beamed into our homes from New York or Los Angeles, I could not imagine television (though it had actually been invented some years before by a fellow who never got much credit or compensation for it) or the coming age of VCR's, DVD's, cable programs, news stations that would operate around the clock and personal computers.

And I certainly could not have imagined a time when traffic jams would be an everyday fact of life in the region. That hardly seemed possible given the rural nature of living.

One thing probably remains consistent. Young people who want good paying jobs cannot work in the area to obtain them generally unless they are professionals such as doctors, lawyers, architects. They can commute out of the area, mainly to Northern Virginia, and Washington and do so by the thousands every day. In parts of the region, notably north Stafford, people live there only because it is cheaper than Northern Virginia and they have little connection with the county in which they live.

CHAPTER SEVEN

A Plane Falls

I have two grandsons, Corey, now 17, and Cody, 14, and I'm proud of both of them and take every opportunity to be in their company.

My wife and I had just one daughter, Lisa Cole Goolrick who was born Sept. 8, 1961 and today is a cardiac nurse in Richmond. We probably would have had more children except that back in those days of the 1960s there was something called the RH factor. My blood was O-positive and hers O-negative and Dr. Bill Liddle, my daughter's pediatrician, said should we try to have another child, there was a high risk the pregnancy might be dangerous. I am told that medical science has practically eliminated the RH factor as a risk.

Bill Liddle operated a practice with Dr. John Painter and they were both highly professional and popular men and dedicated individuals. Our daughter and other children got the best of care from them.

She was grown up and going to nursing school in January 1982, and I was in Richmond on the second Wednesday of the month when the General Assembly convened for the first day of its session. The day was bitterly cold and it would remain that way through the inauguration of Charles Robb as governor on Saturday.

When I got back to my hotel room there was a message to call an editor at the newspaper. I made a call and was told the shocking news. An Air Florida plane taking off from National Airport that afternoon had plunged into the frigid waters of the Potomac River killing most of those aboard, including two area residents. The area residents killed were Dr. Bill Liddle and Mrs. James Blake, who was a secretary to the Fredericksburg Medical Society. They had been heading to a medical conference in Florida.

The news was distressing since I knew them both as fine people. It was even more distressing when I read that Air Florida personnel had been less than meticulous at making sure the plane's wings were not coated heavily with ice as it was taking off.

That night I went to the dining room of the Holiday Inn Downtown in Richmond and saw Mr. and Mrs. Jack Bess sitting at a table. Jack was a veteran lobbyist for the tobacco and vending machine industries. I joined them and we talked about the plane crash. As it turned out Jack had been on an Eastern plane that came in to land at National just as the Air Florida plane was taking off. He described the scene at the airport as very sad.

Long after the crash I heard something I have often thought of as an example of how seemingly small decisions can sometimes affect whether we live or die. It had been snowing that day and was bitterly cold and Bill Liddle had about given up on the idea of taking the afternoon flight to Florida. His thought was to wait until the next day. But Mrs. Blake called and said that she had found a van service from the Sheraton Inn was still making trips to National and that if they could get to the Sheraton then they would not have to drive their own cars to the airport. And once they got on the plane a few hours later they would be in sunny Florida with all the bad weather left far to the north of them.

They met at the Sheraton and went to National Airport, never to return home again. It drives home the point that every day when we walk out of the door of our home, there is no guarantee that we will pass through that door again. That is a lesson we should keep in mind every day we are fortunate enough to live.

A Diverse City

It is fashionable these days to talk about multi-culturalism and diversity as if it had never existed before. But Fredericksburg was a diverse even in my youth.

I can still remember the overpowering aroma of Ferrara's roasted peanuts as I walked down Main Street. Mr. Ferrara was the father of Nunra Ferrara, a man who later became a friend and racetrack companion. Nunra himself ran a restaurant later in downtown Fredericksburg and did so with an iron fist. If someone came in he didn't like, Nunra would refuse him service.

Nunra's parents had come over from Italy and had taught Nunra that pennies make dollars. I can see him now carefully running draft beer into a glass. "Some people let it run over the edges," he told me, "but you don't see me doing that. That's your profit."

Once when a person came in around noon and ordered a tuna sandwich, Nunra told him, "We're out of tuna. I can give you a hot dog."

The man said, "I don't like hot dogs."

Nunra said, "You don't like hot dogs. That's un-American. What are you, a Communist or something?"

Nunra was a first-rate horseplayer who had been known to even book a horse or two in his day. When we went to the track, he would insist on going to the paddock and watching the horses being saddled, a practice I had never found useful in picking winners.

Nunra said, "You look at those horses, they can tell you something if they're too fidgety or sweaty, lay off because they don't want to run today. And you never want to bet a horse if you see foam coming out of his mouth. It means he's off his feed."

I'm still not convinced he was right, but I do know he always managed to pick more winners than me.

The Ventura's were another prominent family of Italian extraction in Fredericksburg. Solly Ventura, the patriarch, had founded Fredericksburg Distributing Company and his sons, Paul, Jimmy and Al ran it later on. Paul Ventura, who always had a big cigar in his mouth, was a short but muscular man who loved the races and more than once I went with him and Nunra to Pimlico and Bowie in Maryland. Then we would ride to Charles Town, West Virginia for night racing in a ritual that was called 'going around the horn.' Along the way we would have a shot of bourbon or two. Paul had a heavy foot and got stopped frequently for speeding, but those tickets never seemed to slow him down.

You couldn't find a more generous person than Paul Ventura. He was a soft touch for any good cause that came along. He sold Schlitz beer when Schlitz was the most popular brand in the Fredericksburg area and when Schlitz began to fade in popularity for various reasons—some claimed they were using a different kind of water—Paul and his brothers got the franchise to sell Coors and the business continued to prosper.

There were a number of persons of Greek descent active in the area. Paul Virvos ran the Mayflower Restaurant, though in later life he returned to Athens and stayed there until he died. Jim, his brother, owned the Recreational pool hall on William Street (with the famous chili dogs) and did well for himself, and Steve Zapantis took it over later. One of my favorite eating places was Pete's Restaurant at Spotsylvania Courthouse owned by Pete Poulos. He had come to America from Greece and worked long and hard to succeed. Every day at noon at the Spotsylvania Courthouse a crowd would be in his place.

The Jewish community was also sizeable. Julian Levy (Carley's) and

Jerry Miller (Fashion Plate) owned clothing stores downtown as did Frank Levinson (Washington Woolen Mills). The local junkyard was owned by Max Klotz and later Alex Klotz. One of my favorites was Rabbi Franzblau of Beth Shalom Temple. He loved journalism and he often came by the paper to talk about it.

    One interesting story was that of M.S. Belman who came to the United States in 1914 from Lebanon at the age of 16. He took a job, after several other jobs, with M.J. Gately who owned and operated a small grocery store located at 501 Main Street, the John Paul Jones house at the corner of Lafayette and Caroline Streets.

    Gately thought highly of the young man and when he retired sold the business to Belman who was then 21. He gave Belman a one year lease at $30 a month rent and a five year option. This included use of a horse stable and outhouse. At first the store was named The Sanitary Grocery but when the Sanitary Grocery chain (now Safeway) located in Fredericksburg, the store's name was changed to Belman's Grocery. Later Belman changed the location of his store to 508 Caroline Street. Son Ferris Belman ran that store for years, as well as others, and a grocery still remains in that location today. (Ferris served for years on City Council and then the Stafford Board of Supervisors. We old timers communicate these days quite often by e-mail. And his son, Robert, a member of the Stafford School Board, is an occasional e-mail correspondent).

    But though we were really multi-cultural in some respects, we were not ethnic in any way to the extent of New York City. I remember the shock of going there at age 12 and hearing people talking all sorts of different languages. You never heard that in Fredericksburg. English was spoken and for the most part everyone spoke the same kind of English. Thus even a thick accent, such as Jimmy Vievos had, seemed a bit strange.

    And then there is still Nick the Tailor—Nick Lopomo, a local legend who has been at his trade forever, although by the time this is published he has probably retired. When you entered Nick's shop there were clothes scattered everywhere and if you left something, you wondered how on earth he will ever find it when you went to pick it up. But amid what seemed an ocean of chaos, Nick invariably reached into a pile and picked up your tailored pants and returned them to you. Another downtown business of bygone days was Vizzi's Tailor Shop ran by Joe Vizzi, a close friend of my father's.

There were and are others of Greek descent who helped make the community what it is. Nick Calamos ran the Liberty Café at the corner of Caroline and Lafayette Boulevard, a favorite watering spot for servicemen during World War II. A lady named Mary Calamos used to operate the Victory Diner on Liberty Street adjacent to the old James Monroe High School (now the Maury property). Trephon Calamos was one of the most dedicated veterans in the area and had been very prominent in the American Legion. His brother, Nick, who sold and repaired vacuum machines for years, served in Italy with the Army during the war and was one of the card playing mainstays at the Elks. He was one of my favorite people. Nick told a story of going to a home and putting sawdust on the floors to demonstrate a vacuum cleaner and then being told the home had no electricity. During World War II while serving in Italy he had buried a machine gun under a tree and said one day he was going back to dig it up, but he never did.

CHAPTER EIGHT

Getting By

I made decent grades in high school although it occurs to me that I didn't work very hard at it. Unlike my brother, nearly a year and a half older than I and destined to be his class Salutatorian, I felt there were too many important things to do other than homework.

The important things included hanging around Eddie Mack's Grill or the Hot Shoppe's parking lot passing the time with contemporaries, both boys and girls. There was no finer cheeseburger ever made than put out by Charles and Virginia Hart who had named the place in honor of their first son. They were surrogate parents to many of their young customers and would cheerfully dispense advice. Years later after his parents died, I would buy their home in Fredericksburg from Eddie Mack Hart.

Teenagers were not indulged nearly as much as the youngsters of today. I can't remember any of my classmates wearing designer clothes or shoes and few of them had their own cars even when they became old enough to drive. My first car was not to come until I left college.

I did have one friend whose indulgent and affluent parents bought him a car, a convertible, and I would often go with him to such places as Fairview Beach and Colonial Beach where we could watch older folks play the slot machines and drink beer. My friend must have been fascinated by the experience because later in life he lost thousands of dollars on slot machines and other gambling.

For those who don't remember, slot machines were legal in several counties in southern Maryland and since the Potomac River is part of Maryland, piers were built over the water at Fairview and Colonial beaches. The piers at Colonial Beach, including Little Reno, the most popular, were open 24 hours a day the year around and attracted thousands of patrons, most of them from Virginia. There was a certain spin off effect for the town since many people spent the night in hotels and ate in restaurants there, but most of the money flowed to the casinos and the state of Maryland was the main beneficiary.

Led by the Rev. Earl Cox, who had been at the University of Richmond while I was there, a group of citizens challenged the offshore casinos. The case went all the way to the Supreme Court and that court upheld a Virginia court ruling that the offshore casinos were illegal. Thus ended the era of gambling at Colonial Beach until many years later when an off-track horse race betting facility was located in what had once been Little Reno.

JM Days

I wish I had more vivid recollections of high school days but I actually recall little that would hold any interest to whomever might read this material.

I must have been the class cutup since my classmates voted me the kid with the best sense of humor when our senior year came around. I can't recall the brilliant lines I spoke to deserve that accolade, although I did put out a mimeographed publication called, 'The Weekly Mistake,' which was full of sophomoric phrases. I was hoping all copies of it were gone until Bill Hall, who now lives in Arizona, presented me one at our 50th year high school reunion. Reading it made me cringe. (Example of the brilliance of those who put out this publication, including Tom Mann, Jerry Bird, Dick Cloe, and James Carter Rowe: 'Nine out of ten girls are pretty and the 10th goes to James Monroe'). I do recall that we constantly derided the official school newspaper The Spotlight and they denigrated our unofficial publication in return.

Along the way there were innumerable teachers who, in retrospect I realize, were utterly devoted to their profession and those they taught despite their meager salaries. People like Emma Euliss, Emiline Stearns, Mildred Chick, Bruce Neill, Elsie Allison, Arthur Schwartz, Mildred Lapsley, Frances Armstrong, and more. (Once when I showed up in her class in a T-shirt, Mrs. Euliss said, 'Young man, people are not permitted to come to school in their underwear' and I was sent home to get a shirt. I shudder to think of how she would react to today's student garb).

Perhaps I am being unfair and crotchety when I voice the belief that teachers of this modern age aren't as devoted as they were in former times. (With such notable exceptions as the former Betty Jo Gayle and Kylene Heubi). I suppose that is just the view of a cynic who has grown to feel nothing is as good now as it was then. I can recall listening to Grover Gouldman who was up in age when I was relatively young.

Grover swore that major league baseball players who came after the likes of Ty Cobb and Nap Lajoie and Rogers Hornsby and Honus Wagner were all a bunch of bums, a view I did not share since my heroes were Joe DiMaggio, Phil Rizzuto and others. I recall also Ikey Middleton, the press room foreman at the local paper, waxing nostalgic about the good old days in Fredericksburg where he played as a boy at some place called Prettyman's Camp which was apparently along the Rappahannock River. He also described carnivals they once held on Lauck's Island on the river. Sometimes we snickered about Ikey's propensity to constantly prattle on about things he had done as a young man decades ago, but now as I find myself doing the same thing I can understand the compulsion and look around anxiously to make sure none of the younger generation is snickering.

I have heard the tales of folks who say they had to walk miles to school each day. That was never the case for me since Fredericksburg was, and is, a small town and all the schools I attended were within easy walking distance. I have also heard exaggerated tales about the supposed bitter rivalries that existed between young people from Darbytown (most of the area below the railroad tracks and called 'Dobbytown' by most in those days), those who lived along the Boulevard (that area from Lafayette Boulevard to roughly William Street) and those who lived on Doswell Field (from the Canal on Fall Hill Avenue to what became the Bypass).

But I can honestly say I have no recollection of ever feeling the least bit apprehensive when I wandered into any territory other than my own. Life in the city was entirely peaceful so far as I was concerned and while delivering telegrams for Western Union I rode my bike where I pleased with never a hint of interference. Telegrams, practically extinct now, were very popular in those days as a means of rapid communication. I carried them on a part-time basis all over the city and picked up a tip of a quarter or so on the average. Sometimes George Nance, who ran the telegraph office, would warn me that a particular telegram to an individual contained such bad news as the death of a relative and in those cases I did not linger once I had put the message in proper hands. I often thought of those times when I was the bearer of bad news. But somebody had to do it.

Philly

A close high school friend was Bill Bullock. His parents, Elizabeth and Charles Bullock, were like second parents and his brother, Travis, works for Union Bank and Trust in this area. For some unknown reason

We decided to apply for entrance to Temple University in Philadelphia. It may have been because Bill had heard it had a good business school and I just went along. We both got accepted and then went up to Philadelphia for some additional testing a few weeks before we were to enter into our freshman year.

During that time we stayed in a drab room in a very drab neighborhood which was where Temple was located. It was a far cry from what we imagined it would be. Everything seemed dirty and depressing and Philadelphia was not our idea of a great place to attend college. By the time we got back home we had agreed to forget about Temple, but it was too late to go anywhere that semester.

Thus we did not enter the University of Richmond until the following January. It was a wonderful place with a scenic campus with a lake dividing the male University and the all-female Westhampton College. The only drawback was that freshmen were housed in military barracks leftover from World War II when ROTC cadets had trained there. The barracks were drafty and gloomy and real firetraps, but we managed to survive.

The Dean of the school was a friendly man named Pinchbeck who always said, "Howdy neighbor," when passing a student on campus. He was one of the role models for Earl Hamner Jr., a U of R graduate, when he wrote his book, 'Spencer's Mountain,' which subsequently became the hit television series, 'The Waltons.'

Pinchbeck died of a heart attack when we were sophomores. By that time we had moved to a room in the tower of Thomas Hall where we remained for the rest of our stay at the University. Bill Bullock was a business major and pursued a career with the Internal Revenue Service. He lives in Charlottesville now but is in bad health and was unable to attend our 50 year high school reunion held in June, 2003. Ours was the first class to graduate from the new James Monroe High School that is now, like us, a half-century older. But we spent only about six months there and I will always consider the present Maury School as the real James Monroe of my memories (at the reunion I noted that if a new James Monroe High is built as planned, then most of us will have lived through three Mary Washington Hospitals and three JM's.

At the University I took about every English course they had to offer and made A's in all of them. But a semester each of Algebra and Trigonometry were required and kept me more than once off the Dean's List. To this day I have not the vaguest notion what either of them are about and am far too old to be concerned about it.

College days were fun and fleeting. I made many friends that I still see occasionally, including one young man who frequently mixed up a concoction he called 'Sledgehammer' which had various kinds of alcohol in it although no drinking was allowed on campus. Several drinks of 'Sledgehammer' would make one realize that it was aptly named.

I quickly fell in love with Richmond and it has been my second favorite American city ever since. In those days there were no high-rise buildings as there are today with the possible exception of Hotel John Marshall and the Hotel Jefferson and the city retained the southern charm it had possessed from its origins. Confederate flags flew everywhere, including the State Capitol, and segregation was the way of life. (Black riders of city buses had to go to the back of the bus for seating). And anywhere you went you saw monuments and statues to the memories of Confederate heroes such as Jefferson Davis or Lee or Jackson or A.P. Hill.

The Gathering Storm

And yet storm clouds were brewing. The 1954 Supreme Court ruling that southern schools must be desegregated with all deliberate speed struck Richmond like a bolt of lightning. As time went on the state legislature, meeting often in emergency sessions, endorsed the so-called 'Massive Resistance' policy enunciated by James J. Kilpatrick of the Richmond News-Leader and promulgated by U.S. Senator Harry F. Byrd Sr. who ran the vaunted Byrd Organization that had controlled state politics since the early 1920s. Kilpatrick's theory that a state had a right to 'nullify' any federal edict it felt unjust stemmed from Thomas Jefferson's notions advanced after the Federalist administration of John Adams passed the infamous Alien and Sedition Act. But nullification did not work then or now.

A little more about Byrd and his much-touted machine. From around 1921 until Byrd's death in the mid-1960s it generally ruled Virginia politics with an iron grip. Though Byrd was the final arbiter, he was not a dictator and gave fellow Democrats who shared his conservative views some latitude in their actions and decisions so long as they did not violate the crucial tenets of the organization such as pay as you go financing since Byrd hated public debt.

The goal of the organization was to maintain power by keeping the electorate mainly confined to those who shared its philosophy. The last thing it wanted was a system where every eligible voter was encouraged to cast a ballot. A poll tax of $1.50 a person a year had to be paid by anyone who voted and it had to be paid six months before a primary or general election. The Democratic primary was tantamount to election since, except in a few regions of the state, there were barely enough Republicans to fill up a phone booth.

In the Fredericksburg area the most prominent Republicans were Nile Straughan, who became a national Republican committeeman, St. Clair Brooks, Ryland Heflin and the parents of Pina Brooks Swift. When I first started covering politics attending a GOP 'mass' meeting was to look upon an event with few present. Yet by then Virginia Republicans were taking heart since many prominent state Democrats in 1952 had endorsed Republican Dwight Eisenhower for President rather than Democrat Adlai Stevenson, and Virginians were increasingly turning to Republican candidates on the federal level but remaining staunchly loyal to Democrats on the state and local levels.

Pina Swift who died of a sudden heart attack in spring, 2001, was a good friend. She always called me by my Goolrick surname and was a woman of very strong opinions and active throughout her life in Republican Party politics. She was someone with drive, determination and energy but also had a terrific sense of humor and was always loyal to her friends.

Vernon Edenfield, director of George Washington's Fredericksburg Foundation and a true visionary, and I were often invited to her home for Pina's delicious oyster stew. Vernon discovered her death when he went to her home one evening for some stew and heard the dogs Friday and Toby barking loudly. Sheriff Charles Jett of Stafford adopted the dogs. Friday passed away but Toby is still living. Pina kept them on strict diets, but whenever I was around them I would slip them a piece of meat or two without her knowing it. They were always glad to see me.

In times past, elections were much less regulated and hard liquor flowed freely at polling places where the right kind of Democratic votes were rewarded with shots of whisky or a dollar bill folded inside campaign literature. Liquor stores were closed election days. Republicans complained for years about the poll tax and alleged election chicanery by Democrats, but to no avail. A little so-called 'walking around' money could work wonders.

While dramatic events were transpiring at the Virginia State

Capitol during my college years in Richmond, I must confess, despite my budding interest in politics, there were other pursuits that took priority.

Among them were dating young women attending the Richmond Professional Institute (RPI) that has long since become a part of Virginia Commonwealth University.

The girls at Westhampton had reputations of being snooty and the daughters of the affluent so young men like me who had only a few dollars in their pockets invited out RPI ladies who would be content with less lavish entertainment. As a college student I made a little extra money giving out sample cigarette packages to students and I think they were courtesy of R.J.Reynolds. Practically every cigarette manufacturer gave out samples on campus..

Blueberry Hill

I have never been a much of a music fan, but I know enough to realize that I lived through and participated in one of the greatest cultural revolutions in American history. The true era of rock and roll music began in the mid 1950s and Bill Bullock and I went early on to The Mosque in Richmond to see Bill Haley and the Comets who with their 'Rock Around the Clock' were the fathers of rock and roll—or at least the rock and roll that became so commercially popular. We saw show after show at The Mosque, listening to and watching performers such as Chuck Berry, Fats Domino, The Everly Brothers, Buddy Holly, Richy Valens, The Big Bopper (Holly, Valens and the Bopper all died in an icy plane crash in some Midwestern state while en route to a concert in the next town) and many more just as they were gaining fame. At the Mosque, young people often started dancing in the aisles and on one occasion when I was there police came in and threatened to physically clear the place. The older generation decried the advent of this primitive new music, contending it would be a great corruptor of the morals of young men.

Now in an age of so-called rap music with filthy lyrics, that era seem tame and mild. Just play Fats Domino's 'Blueberry Hill' and you may agree.

CHAPTER NINE

Fort Knox Tanker

After college days, I was mainly interested in getting on with my life. I had been working part-time at the local paper in Fredericksburg and they had tentatively agreed to give me a full time position as a reporter. The job would not pay a great deal, about seventy bucks a week but that was in 1957 and I could manage to get by on it.

I had gotten started only a short time when the military draft loomed large. That was not surprising since the draft was going strong in the country with memories of Korea not that far behind and the Soviet Union still very much a world menace.

As I watched people just slightly older than I getting called up, I inquired of Conrad "Jiggs" Brennan, a local policeman, what the National Guard offered. The most important thing is that by enlisting I would be sent off for six months training and then return home to complete my military duty by drilling one night a week and going off for a two week summer camp period annually for six years.

While on active duty I would be paid about $70 a month. The National Guard Armory was located in an old building on upper Caroline Street that had formerly been a shoe factory. On the day I signed up I had no idea the Guard would play a major role in my life and that instead of merely fulfilling my six-year obligation, I would remain a member nearly twenty-five years.

I had no great interest in things military up to that point except that I found fascinating the influx of uniformed men into Fredericksburg during the height of World War II. After taking a physical examination and being found fit for duty, I was informed that I would be shipped off to Fort Knox, Kentucky to spend the six months of training.

Accompanied by Charles Hall, Floyd Cooper and Jim Brown, friends from Fredericksburg who had joined the Guard, we embarked from Richmond by train to Louisville, Kentucky, the location of Fort Knox. It was a long trip through West Virginia and we got there the next day and were immediately bused to the military base. Recruits then—and I suppose now—were put into a Reception Center where I spent what seemed the three longest days of my life. We were herded into sloppy formations, given uniforms that were ill fitting, stood in line to take various shots, asked hundreds of questions by surly processors, fed on the run and barely given time to sleep. It did not take me or long to realize that the transition from civilian to soldier was not going to be easy.

But then I got a lucky break. After the interminable three days, we were divided between training units and my friends and I were assigned to Company D of the 9th Training Battalion, an outfit that existed solely to provide basic training for newcomers. The break came when I was assigned to a platoon run by Sergeant Collier who came from southwest Virginia and talked with the distinctive drawl of that region.

When Sergeant Collier asked if anyone from the group had any prior military experience, Charlie Hall, jokingly told him I had gone to Fork Union Military Academy. I suppose I should have confessed that the closest I had ever come to the Academy was driving by it, but by that time Sergeant Collier had decided to make me a squad leader.

The best part about squad leader was that you transmitted the orders from the dozen men in your squad when given orders by the platoon sergeants and squad leaders did not have to do such noxious duty as KP (kitchen police) or guard duty.

Sergeant Collier inevitably learned that I probably couldn't find the parade grounds of Fork Union on a map, but for some reason he took a liking to me and let me continue as squad leader though he told me one day in a good natured way, "Goolrick, you wouldn't make a soldier if you stayed in this outfit a hundred years."

Such criticism didn't bother me nearly as much as the necessity of marching with my squad with full pack and M1 rifle five or ten miles up such places with the forbidding names of 'Misery Hill' and 'Agony Hill.' I must have been in the best shape of my life for I managed to make those incredible journeys without falling out as some did, although I admit that at the end my feet were one big blister.

Many years later, when I was working for Congressman French Slaughter, State Senator John Chichester, who had taken basic at Fort Knox a few years after me, suggested that we fly down in his plane to the base and take a tour. When we got there, we were given VIP treatment and the tour included jeep rides up and down Agony and Misery hills.

Seeing them again, I could not believe that as a much younger man I had climbed to the top of them weighted down by all sorts of equipment. So far as I was concerned it had been the equivalent of climbing Mount Everest.

After miraculously finishing basic, I was sent for advanced training in Armor since the unit back home had been a tank company when I left but, due to a re-organization, would be an anti-aircraft battery by the time I returned. I was not one of the best tank gunners to ever come out of Fort Knox, as some later believed. Actually, I never really fired the tank's primary 90mm gun for official scoring purposes.

What happened is on the day I was due to fire, there was some accident on the firing range that delayed the proceedings for hours. By nightfall, the range instructors were anxious to get away and one of them, a Corporal, came over to me, handed me a scorecard and said something like, 'Here Goolrick, fill this in and turn it back in for me to sign. And don't let anybody know you didn't fire.'

That suited me fine and I filled in what I thought would be a reasonable mediocre score, one not too good but sufficient to pass. I must have misinterpreted the scoring system for when range firing results were posted a few weeks later as training neared an end, my name was at the top of the list. My fellow trainees were undoubtedly aware that I hardly knew one end of a 90mm tank gun from another, but it made little difference to them when final ceremonies were held and the Battalion commander called me front and center and presented me a handsome certificate designating me 'Tanker of the Cycle,' because of the great prowess I has shown in tank gunnery. I suppose the outstanding score is still recorded on my records that I presume are stored in St. Louis, Missouri unless they burned up in a disastrous fire in the early 1970s.

I felt embarrassed when Alvin York Bandy-an outstanding tank officer-congratulated me. With relief I realized since the unit no longer specialized in tanks, I would not have to demonstrate my abilities to Bandy or others.

(During basic training, Floyd Cooper and I were due for night firing of the M1 rifle. It was a terribly cold night and when we saw one group that had just finished firing marching out, we fell in behind them and returned to our barracks and nobody was the wiser).

Our Guard unit commander was Captain John Pavlansky in civilian life was sales manager at Young Motors Inc. He had been in the regular

Army and was an excellent commander, one who always looked out for the morale of his men. Since I worked for the newspaper, Pavlansky called me in and said he was going to designate me as the unit's public relations person. We went to summer training at the State Military Reservation located smack on the ocean at Virginia Beach. The men had the enviable job of firing 40mm guns from M42 tracked vehicles positioned on the beach at so called Radio Controlled Anti-Aircraft Targets (RCATS) flying over the ocean. It was great duty and there were few complaints. When duty was over, the men would head into Virginia Beach for a dip in the ocean followed by an evening of beer drinking and entertainment. I pulled off somewhat of a coup when I got Gov. J. Lindsay Almond, who had a cottage at the State Military Reservation (one reserved for use of state governors) to pose for a photo with Capt. Pavlansky and Sgt. Brennan that was published in the local paper.

I was a lowly Private but my main job wasn't tough and subject to few controls. A couple of men had not shown up to go to camp as required so Captain Pavlansky sent a detail back home to round them up. One day I walked in the barracks and there were two men literally chained to a post. I knew both of them and they said they had just been brought back because of their failure to report for duty. One of the men was desperately thirsty and I fetched him a glass of water. They were kept chained like that for several hours until they were finally taken to battalion headquarters. Each of them was busted one rank and had to forfeit pay for the first week of camp.

During our second summer camp at Virginia Beach in 1961 Captain Pavlansky asked me to organize a party at the end of the two-week period. I wanted to do something unusual so I went to the office of the Virginia Beach City Manager and asked if we could use a strip of city owned oceanfront property that adjoined the State Military Reservation.

Since the beach people appreciated having the Guard installation within their midst, he gave me an official permit. The day before the beach party I assigned a detail to go to various hotels and motels on the beach to post signs in prominent places inviting young women to join the party. The signs explained they could get transportation at certain pickup points.

We bought several dozen cases of beer, got appropriate food and rented a jukebox which we mounted on the back of a quarter-ton truck hooked to a generator. We recruited various unit members with sports cars, preferably convertibles, and the next evening a parade headed by the quarter-ton truck proceeded down Atlantic Avenue. We let the jukebox play at full volume as I sat in the truck with Motor Sergeant Charles McLeod and driver Benny Skinner. (Benny and I often laugh about this when I see him). Behind us I could see young women hopping into cars at various points along the way. People walking along the boardwalk stopped to stare at this strange procession. At one point the Virginia Beach police pulled alongside and I felt certain they were going to rain on our parade, but after a few moments they pulled off. I learned later that the National Guard had just finished a project to help repair the oceanfront after a hard storm had devastated it and the cops, thinking we were Guardsmen who had participated, didn't want to hurt our feelings.

But by the time we got to the beachfront where the party was to be held all hell was breaking loose and military police were everywhere. As the organizer of the event, I realized it was my head that would be on the chopping block so I told McLeod to slow down, jumped out of the truck and hid behind some nearby bushes. I stayed there about a half hour before the MP's finally pulled away.

When I reappeared on the beach, First Sergeant Brennan was furious. "Who in hell told you that you could parade down the main drag like that!" he exclaimed. I said as calmly as I could, "Nobody said we couldn't." After that the sun went down, people drank cold beer and ate and there was dancing on the beach. When I saw Captain Pavlansky the next morning he said not a word about the parade, but complimented me on putting together an excellent party.

One of my buddies in the Guard at that time was Robert Williams, who led a band called The Groovers. He and I managed to get a jeep and cruise up and down the oceanfront to while away the daytime hours. We could tell stories for hours about our military exploits. As could three of my latter day associates John Cole 'Root' Thomas, Lehmar Sullivan and William Bourne. As Williams and others will tell you, I sometimes carried a camera with no film in it and would pull up to a conference where Generals and other officers were planning maneuvers and started clicking away. Nobody ever asked why none of the pictures I took ever got published.

I still occasionally see fellow Guardsmen from those days, including Wally 'Mr. Fixit' Powell, Ed Allison, Wes Hall, Chip Reamy, John Cowan and Mike Martin. Mike worked full time for a while with our Guard unit and when I see him at the Elks we talk of some of the exploits of

First Sergeant Brennan and others.

From the time of the party I was designated in charge of troop morale. I may be the only person in military history to have sold cold beer to troops engaged in combat.

We had formed a club in the unit to which many would repair after a drill to have a beer or two and engage in some good-natured ribbing. During summer training periods, we were given the use of a quarter-ton truck and from the truck sold cold soft drinks and snacks to troops in the field taking breaks from training.

Several times in the midst of large-scale exercises we sent the truck out to the field in the dead of night to sell beer to the troops, although we had an ironclad policy that no beer would be sold until all training was through for the day. Even so, it was highly unorthodox, though quite profitable, for our club to provide such badly desired refreshments to parched soldiers who were bone tired, dust-laden and covered in sweat. The Poly-X Ray Truck (standing for PX truck) was an immense favorite with such troops.

Some time in the 1960s I got a call from a man named Phil Zako who lived in Baltimore. How he got my name I don't know, unless he called the Armory first and they had suggested he contact me. Zako was a prominent professional wrestling promoter in the Baltimore-Washington area.

Zako asked if our Guard Club would like to make some significant extra money and I told him we were certainly willing to talk about the prospect. Zako came down and took to lunch two of us, Jimmy Jones (who later became athletic director at Stafford High School) and me. He was a short rotund man with a big unlighted cigar perpetually dangling from the corner of his mouth. He explained that he was looking for a place to hold wrestling matches in the Fredericksburg area and the Armory was perfect. He wanted our club to sponsor the matches. He would pay all expenses, including whatever the wrestlers were owed, and we would get about thirty percent of the net.

We accepted the deal and Phil Zako was as good as his word. Wrestling is associated in the minds of most with that of a sleazy sport (if, indeed, it can be called a sport) and I have to admit that it certainly does not compare in class with the ballet or opera. But Zako told us from the outset that he did not want any of our club members bad mouthing his wrestling matches or hinting in any way that it was not legitimate. His words to me were, "You tell your folks this is a business. It pays me good money and it'll pay you good money. If you've got a business that works, you don't knock it."

I was amazed at the response we got to the wrestling matches that we sponsored. We had sell out after sell out and our club was making as much as $1,200 a night, a fortune in those days. We had one locker room that all the wrestlers shared, heroes and villains alike. We had over a period of time all the big name professional wrestlers on the East Coast. Argentina Rocca, Haystacks Calhoun, The Golden Terror, Gorilla Monsoon, Bruno Sammartino and many more, as well as midget wrestlers such as Sky Low Low and women such as Slave Girl Moolah. I got to know many of these folks as they sat quietly playing cards with each other in the locker room before it was their turn to climb into the ring and act out their roles while hundreds cheered or jeered. Often when the evening was over, men who had just given the impression they were going to kill each other would ride off together in their cars once Zako had paid them off in cold cash. These folks wrestled somewhere nearly every night of the week and had to be in outstanding physical shape and have acrobatic ability to do what they did, even if their wrestling routines might have been scripted. No matter where they wrestled, the feature event of the night was always billed as being for the heavyweight championship of the world.

One footnote. Gorilla Monsoon was advertised as a giant from Outer Mongolia who spoke no English but gave opponents no quarter. After he got too old to wrestle, he became a TV wrestling commentator, spoke as fluently as a Harvard graduate and was always on the side of the good guys.

Our club members lived lavishly while we were raking in money by the sponsorship of wrestling. We had many parties where food and drink flowed freely. I think some people remained in the Guard just to enjoy the advantages of belonging to the club. But the bonanza came to an end when a Washington TV station took weekly wrestling matches, the main promotional tool, off the air as being too undignified for their viewers.

At one summer camp at A.P. Hill a young man who could not attend camp with his own unit was assigned to us and became the jeep driver for First Sergeant Brennan who was known to use a bit of colorful language. I made friends with the man who was from Rocky Mount, Va. near Franklin County sometimes called the 'moonshine-capital of the world, and he told me that the First Sergeant used swear words he had never heard in his part of the state. The man was Virgil Goode who later became the youngest state Senator in Virginia history and now represents the

5th District of Virginia in Congress. Before Jiggs Brennan died, he always used to ask me how he was doing every time I saw him.

Why I stayed in the Guard I am not certain. When I first joined I had every intention of putting in my time and getting out. But I found to my surprise I enjoyed wearing the uniform and being part of a military unit. When we went from anti-aircraft to Armored Cavalry easy summer camps at Virginia Beach came to an end and we were sent to Camp Pickett near Blackstone. Virginia. By that time the commanding officer was Captain Alvin Bandy, a man totally dedicated to the best performance he could get out of his unit. He was a superb leader of men and a man of great integrity who served with distinction on both the Stafford School Board and the county Board of Supervisors. I considered it an honor to serve with him and we became friends for life. His contributions to his nation, state and region have been immeasurable.

Bandy was fearless. Once he told a tank driver to drive the tank toward him until he gave the signal to stop. The driver did as instructed and Bandy gave the stop sign only when the tank was bearing down on him and only a few yards away. The tank stopped just inches from Bandy and those watching the episode, including myself, got white knuckles from the experience.

When the era of Vietnam dawned, the Guard changed immensely. Young men were being drafted and put into infantry units destined for duty in that far-off country in a war that increasingly divided the nation. Soon we had a long waiting list for membership in the Guard. More than once some politician approached me or Chili Cox, the full time guard technician, and asked if there was some way to move a particular young man up on the list (probably the son of a prominent supporter). We always told them nothing could be done since the practice was against the law. Some administrators in other Guard and reserve units later were charged with taking bribes to get young men who wanted to avoid being drafted into the Army into the reserve.

Don't get me wrong. There was absolutely nothing wrong with what people such as Dan Quayle did in joining the National Guard and serving their time there. What was wrong was that President Lyndon Johnson never had the guts to call the National Guard and the Reserve to active duty during the Vietnam War. He feared the political consequences but it is possible that had acted the war would have ended sooner.

By no means was I hoping to be called up. In 1961, shortly after President Kennedy took over, the Berlin crisis developed and while our unit was away at camp, our name was listed in the Army Times as one of those the federal government would likely summons to active duty. Since I had been married only a short time the notion didn't set well with me, but I was prepared to go if the call came. As it turned out by the time we got back to Fredericksburg the government had decided to call up instead the other Fredericksburg unit, a combat engineer company, which subsequently spent its nine months of active duty at Fort Belvoir.

Captain Bandy made the troops nervous when he addressed them and said he was hoping against hope that the government would put our unit on active duty and let us fight the Viet Cong. I must say frankly that not many in the unit shared that sentiment. Most had very mixed emotions about the Vietnam War. It seemed stupid not to win a war we obviously could have won in a few weeks if we had let the military have its way. Instead, American soldiers were asked to fight with one hand behind their backs while protesters at home, such as Bill Clinton, were rallying against their own country and often burning the American flag. Bill Clinton (or Hanoi Jane) could never live long enough to command an ounce of respect from me. Like him, I did not want to go to Vietnam and am thankful I never did, but neither did I turn my back on my own country. I would not walk across the street to shake Clinton's hand and if BroomHillary is ever elected President and I am living, I will probably have to leave the country.

Hal James, who succeeded Alvin Bandy as commander of the Guard unit, was did an excellent job and later went on to make the Army his career. He and his wife, Raynor, are friends.

European Tours

In the late 1970s at the invitation of General John Castles, the Adjutant General of the Virginia National Guard, I transferred from the Fredericksburg Guard to the 2120th Public Affairs Detachment in Richmond. The 2120th had about 14 members, most of them connected with journalism. The unit's duty was to publicize the Virginia Guard, including publishing a quarterly magazine.

I transferred over because the 2120th was being sent to Germany to help publicize annual Reforger exercises and for other duties. We were stationed at a place near Fliegerhorst Kaserne near Hanau and were billeted in a German gasthaus operated by a man named Bruno Techner who during World War II had been part of a glider unit and had been captured and spent six months as an American prisoner of war in the states.

Bruno was an outstanding cook and I loved everything about German food and German drink, including beer, schnapps and the fine wine. A photographer and I were assigned a regular Army driver and we set off on our own to watch the Reforger exercises sponsored by the NATO countries. Tanks, infantry carriers, huge trucks and other military equipment rumbled through the streets of towns and villages, sometimes hitting parked cars or running into buildings. And out in the countryside they would manage to tear up crops planted in fields by German farmers. Coming behind the troops were administrative personnel with checkbooks who were authorized to make settlements with Germans for damages caused by the exercises. Try to imagine war games being run through the heart of the city of Fredericksburg with tanks and trucks racing down the streets in mock combat and you may get some notion of what the Germans endured. They did it because they wanted NATO protection against the Soviet Union and there was so little space in Germany and other western European countries to conduct large scale military maneuvers. I was pleased that a couple of my dispatches got printed in Stars and Stripes, including one dealing with an incredible sea of mud that mired down the troops.

Once the exercises were over, General Alexander Haig, wearing four stars, came to Fleigerhorst for a briefing. Haig, who had gone back to active duty as NATO commander following his stint as chief of staff to Richard Nixon and his crucial role in the waning days of the Watergate crisis, was friendly and effusive. I saw him years later at a political rally in Culpeper, Virginia and told him how amazed I'd been at the Reforger exercises and he chuckled and said, "We'd never had been able to get away with that over here."

I spent two more overseas tours with the 2120th, one in Wales and another in Germany for another Reforger, and those years were a fitting climax to my National Guard Service. I did come up with what became the unofficial motto of the unit (a MASH type outfit if there ever was one.) It went:

'The Fighting 2120th. We will go anywhere, face any foe, make any sacrifice to accomplish the mission . . . so long as it involves no personal inconvenience.'

It was with mixed feelings that I left the Guard after 24 plus years. I had never figured on staying anywhere near that long and I had gotten tremendously attached to the Guard and its role in the national defense. But I was getting long in the tooth and it was harder and harder to find time to do all the drilling that the modern Guard required. So I left quietly, storing my uniforms away carefully just in case I might need them again. I haven't and these days I don't know where the uniforms are.

In the early 1980s Virginia Governor Charles Robb appointed me as the first enlisted member to serve on the Virginia Board of Military Affairs. Once my terms expired, Governor George Allen named me to the Virginia Military Advisory Council. And while my name will never go down in military annals, the Guard gave me the realization of how essential to our freedom are the sacrifices made by the brave men and women who comprise our military forces.

CHAPTER TEN

Richard Feldman, Prophet

When I went to work full-time for the local paper in the late 1950s (I had worked there part-time during college), its daily circulation was less than 10,000 and life in the city and environs was still bucolic.

There wasn't much deadline pressure for a young reporter. I could get lunch at Cotton Lewis's drug store next door or fetch a couple of pool room chili dogs and return to the office to finish a story for that day's edition.

One of the first duties assigned me was that of farm page editor, a task given to the most junior member of the news staff. I couldn't tell an eggplant from a squash, but, remarkably enough, I found myself enjoying the job. I got to spend lazy afternoons riding far out to some farm in Spotsylvania or Stafford to do a story and coming away with not only my notes but a bagful of corn or cucumbers. I'm afraid I didn't learn much about farming except that farming is a heck of a tough way to make a living because you're always at the mercy of so many things you can't control. Wind, rain, droughts, even the interest you have to pay on loans to buy essential machinery.

You could drive along Route 3 west, a two-lane cow-path, all the way to Culpeper and meet practically no traffic while you were passing mainly scrub farmland on both sides of the road. When a man named Richard Feldman, who lived on the road, warned the Spotsylvania Board of Supervisors in the 1960s that they needed to properly zone Route 3 so that future growth would be controlled and orderly, I felt here was someone ready for the funny farm. Wherever you are, Mr. Feldman, I humbly salute your prescience. Those who bought the scrubland I snickered at got rich putting in malls and subdivisions.

When I first went to the paper, it hadn't been many years since the Fredericksburg Bypass caused consternation among downtown merchants who felt it would wreck their businesses. Before then, all traffic going north and south on U.S. 1 had come through town on Princess Anne Street. Imagine if today all north and south traffic had to come smack through the city. Traffic would probably be backed up north to

Baltimore and south to North Carolina.

The Civil War had been over less than a century and there were still many folks living in the area who had grandparents who fought in that war or witnessed parts of it, including the great battles of Fredericksburg, Spotsylvania, Chancellorsville and the Wilderness. I regret that I didn't seek them out and jot down all the memories passed to them about those terrible times of the 1860s. Like most folks, my appreciation for history has grown much deeper with time.

The first feature story I did for the paper was about an elderly lady who was famous for making homemade spirits that she sold clandestinely. I was fascinated by her tale of meeting Frank and Jesse James when she was a young girl (in Missouri, I think) and having the famous outlaws pat her affectionately on the head.

City Editor Jim McKnight insisted that I rewrite the story not once but twice even though I felt the first draft was perfectly good. But looking back, despite the fact I've always had some antipathy toward editors, he taught me a lot about the importance of compact writing.

McKnight always had on his desk a tall, dreaded pile of paper that he would pass around with glee to junior reporters. In this fashion I believe I rewrote every one of the press releases the Army sent out about Arnold Delosh's promotions from buck private to bird colonel. McKnight never let you forget we were a local paper and we specialized in local news.

Fredericksburg was the region's hub. On Main Street were the big stores such as F.W. Woolworth, J.J. Newberry, W.T. Grant, Montgomery Ward and J.C. Penney, Bell Brothers and E.C. Ninde furniture stores, Young Men's Shop and Washington Woolen Mills clothing stores as well as People, Bond, Goolrick's and Morton's drug stores and the two movie theaters. (As I recall J.C. Penney had a strange system of tubes on wires that transmitted orders and money from downstairs to upstairs. To this day, I have no idea what it was all about). In the city were popular restaurants such as The Southern, the Mayflower, The Blue Mirror and Gulla's, and fast food places like Eddie Mack's, Scotty's, the R & S, Busy Bee and the world famous poolroom with its stomach-eating chili dogs. If there was anything in Stafford or Spotsylvania except farms and country roads I can't remember it. The only shopping you could do in those counties was at stores whose centerpieces were cracker barrels.

The paper was located in cramped quarters in the 300 block of William Street and there was a feed store just across the street. The place was incredibly noisy, particularly when the ancient press started its run in mid-afternoon. In the composing room linotype machines operated by people such as Harold Ballard (Colonel Ballard as we called him) and Bernard Jackson set type into hot lead. One day I had more type for the farm page than the composing room boss Clarence "Rats" Lewis could squeeze onto the page. He asked me what I wanted to take out and without a word I picked up several handfuls of type without trying to read their content and threw them into what was called a hellbox. Rats looked at me with a cigarette dangling from his lips, shook his head and said, "Boy, you oughta find another line of work."

Another day I was in the newsroom when someone came in and said that famous movie actor Tyrone Power and his wife movie star Linda Christian were having lunch at the Southern Restaurant on Princess Anne Street. City Editor McKnight asked star reporter Frank Trippett to go over to interview them, but Trippett allowed as how he didn't give a damn about either of them so I was sent over instead. Power, who had been stationed at Quantico once, had dropped back by there for old time sake and then had come to Fredericksburg. He allowed me to interview him about ten minutes once they'd finished lunch. I haven't got the slightest recollection of anything I asked him.

Every afternoon the paper would post the latest New York Stock Exchange prices on the building's window and people would drop by to look at it. One of the regulars was Dr. John E. Cole, a physician who brought me into the world. Dr. Cole would point to various stocks and give me tips. One day he looked at a stock called General Foods selling for about seven dollars a share and whispered confidentially, "That's a good one because everybody eats but the dead man." I'm sure that if I'd followed his advice and put a modest amount of money into the market I would be quite well off today. Trouble is I'd just gotten married and could barely pay the rent.

On election nights the paper's newsroom became a gathering place for those who wanted to keep up with the results. Some of those who dropped by would bring flasks of whiskey with them to sip on while waiting to see if their candidates had won or lost. And every election night Ikey Middleton, the veteran pressroom foreman, would call the newest member of the staff and ask in a disguised voice how Mr. Warren Harding was doing in the election. When the young reporter complained that he had some nut on the line, others around him would burst into laughter.

The late 1950s and 1960s were a time of turmoil in many southern localities because of a number of federal court rulings outlawing segregated schools and public facilities. Looking back I'm amazed at how little trouble occurred in Fredericksburg during that time. Though local society was highly segregated, there had always been a feeling of mutual respect between the races, perhaps going back to the terrible and shared deprivations of the Civil War.

There were some incidents, but for the most part desegregation was accomplished quiet peacefully here. City Council had wisely formed a Biracial Commission to promote such an outcome and I think its first chairman was a black man named Clarence Todd who was not only intelligent and articulate, but a born leader. He did as much or more than anyone to promote racial harmony and if they haven't already named a bridge, street or building in his honor, it should be done.

A young black minister named Lawrence Davies, who served for years on City Council and then as Mayor, should be credited with averting trouble within the city. In some Virginia localities, most notably Prince Edward County, public schools were actually shut down rather than allow their desegregation. But the Rev. Davies was always a voice of reason and a bridge between the races.

I think there may have been a 'sit in' at the lunch counter of the F.W. Woolworth store downtown since that counter was forbidden to blacks, but I don't recall much about it except that it occurred peacefully. There were some incidents in adjoining counties relative to school desegregation but nothing of a serious nature.

There was little crime in our area unlike the present when we are awash in it. I was shocked, like everyone else, when the Jackson family abduction happened in Louisa on a winter's night in 1959 touching off the biggest police manhunt in Virginia history.

Carroll Jackson, his wife, Mildred, and their two young daughters were missing. When the bodies of the father and one daughter were found buried beneath trash near a lonely road on what was then called Cherry Hill Hatchery Road but is now Bragg Road and part of Central Park, there was a run on gun stores as people tried to arm themselves against danger. Later the bodies of Mrs. Jackson and another daughter were found in Maryland.

When I returned from military duty at Fort Knox, I helped Paul Muse cover the trial of accused Jackson family killer Melvin Davis Rees in Baltimore. The trial, presided over by an incompetent federal judge, turned into a circus because of the judge's refusal to keep defense attorneys under control. Rees got a life sentence in Maryland and the death penalty after a two weeks trial in Spotsylvania where Circuit Judge John Butzner Jr. ran a tight ship and later became a federal judge. The prosecutors were Commonwealth's Atty. Stokely Coleman and special assistant William Scaife and the defense attorneys were Joseph Savage Jr. and Alfred Garnett.

I was in the courtroom every day and will never forget how cool and detached Rees, a former jazz musician who had lived in Hyattsville, Maryland, appeared. He was undoubtedly guilty of many heinous crimes and yet his cold hard eyes never showed the slightest hint of remorse. It was my first glimpse of a psychopathic serial killer. His grief-stricken parents seemed nice hard working people who simply could not believe, despite the overwhelming evidence, that their son could have done such despicable acts. They would have little to do with the press but I often talked with the parents of Carroll and Mildred Jackson.

Rees never kept his appointed date with the electric chair. He was judged insane and spent the rest of his life behind bars until he died in 1995. I often thought of writing a book about the fascinating case which had every sensational element from strip teasers to psychics, but it was another one of those things I never got around to doing.

The Jackson murders, combined with the brutal killings of two Fredericksburg police officers behind a shopping center in 1964, seemed to bring a new element into life here. The slain officers, Frank Mines and Roy Wright, were both friends and years later I became the first reporter ever allowed to sit in the dining room of the state penitentiary and have lunch with a prisoner. The prisoner was Bruce Leikett, a habitual criminal, who had been convicted of killing the officers. He never admitted his guilt and yet he let me know very subtly that he was the killer and that he had become a changed man and was remorseful. He even showed me some of his atrocious poetry. I left with the feeling that he was a person, like Rees, incapable of remorse.

I could not know it then, although Richard Feldman apparently did, but such events and the opening of Interstate 95 in the mid 1960s foreshadowed the end of tranquility in an area that had, by and large, remained tranquil and poor since Lee's surrender at Appomattox in 1865. The age of the superhighway and explosive development had dawned and, for better or worse, the era of my birth in 1935 would never return.

CHAPTER ELEVEN

Lots of Copy

One thing I learned quickly as a young reporter is that you were expected to do just about everything with the exception of sweeping the floors. For instance, Thursdays were 'double run' days and everybody, including the editors, gathered in the front office to 'slip' papers, that is put one section inside another since it had to be done manually.

There were just a couple of editors, four or five reporters and a sports editor and a lot of news space to be filled. You were expected to produce two or three stories a day that could be published.

I'd like to have a dollar for every obituary, church notice and other such material I churned out during my first few years. I had it down to a science and could have written copy of that kind with my eyes blindfolded.

Churches have something called homecoming every spring and they all pretty much follow the same format. There are guest preachers and Sunday morning services are followed by lunch on the lawn. Obituaries are not difficult to do, but it is essential that they be accurate in every detail because it is a time of family stress when relatives of the deceased get easily upset if anything is amiss. I believe that I once attempted to bury the lately departed in the wrong cemetery and everybody seemed to be mad at me except the poor fellow who was to be buried.

The apprenticeship I served under the tutelage of City Editor Jim McKnight was valuable to an appreciation of the diverse interests of the readers we serve. Too often these days kids graduate from journalism school and don't want to wait more than a week before they are given top notch investigative reporting assignments so they can be nominated for Pulitzer prizes before any dust gathers on their J-school degrees.

In the early 1960s I covered the Spotsylvania Board of Supervisors and they were a good group of people that included Solon Marshall, Buford Carr, Andrew Seay, Wilbur Wallace and one or two more. They did their jobs diligently, though at that time Spotsylvania was so sparsely settled that oncoming cars I encountered on Route 208 on my way to night meetings at the courthouse were practically non-existent and the board's agenda might include such hot items as whether to replace the screen doors on the county jail or how to respond to Farmer Brown's complaint about mud collecting holes in the dirt road that ran past his farm. I often found myself returning home late at night from meetings and wondering how on earth they had managed to spend hours and hours talking about largely inconsequential matters. This was before I discovered that politicians of any kind, no matter whether they are debating screen doors or nuclear weapons, will always far exceed the time any otherwise rational person might devote to the discussion of a particular subject. If you don't believe me, just watch C-Span some time and see how it works.

Procrastination

I covered City Council a while during the 1960s and so long as I have been aware of its existence our Council has turned procrastination into a fine art. It took the city fathers twenty years to finally decide not to build a firehouse in the city park and if all the studies of subjects commissioned by various Councils were taken off the shelves where they have gathered dust and the dust were collected, it might be enough to fill the Grand Canyon.

Yet there is something to be said for the way the City Council has operated. Being one who believes, like Jefferson, that government is best which governs least, I think he, perhaps, had City Council in mind since it seems from generation to generation to hardly govern at all.

Nevertheless, there were many members of Council during my time who were dedicated servants. Sam Perry, Arthur Smith, Tuffy Hicks, Walter Lowry, Bill Greenup, Mac Cowan, Sidney Armstrong, Lawrence Davies, Ed Cann, Joe Rowe, Eldred Lee, Stacy Lloyd, George Van Sant, Gordon Shelton, Ferris Belman, Weldon and Ambrose Bailey, Roger Moure, Jimmy Ventura, Charles McDaniel and his son, Charles G., and more. From time to time, particularly, since leaving the paper, I have been asked to run for Council but having watched it from the press table I always let it be known that I have no intention of doing so. And if pressed further by anyone, I tell them that I will commission a twenty-year study to help reach a final decision and then perhaps commission another 20-year study.

Highway Jerks

I try to be a cautious driver and one of the major reasons is that I was assigned early on to the police beat. In those days reporters were required to take photographs and we used the old Speed Graphic cameras that weighed approximately as much as an M-48 tank. I think I managed to mess up more pictures than actually came out right and the whole experience turned me so much against photography that I seldom again used a camera. Photographs take up valuable space that could be used to print words.

Covering the beat, I listened to the police radio and went to the scene of fires and car crashes. U.S. Route 1, before I-95 finally opened, was a hellhole with far too much traffic and four lanes undivided. There were frequent horrible accidents, particularly on weekends, and I saw more than my share of dead bodies and maimed people. I can recall watching as they fished six victims from a crash out of Coleman's Mill Pond near Thornburg, three of them young children. Sometimes State Police would ask me to go to funeral homes and take pictures of the corpses and I did. It did not upset me then, but I know that I would not only never want to do it again, but could never do it again.

I think of those sad sights every time some jerk, and there are legions of them, drives recklessly down a highway weaving in and out of traffic and endangering lives of innocent people just to save a few minutes when from the looks of these people they probably never have anywhere to go that could be really considered important. Most of these morons who run red lights and far exceed the speed limit are probably rushing to get to the 24-hour Laundromat before it closes.

Fredericksburg's premier funeral home was operated by the Thompson family on Princess Anne Street where a juvenile court facility now stands. (The other was Elkins Funeral Home in the 600 block Caroline Street.) I remember Mr. Wheeler Thompson, the owner, coming into the office one Monday morning with a fistful of obituary material and remarking, "Well, we've got 'em stacked up to the ceiling today." He had been called to collect ten bodies over the weekend.

On November 22, 1963, a Friday, I was at the office of the Spotsylvania county administrator when someone called and told me to return to the office. I learned on the way in that President John Kennedy had been shot in Dallas, Texas although nobody knew yet how serious it was. By the time I got back to the office the official announcement was made that Kennedy was dead and I helped Paul Muse rush out to Main Street and get a man-on-the-street reaction story that appeared in an edition of the paper published a few hours later. That weekend, like everyone else, I stayed glued to the television set all weekend and saw on live TV the shooting by Lee Harvey Oswald by a sleazy strip club operator named Jack Ruby (Jack Rubenstein) who had connections to the mob. I believe to this day that Osward did not act alone and there was a conspiracy involved.

In the 1960s Judge John Butzner Jr. called and asked me to go with him to a place where a special announcement would be made. We traveled to Chatham, the home of John Lee Pratt overlooking the Rappahannock River. (Brother of Dr. Frank Pratt who made enormous contributions to the city). Pratt, one of the original founders of General Motors, was one of the wealthiest men in the nation and had originally come from King George. He had his servant fix bourbon and water for the Judge and me and then said he was donating land for a park to serve Stafford and Fredericksburg. This became St. Clair Brooks Park, named after an old and dear friend of Pratt's, and as time went on he donated even more land that became Pratt Park.

Pratt, dressed in wrinkled old clothes, looked anything but one of the wealthiest men in America. With the Judge driving, we rode out to inspect the land he was donating and it was magnificent. At one point Pratt took a pocketknife from his pocket and sharpened a pencil to write something he wanted to go along with the story. He told me he never failed to carry a pencil, paper and a sharpener just in case an idea popped into his head. Years later I wrote his obituary and it took up nearly a whole news page, the longest I had ever done. In a magnificent gesture Pratt left his historic Chatham Manor to the National Park Service and it is used as area park service headquarters today. Much of his fortune also went to various worthwhile causes as he did not believe large fortunes should be passed along from one generation to another. Pratt often walked across the Chatham Bridge and sometimes motorists feeling sorry for the old gent would stop to offer him a ride. Pratt would thank them but politely decline.

When I went to work for the paper part-time in the early 1950s I met a man who was destined to play a leading role in changing the face of the area.

His name was Carl D. Silver and he owned a car dealership on Princess Anne Street. The son of a Polish immigrant, Max Silver, who was a scrap metals dealer, Carl had come to Fredericksburg from Tappahannock after European combat Army service in World War II (he was wounded and earned a Purple Heart) and quickly made a name for himself. As he recalled later, it was easy to sell cars in those days because of the pent-up demand. The hard part was getting cars to sell.

Silver was a huge success in the car business and when he decided to leave it in the 1960s to pursue other interests people were puzzled. He went overnight from having 60 to 70 people working for him to a one-man operation.

But he knew what he wanted and that was to develop real estate. He bought many tracts of property and put together shopping centers. Today he is the best known developer in the region and his Central Park project at the Sheraton property on Route 3 west is the crown jewel of his development career, although a current ongoing project called Celebrate Virginia conceived by his son, Larry, (contrary to what many believe, Carl Silver does not have a single dollar invested in Celebrate Virginia) may well be the instrument that finally makes the historic Fredericksburg region an authentic tourist destination instead of a mere stopover.

I had the pleasure of writing, along with Larry Silver, a biography of Carl Silver some years ago and it was an enjoyable experience. He is an aggressive businessman who is the master of the deal and yet he is also a person who has given huge amounts of money to worthwhile causes and who never forgets a friend or former employee. He will be remembered long after he is gone for his many accomplishments. Some will argue that his developments helped destroy the quality of life in a once tranquil region, but that tranquility was doomed from the moment the Interstate road sliced through the region.

I have worked with Larry Silver on several projects and he is both a fine human being and an astute businessman. He learned much from his father, but Larry made it on his own. While in high school, he was running his own business and became the most successful homebuilder in the area. Growth was inevitable and those who might be critical of his role in it should accept the fact that in our geographical location its demise of our rural nature was preordained. Larry divides his time these days between homes in Northern Virginia in Florida. He and his wife,

Deborah, have two children, Spencer, now 6, and Madison, 5. (Madison is a great Virginia name). And Silvers Companies does business now not just in Virginia and Florida but all across the nation.

Maniac Editor

As noted, I covered the police beat for a few years in the 1960s, though in those days the incidence of crime was far less than today. But there were a few juicy murder cases and I found a way to help supplement my meager income by writing stories about the cases for a detective magazine located in New York.

The editor I dealt with was a complete maniac who spoke like a gangster. There was an ironclad formula in writing stories for such magazines and probably still is. First, there had to be a murder involved and someone must have been at least indicted by a grand jury in connection with the murder. The police investigating the crime must always be made to look like sheer geniuses even if they were hopelessly incompetent. The reason for this was that it made it much easier for such sleazy publications to get police cooperation.

And finally there had to be a female involved either as victim, kin to the victim or accused and no matter if this female was ugly as sin, she must be described as sexy and voluptuous in order to titillate the reader. I wrote under the pen name Caldwell French, probably had six or seven such stories published and was paid around $250 per story, an astronomical sum in those days for a young reporter. When I was pulled off the police beat and put on politics, my Caldwell French days were behind me along with the extra money. But it was just as well since I had developed a habit of writing fiction when it came to describing the beauties of some plug ugly women involved in sensational cases.

Hotsy

At the old Star building on William street a local businessman named Robert "Hotsy" Moore would drop by each day, help himself to the newsroom coffee and make himself at home in the chair at the editor's desk.

Hotsy, who was then the owner of the Young-Sweetser feed business (housed in a building still the tallest in town) mumbled his words and, even worse, started all his conversation in mid-sentence. He would say something like . . . "not gonna be able to bring the damn band, very disappointing."

I don't think I ever understood much of what Hotsy was saying, but he was a genuine character with a real talent for organizing. He was prominent in the American Legion and there was a big Memorial Day parade every year and Hotsy was instrumental in putting it together. He had an amazing ability to get top flight marching bands to participate and on one occasion he got former heavyweight champion Rocky Marciano to visit and brought Marciano by the office where I had a chance to talk with him. In this age of blandness, we could use more colorful people like Hotsy even if I could never understand what he was saying.

Hotsy's wife, Mary Frances Moore, was a wonderful outgoing person. Later she married Freeman Funk and I think that took place once he left as Fredericksburg's city manager.

Reporting News

In the 1960s journalism wasn't the glamorous profession it is now thanks to Watergate (and more about that in later chapters) and reporters were in demand by newspapers. I had gotten several offers and was on the verge of taking one with the Richmond News-Leader when Paul Muse, our paper's political reporter, announced he was leaving to become a partner in a weekly paper in Prince William County.

I was greatly interested in politics and the editor agreed to let me replace Muse and I told the Richmond paper that I had decided to stay put. That started a twenty-two year journey of covering Virginia politics and the General Assembly and in ways changed the course of my life. I had always figured after I'd gotten a little experience at the local paper, I would try to move up the ladder to a bigger paper.

But though the local paper's circulation was hovering around 12,000 and it's advertising revenues weren't that great, the management wanted to put out a quality product and I was told I could spend much of my time on political coverage. The paper moved from The Star Building to a new building at 616 Amelia Street in 1965. In 1960 in cramped quarters upstairs Radio Station WFLS AM had started operations with Bill Poole as manager. Bill stayed on many years, was elected to the Virginia Broadcasters Hall of fame and married Betty Burke (Janney) Poole. WFLS FM was started in 1962 and is now the area's most popular radio station. During my growing up years the only station serving the area was WFVA-

AM then located on Princess Anne Street in the city.

I helped Muse cover a primary election in 1966 that stunned political insiders around the nation. Fredericksburg attorney George Rawlings challenged the legendary Congressman from the 8th District Judge Howard Smith, one of the most powerful men in Washington. He was so powerful that as chairman of the House Rules Committee he had thwarted the will of President Kennedy on civil rights legislation and was fighting President Lyndon Johnson tooth and nail on the even broader civil rights package that Johnson proposed.

Over the years the taciturn Smith had been scarcely visible to his constituents in his district that included Fredericksburg and other parts of the area. Every two years he would show up at the district convention in Fredericksburg's Community Center, briefly accept renomination and then go home. And though he did not particularly like the press, he was always kind enough to grant me a brief interview.

But Rawlings wanted a primary and Smith agreed. Few gave the challenger a chance but he ran a stealth campaign by working behind the scenes to galvanize his kind of Democrats, Liberals, Blacks and a number of moderates fed up with Smith, while the Smith forces were complacent.

On Election Day, Rawlings won and the conservative forces that ruled the Virginia Democratic Party were stunned. Republicans had nominated an obscure Northern Virginia lawyer named William Scott and the conservative Democrats, including Governor Mills Godwin, refused to support Rawlings and effectively threw the election to Scott. The defeat of Smith was a clear indication that the old conservative Democrat machine put together in Virginia by Harry Byrd Sr. was on its last legs.

It was during this campaign that I first had a chance to talk with Mills Godwin, though I had occasion later to converse with him often. He had an encyclopedic knowledge of Virginia history and recalled that C. O'Conor Goolrick of Fredericksburg (my uncle) while in the State Senate in the early 1920s had disagreed with Harry Byrd over how state roads should be funded. Byrd wanted pay as you go while my uncle felt bonds should be issued in order to get good roads faster. Pay as you go finally prevailed, Godwin recalled, though by that time as Governor he had come to believe that state borrowing wasn't the great evil that Byrd made it out to be. Byrd's son, Harry Jr., who served in the State Senate and U.S.Senate was a staunch fiscal conservative.

I have an autographed copy of his book 'Defying the Odds' describing the 1970 campaign in which he ran as an independent for the Senate and won, and did so again in 1976. I still correspond with the former Senator from time to time at his Winchester office and recall him telling me the story of Winston Churchill's stay in the Governor's Mansion in 1929 when Byrd's father was Governor. When Churchill was served Virginia ham, Mrs. Byrd asked if he wanted mustard and when he said yes, young Harry had to quickly run across the street and fetch some since there was none in the house. He also recalled that one of the men in Churchill's party, someone with a royal title, ran up an enormous phone bill calling his girlfriend in California.

On that first occasion Godwin spoke of what a charming town Fredericksburg was and how lovely were the surrounding counties, but predicted because of Interstate 95 the area was certain to grow and while this in many respects was desirable, he hoped it would still retain the charm with which it had been blessed for so many years.

CHAPTER TWELVE

Nazis in the Newsroom

Around 1966 or 1967 Nazis began to appear in the newsroom of the local paper.

It was a startling sight. Men dressed in brown military uniforms with black and red armbands bearing the swastika symbol. The black boots were highly polished.

Fredericksburg was an unlikely place to encounter swaggering men who looked like something out of the old 1930s and 40s newsreels showing adoring crowds of Germans cheering as columns of Nazi storm troopers passed in review.

There were four of them, including George Lincoln Rockwell, Fuhrer of the American Nazi Party.

Though the party consisted of only a few hundred misguided souls, Rockwell had become well known with his outrageous antics. He and his band of followers openly proclaimed their allegiance to the racist policies of Adolph Hitler and held rallies to denounce Negroes, Jews and most non-Aryans (including one rally in Fredericksburg's city park). Rockwell often brandished rifles and pistols at such rallies and urged those attending to load up on weapons and ammunition for what he predicted would be a coming war with Negroes and liberals.

His appearances at several college campuses had caused near riots and he had ran for Governor of Virginia, getting about three percent of the vote.

Headquarters of the American Nazi Party was in a tightly guarded private residence in Arlington, Virginia, but a decision had been made to locate the party's printing plant in rural Spotsylvania County. Thus it came to pass that Rockwell and some of his Nazi security detachment dropped by the paper.

Rockwell was a physically imposing man, tall and dark-haired. He had won medals during combat service in Korea and attended Brown University before going on his Nazi kick. He came from a good family but now devoted his life to spreading Nazi racial hatred in the land.

Though when speaking at rallies Rockwell's style was a frenzied one filled with vitriolic speech, he was much more subdued the first time I spoke with him. He said that while the party's philosophical base was an intellectual one that rested on high moral standards and racial purity, it required an appeal to raw emotions to stir the masses.

It seems almost unreal now that I sat in the heart of Fredericksburg talking to people in Nazi uniforms who actually felt that Hitler, one of the most despicable men in history, should be America's role model.

A number of stories I wrote on Rockwell and his followers were published and, Rockwell sent me a note saying we were one of the few papers in the country willing to print things as he actually said them. I was invited to attend a swearing in of storm troopers at the Spotsylvania plant and I witnessed a bizarre ceremony that included crossing of swords and burning of a cross.

Among the people I met that evening was Frank Drager who said he had been a petty criminal before changing his life by joining the American Nazi Party. Drager later ran for sheriff of Spotsylvania County, but got few votes.

I also met a man who called himself John Patler but whose real name was something like John Patsalolous. He was a gifted artist whose savage depictions of Negroes and Jews appeared in various party publications.

I got to know many of those close to Rockwell. Their philosophy was totally abhorrent, yet there was no way the paper could ignore the presence in the region of people who paraded around in Nazi uniforms.

One day word came that Rockwell had been assassinated in Arlington. The astonishing news was that John Patler, who had once worshiped Rockwell, had lurked on the roof of a building and shot Rockwell, killing him instantly. It developed that Patler had become disillusioned with Rockwell and the evil philosophy he preached and decided he must put an end to it.

I drove to Arlington party headquarters where a number of reporters were waiting outside a gate that lead to the private home. Since the others had been denied admission, I assumed I would be too, but one of the guards spotted me and said, "Hey John, come on in."

I felt embarrassed walking past the gate, fearing the other reporters would misunderstand. They let me in because for the past year and a half I had been the reporter they most often dealt with.

The Nazis tried to bury Rockwell in a National Cemetery at Culpeper but a huge brouhaha ensued and federal officials used troops to block the burial. After a tense day recorded for broadcast on national television by Daniel Schorr of CBS and others, the Nazis gave up and decided to have their fallen leader cremated. I won a national award for my account of the non-funeral. Patler was given time in prison but was paroled after a few years. Without Rockwell the Nazis, who had never amounted to much, withered and died. Rockwell had given me an autographed copy of his book, "White Power," but I had disposed of it quickly.

If there is anything at all positive I can say about the whole affair it is that, despite criticism, the paper carried through on its obligation to report the news and defend the right of free speech even if that speech is sometimes deplorable and hateful.

Expense Account Living

I have no complaints about my years at The Free Lance Star. I felt at home there and resisted offers to go elsewhere. Once former reporter Frank Trippett, who was then with Newsweek, arranged an interview for me with someone from that magazine whose name I cannot recall. When I expressed interest in political reporting, he said nothing was open on that front but there was a vacancy in the Hollywood entertainment bureau. And since I seldom watched any movie made after 1960, I was not at all interested.

During nearly twenty years of political and legislative reporting when I spent most of the winter in hotel rooms in Richmond, I lived well.

I did not always agree with the judgment of the paper's editors—in fact, I frequently disagreed, but I have to say they weren't cheapskates. Not once that I recall did anyone question any expense account item.

Not that I padded the account because I never did. But as time passed I decided since I had to be out of town and away from home, I might as well live decently.

Once I drove my car to Newport News Airport to meet Senator John Warner on a campaign excursion. I flew with Warner to various events and then on our return home for some reason the plane landed in Norfolk. My problem was how to get from the Norfolk Airport to the Newport News Airport where my car was parked.

There were various possibilities but all of them involved renting a car for a brief trip in rush hour traffic and I was anxious to make a quick start home. I inquired with a charter plane company how much they'd charge me to fly to the Newport News Airport. The answer was around $135.

I mulled it over and finally said okay. The plane took off and was barely aloft when it started to land. I probably spent less than five minutes in the air, but the bill for the flight was approved with no questions asked.

The newspaper had once been partially owned by my uncle C' O'Conor Goolrick and others and was finally sold to Josiah P. Rowe Jr. Rowe died suddenly in September, 1949

Charles Rowe, the older of two brothers, had completed two years of law school at Washington & Lee at the time, having served in the Navy as an officer during World War II.

His younger brother, Josiah III, who served two years in the Army as an enlisted man and later became Mayor of Fredericksburg, was someone who had an incredible ability to get things done. He knew how to operate every piece of machinery in the building and even in these highly specialized computerized times probably still does. Joe's wife, the former Anne Wilson, and I were high school classmates, graduating in 1953 from James Monroe. In 1952 we had a school mock election and Anne was chairman for Democrat Adlai Stevenson and I was chairman for Dwight Eisenhower. When we had a debate, I packed the audience with students who would ask loaded (and I think now unfair)) questions such as what Presidents were in office when all the wars started that century. Eisenhower won the mock election but not because of any particular thing I did.

The arrangement was that Charles would take care of the editorial end of the operation and Joe would take care of the mechanical process and to a large degree the business end. Both helped supervise the advertising department.

Over the years a philosophical chasm developed between the brothers concerning political and social issues. Joe was a conservative and never changed, but Charles evolved into somewhat of a liberal on some issues. He rose from a small town paper editor to become President of the Associated Press Managing Editors Association and hobnobbed with editors from across the nation.

Charles went on to become a Captain in the Naval Reserve. In 1970

He had the chance to introduce Admiral John S. McCain Jr. (father of Senator John McCain and son of the first Admiral John McCain who served in World War II) to a meeting of the Associated Press Managing Editors convention in Honolulu. Admiral McCain II, who was at the time CINCPAC, (Commander in Chief, Pacific) asked Rowe if he would like to do his annual reserve duty in Honolulu on his staff. Rowe instantly accepted, did the Honolulu duty and subsequently two more active duty tours under McCain, including one in Toyko studying the operations of Pacific Stars & Stripes to recommend ways to cut its expenses. Charles had 32 years of Navy service and was recommended by McCain for promotion to Admiral. He later learned he almost made the final cut of a selection board, something amazing since he'd never had a paid billet in the Reserve which meant that he was never in a slot with command responsibilities.

I always wondered if Charles, who lives in Florida these days but frequently returns to his hometown, had any regrets about not completing law school. I asked him recently via e-mail and he responded that he had mixed emotions since he loved certain parts of the law but was not keen on others. But his father's untimely death left him no choice and Rowe thinks he had much more enjoyment and personal satisfaction in journalism than he would have had as a lawyer.

Several episodes of differences between Charles and Joe Rowe stick out in my mind. Once was when Joe, as Mayor of Fredericksburg, went before a congressional committee to push for approval of the Salem Church Dam. Not long afterward Charles Rowe testified against the dam. Several committee members were startled to learn that the two were not only brothers, but co-owners of a newspaper.

In 1973 Joe Rowe was outraged to learn that Charles had written an editorial endorsing Democrat Henry Howell for Governor over Republican Mills Godwin. Howell was not only a very liberal Democrat by state standards in those days, but Joe Rowe and Mills Godwin were close friends. The Free Lance-Star remains the only daily paper in Virginia ever to have endorsed any of Howell's various runs for statewide office.

There were many people at the newspaper I considered close friends and one was Jim McKnight, the city editor. He was devoted to the paper and his work and sometimes reporters were frustrated by his insistence that everyone under his command do their jobs properly. I was blessed with the ability to write fast-and I hope accurately-and I believe

I did more than my fair share of stories, but that was the way I wanted it. I came into the office usually on Sundays and holidays and when I did I would often find Jim McKnight hunched over his desk poring over a mountain of copy.

In postwar years I also recall school letting out a half day when the Fredericksburg Agricultural Fair began. An afternoon parade was held to mark the event. I used to go to the so-called sideshows (or freak shows) that consisted of such things as fat ladies, men with rubber skins, geeks who ate glass and the like. Carnival people were a strange gypsy-like lot who never stayed in one place for long. In this politically correct age, I guess it would be impossible to stage the kind of freak shows as then. My friend, John Wayne Edwards, (whose talent was recognized even before he started his public school education) has vivid recollections of the fair and has completed some paintings of the kind of garish banners that used to proclaim that for a quarter you could see the bearded lady inside the tent. John held a hometown art show not long again and sold tons of stuff. Malone Schooler, an area developer who has done projects all over the state, bought the original of Eddie Mack's Grill of which I have a copy. For Malone, who played in a band called 'The Prophets' along with Steve Jarrell, the picture had special value because he lived in that building for a time after it was turned into apartments. Steve Jarrell did well down in Nashville and now has a band that plays in many venues.

When Robert E. Lee Baker, who had been assistant managing editor of The Washington Post, returned to the local paper in 1978 as managing editor he was a stranger to most of the newsroom personnel except McKnight and me. Baker, who Charles Rowe selected, had been there as sports editor in the late 1940s and early 1950s and while in high school I had been one of his stringers writing summaries of little league baseball games.

Baker and I shared a habit of memo writing and in my remaining six and a half years with the paper must have exchanged hundreds. At times I disagreed with his decisions, and though he had the last word, there were occasions when he re-examined an issue and tilted in my favor. He had covered for The Post the civil rights era in the South (and had the perfect name for the assignment) and also had been its London correspondent for several years. We got along well for he was intelligent, personable and had a terrific sense of humor. But I was disappointed in his de-emphasis of political coverage. He was probably guided by one of those surveys that showed people would rather read such trash as Ann Landers and other junk than stories about things that actually would affect their lives, so the popular taste prevailed. That is the unfortunate direction in which most papers have been led in this age when television, which is so full of garbage, dictates the direction of American journalism to blend it with entertainment.

Joe Rowe had been frustrated many years about not having any real say in news and editorial policies. After Charles decided to retire, Joe bought his interest and changed the editorial policies of the paper from mildly liberal to conservative. I still hold both Charles and Joe in high regard and see them from time to time.

Joe made strong moves when he acquired the newspaper by adding a Sunday edition and going from an afternoon paper to a morning paper. The Free Lance-Star has a circulation of about 50,000 and is in the major league of state papers.

The newspaper's Editor of the Editorial page, Paul Akers, is also a friend and I agree with his national editorials 95 percent of the time, state editorials probably 80 percent and local editorials about 70 percent of the time. Paul is a nice guy with real talent.

I still have friends at the paper from bygone days including Keith Epps, Robert Hedelt, Jim Toler, Jim Mann, Nancy Moore, Cathy Jett, Gwen Woolf, Ed Jones, Ace Lawson and others. But many I worked with have gone elsewhere or retired, including Larry Evans now writing about environmental matters for a Florida newspaper, Paul Sullivan who, though retired, still writes an excellent weekly column for the paper and Phyllis Lane, one of my all time favorite people. Duval Haynes, was a stalwart in the composing room for years and we often talked. He is the grandfather of my present co-worker Jenny Stein whose grandmother, Peggy, makes the most delicious lemon pie I've ever eaten. Others I knew well included Charles Cassiday, Rats Lewis, Colonel Ballard, Ray Hudson and my high school classmate Gilbert James who worked in the press room

Passapatanzy Pete

During nearly thirty years with the local paper, I wrote countless thousands of words about different things. Obituaries, politics, City Council and supervisor meetings, school boards, farm operations, crimes, sporting events, state government and Congress.

Yet nothing I wrote in all those years elicited the response I got then, and still get occasionally, from just one simple subject.

Passapatanzy.

If you're not in on the joke, it's hard to explain. Passapatanzy is a small settlement in King George County and I do mean small. I had never heard about it until Frank Trippett, who was a reporter at the paper when I started there part-time, remarked one day that he was going out onto the street and ask passerby how to spell Passapatanzy.

He said it jokingly and I forgot about it until I started writing a once a week humor column in the paper's Saturday magazine section a few years later. One day I inserted into a column that ceremonies had just been held to open the new Passapatanzy International Airport at Passapatanzy in King George and the Mayor of Passapatanzy had cut the ceremonial ribbon. The column drew an appreciative chuckle from some readers so I continued mentioning the airport and threw in the University of Passapatanzy. I invented some fictional Passapatanzy characters to talk about. Free Lance-Star reporter Cathy Dyson recently did an interesting story on how some area places got their names. When she inquired about Passapatanzy, I told her that a few folks had told me it was named for a chief of the Potowomack Indian tribe, but I had never been able to gather more than hearsay on the subject, though I am still trying. Entertainer Wayne Newton, who great up in Stafford, believes he is descended from that tribe. The tribe is presently trying to get state recognition.

Nightlife in Passapatanzy

Jim Kutzle came by and introduced himself. Jim was a pilot for Eastern Airlines and had moved to a farm in Passapatanzy about six months before. He got a big kick out of my columns. About the same time Bob Van Valzah, who operated a country store on Route 3 at the entrance to the road that led to Passapatanzy, printed up some Passapatanzy International Airport shirts that sold pretty well as a novelty item.

I declared Van Valzah Mayor of Passapatanzy and Kutzle manager of the airport. The late Earl Copp, a paper editor, once told me I should write about Passapatanzy less, since people might get tired of it. But whenever I didn't write about it, I would run into people who wanted to know when I would be bringing them up to date on Passapatanzy again.

It's ironic that of all the serious things I wrote about over the years, that all of the words I wrote conveying information about the opinions of would-be political leaders, nothin came close to the reaction I got from frivolous off-the-wall prose about Passapatanzy. I even came up with Passapatanzy Pete, a beaver, as a rival to the famous groundhog Puxatawney Phil. Passapatanzy Pete didn't look for his own shadow but for the shadow of a Boeing 747 flying over Passapatanzy International Airport to determine if there would be six more weeks of bad weather.

Jim Kutzle invited me to his place and then took me over to Van Valzah's store where a 'John Goolrick Day' had been proclaimed in Passapatanzy. It was a great event with lots of food and short speeches and I appreciated it. Jim, who now lives in Florida, was a great guy and his wife, Ann, was a wonderful lady.

I suppose that I can tell this now without getting anybody in trouble. Jim let me fly with him and his co-pilot on an Eastern Airlines Boeing 707 shuttle from Washington National Airport to LaGuardia Airport in New York. The view from the cockpit was wonderful and he let me sit in the pilot's seat as we passed over Philadelphia. While I was obviously not flying the plane, I am sure the passengers would have been terrified if they had known where I was sitting.

Though all the political wisdom I dispensed in hundreds of stories was not very well absorbed, I had a lot of fun with Passapatanzy, both downtown and suburbs, and I'm glad it produced people who still remind me of things I said about Passapatanzy and connect me with that wonderful place. People ask if the airport is still there even though they never hear about it anymore. I answer Yes, Virginia, there is still a Passapatanzy International Airport and it will be there forever in those dozens of columns I wrote about it which are now stored on microfilm.

I like to think it was a result of all I wrote about Passapatanzy that the State Highway Department finally put a marker on Route 218 reading simply 'Passapatanzy.' But while it may be suburban Passapatanzy, it is not downtown Passapatanzy which is several miles away where a great lady named Ruby Hawkins lives. Ruby the Realtor has a wonderfully optimistic outlook on life.

Even so, I am hoping that someday the graduating seniors at the University of will ask me to give the commencement speech.

CHAPTER THIRTEEN

Hotel Raleigh

Life is full of twists and turns. Paul Muse was the political reporter for the local paper for years. Then in the mid-1960s Muse decided to join a weekly paper in Prince William County to seize an opportunity to become part owner. Muse had grown up in the Manassas area of that county and his father, Benjamin Muse, had once been nominated by the Republican Party to run for Governor, a hopeless task for Republicans in that era.

So I became political reporter for the local paper for what it was worth for we were a small daily paper and politicians usually judge the importance of a paper by its circulation.

When the managing editor decided I should spend my winters in Richmond covering the Virginia General Assembly, I looked around for a suitable reasonably priced hotel. None was more reasonably priced than The Hotel Raleigh at $9 a room per night and the Raleigh (now the plush Commonwealth Park Hotel owned by Carl and Larry Silver) was superbly located at the bottom of Richmond's Capital Square.

It was fate that landed me on the Eighth Floor of The Raleigh, an eventuality that would have a major influence on my years covering politics.

As I quickly learned, staying on that same floor were Delegate Tom Moss of Norfolk, a future Speaker of the House; Delegate Warren Barry of Fairfax who would later serve as Fairfax Clerk of Court and then return to Richmond as an influential member of the State Senate; Garry DeBruhl of Stuart, Virginia, a member of the House of Delegates then and later to become one of the most influential lobbyists in Virginia; Mel Carrico, the legendary political reporter from The Roanoke Times who spoke with a southwest Virginia drawl so thick you could cut it with a knife and who invariably wore a red baseball cap while working; and a number of others.

Every evening when the legislative session had ended, we would gather in DeBruhl's suite for cocktails. Among frequent visitors were

Jim Roberts who went on to become one of the state's most outstanding attorneys, specializing oddly in both criminal law and insurance law; and Jay Shrosphire, later to become Clerk of the State Senate and eventually to be Chief of Staff to Governor L. Douglas Wilder.

There were many other visitors who were members of the Legislature, including one notorious legislator from the southwest who was convicted of selling thousands of dollars worth of stolen goods. He once offered to sell me a pistol and I almost bit.

The way Carrico and I saw it we were not on around the clock duty and the others found I was a reporter they could trust to confine his quest for news to their public lives. With the exception of Carrico, they, like myself, were just getting started and were not adverse to having a good time while they were helping make the laws of the Commonwealth. And they had a lot more time then because rookie legislators are never particularly busy. After the day was done, there was little partisan bickering among Democratic and Republican members and they often socialized together. Today the Virginia General Assembly has reached the point it is nearly as charged by partisanship as the U.S. Congress.

I sometimes wonder what might have happened had I not wound up on the Eighth Floor. Those early associations I made paid off as these folks became more senior and powerful in Virginia government and I got access to information I would not have had otherwise. I heard subjects being discussed The Washington Post would have printed if they had known.

I was a small fry reporter from what most would consider a minor league paper. Logically, there was no way I could compete on anywhere near equal terms with reporters from bigger papers or any reporter from any television station. Since politicians wanted maximum exposure, they gravitated toward the reporters from The Times Dispatch (Jim Latimer), The News Leader (Carl Shires), The Virginian Pilot (George Kelly), The Roanoke Times (Carrico), The Washington Post (Helen Dewar) The Associated Press (John Daffron) and others. No other paper with a circulation anywhere near as small had a full-time reporter in Richmond covering the legislature.

That I was able to hold my own came about through a combination of circumstances that had little to do with my journalistic abilities. First, I met and became friends with a group of people whose stars—though I did not know it—were to rise quickly in the Virginia political firmament. Second, I was fortunate enough to have a surname that was recognized by many political leaders. When I went to Richmond the Governor was Mills

Godwin who had known my uncle, former State Senator C.O'Conor Goolrick of Fredericksburg, as had many within the Byrd Organization. Thus at gubernatorial press conferences I was able to get recognized to ask the Governor questions and that ability increased my credibility among my colleagues. I think for a reporter with a narrow base in terms of newspaper size I got major stories from time to time that no one else had.

One of my best sources was Delegate V. Earl Dickinson of Louisa, I had known his father, Vivian, while covering the Spotsylvania school board in days past. Earl took me to dinner occasionally at the Commonwealth Club where the wealthy and powerful gathered each evening to make deals over drinks and food. Among those I met there were A.L. Philpott of Bassett who was to become one of Virginia's most powerful Speakers of the House. Another was Senator Hunter Andrews who also wielded great influence. Dickinson, Philpott and Andrews were among the most dedicated public servants I've known.

As for the activities in which a number of us engaged at night suffice it to say the party in DeBruhl's room moved in time to somewhere there was a bar and food and often lasted into the small hours of the morning. Everyone was much younger and resilient and a few hours sleep would put them in shape to do it all over the next evening.

There were nightly lavish receptions hosted by special interest groups for legislators and hangers on and occasionally I would attend one since media people were always welcome. But the most famous party among insiders in Richmond is one that only a couple of journalists, including myself, have been allowed to attend. I was there from its inception. It was called the PuPu Party and was hosted by lobbyist-attorney Jim Roberts at a Chinese restaurant in Richmond's West End. It derives its name from the Chinese words for hors d'oeuvres that are served along with lots of liquid refreshment followed by tons of food.

Traditionally many in the room are called on to make brief remarks. It is still legendary that one night early on I had had a couple too many and when I was called on to speak, instead of addressing the audience I spoke directly to a statue of Buddha in front of me.

Let me briefly reminisce about the Raleigh Hotel. For nine bucks a night one got what one paid for. There were two bellhops at the Raleigh whose names—at least the only names I knew—were Lips and Louie. They seemed to be in perpetual catatonic trances and always asking for shots of whisky. The elevators at the Raleigh were small and ancient and wheezed their way upward. The rooms were cramped, the plumbing bad, the mattresses lumpy and if someone on a floor above you turned on the hot water early in the morning you would find yourself taking an unintentional cold shower. Among those living above us on the Ninth Floor were Del. Vincent Callahan, a nice guy who is now chairman of the House Appropriations Committee, and Del. Ray Garland, among the most erudite members of the legislature.

When Vince ran for lieutenant governor in 1965 as a Republican, he spent only about $10,000 in his entire statewide campaign a figure that these days would barely buy a couple of TV spots in major markets.

Everything was worn out about the Raleigh-the carpets, the furniture, the walls, the ceiling. Since we stayed there only during the winter months, we were spared roaches and bedbugs. The rooms had televison but sometimes you could barely pick up a picture. Eventually it closed, was gutted and a luxury hotel put in its place. We moved to the Downtown Holiday Inn. But despite its faults and rundown condition, I have fond memories of that old hotel because under its roof I spent many pleasant fun-filled hours and met people who remain friends.

End of an Era

When my political reporting career started, the Governor of Virginia was Albertis S. Harrison of Lawrenceville who looked the part. Harrison was a product of the Byrd era and had been an organization stalwart. That was also the case with Mills Godwin who succeeded him as Governor. To Godwin's great credit, he pushed for the enactment of a sales tax to bring educational standards in the state out of the pits where they had been.

Linwood Holton was the first Republican elected governor in Virginia and that happened in 1969. During his campaign I recall the excitement gathering that fall as Holton drew large crowds.

Holton was from Roanoke and a mountain valley Republican who believed in moderation. I sensed that when he won the state would be heading in a new direction.

It is ironic that Holton's worst critics became his fellow Republicans since his goal was to reorganize state government and make it more efficient.

But because all the juicy state jobs had always gone to Democrats, the GOP faithful were expecting their rewards from the political spoils system and Holton disappointed them by essentially ignoring the party stalwarts who had elected him. He went out of state to select a Commissioner of Motor Vehicles, a job sought after by several of his biggest supporters. When his term ended his future in Virginia politics did not seem bright. Now his son in law, Tim Kaine, a Democrat, is lieutenant governor of Virginia and the probable Democratic nominee for Governor in 2005.

Holton was succeeded by Mills Godwin who had become a Republican and narrowly staved off a challenge by liberal Henry Howell.

I often saw John Dalton at the Raleigh Hotel restaurant in the early days. He was a member of the House of Delegates who went on to get elected lieutenant governor and then Governor in 1977. His father Ted Dalton, who later became a federal judge, had made a good run for Governor as a Republican in, I think, 1961, but the time was not yet ripe for members of his party. John Dalton was a friendly person with a sharp mind and excellent political instincts.

It is remarkable that not the slightest hint of official corruption has touched any of the Virginia governors who have served during my lifetime. I have personally known eleven of those governors and worked for one, George Allen when he was a member of the U.S. House of Representatives. While working for Allen, I got to know Rick Richardson who was on his staff and is now a state economic development official. Rick, a close friend, has the same efficiency level as Rick Holcomb, another friend, and that's saying a lot.

The Senators

In 1978 two men who were destined to become highly influential figures in Virginia were elected to the Senate.

One went to the Virginia State Senate and the others to the United States Senate. I played minor roles in their elections.

Representing the Fredericksburg area in the State Senate at the time was Paul Manns of Bowling Green, a veteran conservative Democrat of great dignity and integrity. A funeral home operator, Manns was personable and likeable. But at the beginning of 1978 he was suffering from terminal cancer.

Serving in the House of Delegates from Hague in Westmoreland

County was Calvin Sanford, a Republican who had a simple philosophy. Introduce as few bills as possible, because there were already enough laws on the books, and keep bad laws from passing.

Calvin and I were friends and started a yearly tradition of having an oyster party for legislators and guests.

One evening when Calvin and I were having dinner at a restaurant on Strawberry Street, he noted that Senator Manns was in ill health and probably would not live much longer. He said Northern Neck Republicans were looking for someone to seek the vacant seat if the Senator died.

I told Calvin they might consider John Chichester who lived in Stafford and was a Fredericksburg insurance agency owner. Though Chichester had grown up as a Democrat, he had been forced out of the party by the liberal element. I said he was intelligent, affable and popular. Chichester had previously played a role in state political history when in 1969 as a Democrat he challenged Del. George Rawlings and lost in a primary election. But again conservative Democrats turned on Rawlings and elected Republican Ben Woodbridge, a Fredericksburg attorney, that fall to succeed him.

Sanford asked me to a meeting with a few Northern Neck Republicans and Chichester.

That weekend I called Chichester and reported the conversation. A meeting took place and the folks from the Northern Neck were highly impressed. They pledged their support. A week or so later Manns died and a special election was held.

Chichester easily got the Republican nomination while Peck Humphreys from Kimarnock was nominated by Democrats. Humphreys owned a menhaden processing operation and was wealthy. He was a friendly man that I liked very much and I believe I provided fair and objective coverage.. Humphreys spent more money on the senatorial run than any previous such campaign in Virginia, but lost to Chichester.

In 1999 John Chichester became chairman of the Senate Finance Committee giving him one of the most powerful positions in the state. As I write this he has just clobbered an opponent in a Republican primary and will be returning to Richmond for what may a final four-year term. Though his wife, Karen, has been ill, she encouraged him to seek reelection.

His prestigious position on the Finance Committee and as President Pro Tempore of the Senate, compensate for 1985 when John was nominated for Lieutenant Governor but narrowly lost to L. Douglas Wilder, the Democrat. Chichester could have won that campaign if he had signed off on an intensive 11th hour negative campaign recommended by his campaign manager and others, but he was unwilling to do it. He has had an aversion to negative campaigning throughout his career. While I share that belief, the unfortunate reality is that such campaigning, if properly constructed, works. I have faith in the political system, yet I am still puzzled at the rapidity with which people who cast votes can have their minds changed. I guess if you can persuade people to buy a particular shampoo with a 30 second television spot, you can also persuade them with the same tool to vote for or against somebody. But people who are swayed by such things without taking the time to really learn what the issues are all about probably get what they deserve.

In 1978 incumbent Republican Senator William Scott decided to retire and shortly afterward four Republicans said they would seek the party nomination. They were John Warner, a former Secretary of the Navy; Richard Obenshain, who had been the state Republican chairman; former Gov. Linwood Holton; and State Sen. Nathan Miller of Rockingham County. I met Warner when he came to Fredericksburg in 1976 while was serving as chairman of the American Bicentennial Commission. By the time of his announcement he was married to the movie actress Elizabeth Taylor.

The fight for the nomination was prolonged and spirited. With Liz Taylor at his side, Warner hit the chicken dinner circuit. In the spring of 1978 I found myself in the company of Liz Taylor and Warner at a suite at the Sheraton in Fredericksburg. The glamorous Miss Taylor, one of the most famous people in the world, fixed me a drink of Jack Daniels and water and poured herself one over the rocks. We had a pleasant conversation, though I recognized the somewhat absurd situation of a small town political reporter sitting there sipping on a drink and with a straight face asking the world's most famous movie actress questions about Virginia politics. (I believe, but am not sure that Ed Jones, now managing editor of the paper, was along with me that day).

When the GOP convention was held in Richmond, it went into the Guinness book of records as the largest political convention ever held to that point in time, meaning more delegates and alternates attended it than any other before, including all the national political conventions. It was covered by media from across the nation and from many foreign countries and-I am not making this up-Liz Taylor dressed in a sailor suit led partisans in singing 'Anchors Away' in honor of her husband who had been Secretary of the Navy during the Nixon Administration.

The balloting was close between Warner and Obenshain who had inspired much of the ultra-conservative party element. Holton, though a former governor, had angered many party activists by not being partisan enough and his campaign never got off the ground. Miller didn't have a prayer from the start.

Obenshain finally prevailed and was set to take on Democratic nominee, former Attorney General Andrew Miller. But about six weeks later Obenshain died in the crash of a small plane in Chesterfield County while returning home from a campaign appearance in Winchester.

Warner, who was vacationing in a chalet in Switzerland with Miss Taylor, made a hasty return and was given the party nomination. He waged a vigorous campaign and won very narrowly. My little contribution, as previously mentioned, had been my remark to him that any Republican nominee should run more against incumbent President Jimmy Carter, a weak sister from any angle, than against the personable Miller. (Whose father Francis Pickens Miller, a Democrat, had waged war on the Byrd Organization in the 1940s). Warner did just that and told me a few years later he had taken my advice to heart, particularly when it was reinforced by professional polls.

While he was married to Elizabeth Taylor, I saw them at times in Richmond. I once got on an elevator at a Richmond hotel and there was Miss Taylor with her husband and she said something like, "How are you doing, John?"

Never in my wildest dreams as I watched such films as 'National Velvet' and 'Cleopatra' and many others did I think the famous Elizabeth Taylor would someday greet me by my first name. I was in Grundy, or whatever little Southwest Virginia town, the night she got a chicken bone stuck in her throat and had to be rushed to the emergency room. Looking back there is something almost surrealistic about it for when I see Miss Taylor's face on the tabloids as I go through the line at the supermarket I find myself thinking did what I remember actually happen, did the Liz Taylor actually take time to say hello as she helped her husband campaign for political office from Fredericksburg to Grundy.

John Warner is a man of courage and conviction who stood against his own party when it nominated for Senate in 1994 one of the few people in Virginia who would be unable to beat incumbent Democrat Charles Robb. That man was Ollie North. I had nothing against North personally, had met him on several occasions and found him articulate and charismatic. He had once lived in Stafford County and worked bingo at Montfort Academy in Fredericksburg while a Marine lieutenant, but by now he had transcended all that. The Iran-Contra business had made him famous. The trouble was, and I felt it from the outset, he would not be able to beat Chuck Robb because there were many Republicans like Warner who would not vote for him. There is no question that Ollie North was a fearless leader, an authentic American hero who served his country bravely and richly deserved every medal he got. There is no question he loved his country deeply and sincerely. (And I enjoy his television show on Fox News). But the machinations of Iran-Contra tainted his political viability and he was not destined to be a U.S. Senator.

CHAPTER FOURTEEN

BEING THERE

Though the hours are sometimes long, the work often grueling and the pay atrocious, someone who works as a political reporter is accorded a front row seat as history is made.

The reason is simple. While those important people making history know you drive around in a beat-up old car and live from payday to payday, you, in effect, have a big printing press in your back pocket and their lifeblood is publicity.

I have met few politicians who did not want their names in print, their voices on radio or their faces before the cameras cast in a favorable light. Thus they give members of the media, whom they may privately regard as unkempt idealists too stupid to get jobs making real money, the red carpet treatment, calling them by their first names, flattering them, whispering confidential matters in their ears. It is often difficult for a political reporter to remain objective when he or she is being skillfully cajoled by a well-known politician whose basic aim is to get the reporter to reflect his own exalted view of himself or herself. One of the great practitioners of the art was John Marshall Coleman of Augusta County, a born glad hander who ran unsuccessfully for Governor twice and served four years as Attorney General of Virginia. It was said of Coleman that while he was shaking your hand he would look over your shoulder to see if there was anyone more important in the room to whom he should turn his attention.

I first met Coleman when he got elected to the Virginia House of Delegates in the early 1970s. He was a Marine who had been seen service as an officer in Vietnam and he was tall, ruggedly handsome, intelligent, articulate and witty. He had all the attributes to succeed in politics.

But more than anything else he had ambition written all over him. He intended to go places and do whatever he had to do to get there. He cultivated reporters like gardeners cultivate crops. I could hardly get through the halls of the Capitol without Coleman stopping me and giving me a news release about the latest bill he had introduced. He was a relentless self-promoter, but had such a gracious self-effacing manner about him that it was hard to resist the charm. It was as if he was on the one hand buttering you up but on the other mocking his own upstart ways.

He got loads of publicity, soon got elected to the State Senate and was a rising star. But when he was nominated for Attorney General in 1977 he made the mistake of blasting Democratic nominee Ed Lane's past support of massive resistance policies. Mills Godwin, still governor, did not like Coleman whom he considered too brash and self-serving and Coleman's dredging up of massive resistance rankled Godwin greatly.

Godwin's enmity did not hurt Coleman that year since he won, but it sent a signal to the conservative establishment that the young mountain valley Republican was not of their ilk and in 1981 when Coleman ran for governor against Democratic nominee Chuck Robb the support he got from conservatives was lukewarm at best.

Not that anybody could have beaten Robb that year. In 1977 Robb, the son-in-law of former President Lyndon Johnson, parachuted into Virginia to run for lieutenant governor and won. I had watched him campaign and he didn't seem very good at it. When he walked into a grocery store he seemed reluctant to step up to shoppers, introduce himself and ask for their votes. In a quick sound bite age, his answers to questions seemed extraordinarily long and often minutiae-filled. As the old joke goes, if you asked him the time, he'd tell you how to make a watch.

And yet I sensed instinctively that here was someone who was going to be a major political force. He was not, like Coleman, at home in a crowd, but he had that All American boy image. He had no trouble getting elected lieutenant governor, became better campaigning as time passed and was one of the most polite and considerate people in public life I have ever met. While he was lieutenant governor, I sometimes stopped by his office in the Bell Tower for long talks.

The Robb Style

I began to hear the rumors about Robb shortly after he left office as Governor of Virginia in January, 1986.

I didn't believe them. A few persons were alleging that while Governor, Robb often associated with unsavory folks in Virginia Beach.

Robb, so they said, had frequently attended parties where cocaine was used. He had socialized with a number of bimbo type women to the point of partying with them on yachts owned by questionable figures. While in Virginia Beach Chuck Robb had, I was told, been the life of the party and that he was warned by the Attorney General and by State Police to stay away from the undesirables with whom he was socializing.

I found this preposterous. Robb was a former Marine who was straight laced and sipped on ginger ale at cocktail parties. I liked the man with his old fashioned emphasis on values, something that sounded a bit naive in the 1980s but was nevertheless appealing. He had a handsome family and he had served his country in Vietnam at a time many of his generation were rebelling against that unfortunate war.

Chuck Robb, philanderer, party animal, womanizer, condoner of illegal substances? No way. Many thought he would eventually become President of the United States. My initial reaction was that someone was out to destroy him politically by spreading nasty unfounded rumors.

But they not only persisted, I soon came into contact with those who had personal knowledge of Robb's Virginia Beach activities, people with no political axes to grind. Reliable people who had reputations for truth and veracity.

As bits of the story started to leak, I went to the managing editor of the paper and suggested they give me the time and resources to look into the matter. At that point I think I probably knew more than any other journalist about the allegations. Given four or five months, I might have come up with evidence proving that Robb had lived a secret life at Virginia Beach.

I liked Robb and still do. But if a he had clandestinely done such things the people should know about it. Certainly he should not be given another moment's consideration as a future President or Vice President of the United States.

The managing editor mulled it over and but never gave me a definitive answer. Just about the same time Rosellen O'Connell, a reporter with the Norfolk Virginian-Pilot, was getting into the Robb story. She spent months working on it and had tons of information (the same information I had or could have obtained). Then Robb put heavyweight lawyers to work on his side who quietly threatened the Norfolk paper with numerous lawsuits. The ploy worked and O'Connell, over her vigorous protests, was forced to water down what she wrote. About the same time Robb was cruising in 1988 to an easy win for a U.S. Senate seat. It would be a few years before the full story of his covert activities emerged and he reportedly came within a hair of being indicted by a grand jury for what some federal prosecutors regarded as a cover up. Three of his Senate aides suffered sanctions for their part in the

HANDLING OF AN ILLEGALLY TAPED CONVERSATION BETWEEN GOVERNOR DOUGLAS WILDER AND A VIRGINIA BEACH BUSINESSMAN.

ROBB WAS RE-ELECTED TO THE SENATE IN 1994 ONLY BECAUSE THE REPUBLICANS IN VIRGINIA NOMINATED AS THEIR CANDIDATE OLLIE NORTH WHO WAS UNELECTABLE. ROBB, WAS AN HONEST AND HARD WORKING PUBLIC OFFICIAL BUT EVEN HE ACKNOWLEDGED THAT MANY OF THE DECISIONS HE MADE IN VIRGINIA BEACH WERE UNWISE AND UNWORTHY OF THE OFFICE OF GOVERNOR.

CHAPTER FIFTEEN

Conventional Wisdom

I have attended more politician conventions than I can remember. There were congressional district conventions, state conventions and national conventions. During my days as a political reporter, I attended conventions of both parties and got to know the key players on both sides.

For years, Judge Howard Smith was the Congressman from the 8th District of Virginia that came down from Alexandria to take in Fredericksburg and the area. Judge Smith was not one who believed particularly in staying in close touch with his constituents and despite its proximity to his home in Fauquier County, he seldom made forays into the rest of the district.

In 1966 Smith had long been a figure on the national political scene. Almost single-handedly as head of the House Rules Committee he had bottled up Civil Rights legislation desired by both Presidents Kennedy and Johnson until finally Kennedy had pressured the Congress to change the rules so that Smith could not be such an obstructionist. Nevertheless because of his seniority he remained a powerful figure in Washington, one not to be taken lightly.

Every two years Smith used to stride majestically into a nominating convention usually held in Fredericksburg at the Community Center. At such conventions the party's nomination for Congress was routinely bestowed on him again. Smith would stay around to make a few comments accepting the nomination and then leave. He commanded respect, but he was not a glad handing politician and had not much truck for the scut work of campaigning. But since he never had opposition, there was no need to get his hands dirty.

That was the case until 1966 and Democratic lawyer George C. Rawlings Jr. of Fredericksburg, then a member of the Virginia House of Delegates, announced plans to challenge him.

A Huge Upset

Rawlings is an interesting case study. He got elected to the state legislature in 1963 by taking on veteran Delegate Francis B. Gouldman in a Democratic primary. Few gave Rawlings much of a chance at first, but he came up with a great campaign gimmick. At the time the Salem Church Dam was a hot topic and people felt its construction would bring progress to the area as well as flood control. Gouldman, who favored the dam, had said in frustration over its slow pace that he didn't think he would see it built in his lifetime. Rawlings seized on the statement as evidence that Gouldman didn't want the dam. He called Gouldman a tool of the Byrd machine and managed to get some Democrats who were moderate conservatives to go along with him.

He pulled off an upset of Gouldman against the odds, yet when he ran against Smith three years later people were still not ready to believe he could win. Here was an upstart young lawyer with little campaign money up against one of the most powerful men in the nation, an incumbent who would have no trouble raising all the money he needed to wage his re-election campaign. Not only that, but Smith would have the absolute backing of Virginia's ruling old Guard Democrats, including Mills Godwin, the Governor.

But there were factors at that increased the underdog's chances. First, Smith had decided to run for re-nomination in a primary instead of letting a convention choose the nominee. He and his advisors apparently feared that Rawlings would be able to pack a convention with his people, but since the Organization was well experienced in turning out its people, it was likely that Smith would have prevailed.

The primary was a horse of a different color, mainly because the Smith people were the picture of complacency. They proclaimed that there was no way the elderly Judge could lose, that he was a shoo-in. While Rawlings made up for his lack of money by grueling campaign trips around the district to meet as many voters as he could, the Smith forces were practically moribund unless you counted newspaper advertisements that attracted little attention.

George Rawlings defeat of Judge Smith in the primary was historic in that it augured the end of the Byrd era in Virginia and the beginning of a factional fight among Democrats that would eventually see hundreds of prominent conservative Democrats switching to Republican ranks and making Virginia essentially a Republican state.

The victory that the Rawlings forces celebrated that June was short-lived. Rawlings was despised by the conservative forces that controlled the General Assembly. Speaker of the House Blackie Moore, a Byrd stalwart, put him on committees that never met. When Rawlings was first elected to the House of Delegates, he put out a news release noting he had been appointed to the prestigious Committee on Interstate Cooperation. I learned it had never had a meeting throughout its existence.

When Judge Smith lost, I attended a testimonial dinner for him in Manassas arranged by Godwin and other conservatives to send a signal they weren't about to let Rawlings go to Congress. Thus it became all right for such Democrats to back the Republican nominee, a man named Bill Scott who had to be one of the luckiest people ever to run for high office.

I followed the Rawlings-Scott campaign closely. It became obvious that conservative Democrats were out for revenge and would take it even though some of the Rawlings brain trust still confidently predicted that when the time came, nearly all Democrats would loyally support the nominee. When I wrote that they were wrong, they resented it.

On Election Day Rawlings was solidly beaten and the defection of his fellow Democrats who disagreed strongly with his liberal philosophy was the key reason. But though Rawlings lost, he was not one to give up easily and would eventually get his revenge when the liberal element took over the Virginia Democratic Party, thus giving the Republican Party in the state a huge boost. After Harry Byrd Jr., the incumbent U.S.Senator, turned independent in 1970, Rawlings was nominated by Democrats and Del. Ray Garland of Roanoke by Republicans. It wasn't even close as Rawlings finished a distant second and Garland far down the track. After the election results were clear, I had a drink with George's father in his room at the Jefferson Hotel where he lived. He asked if I knew of any way George could be persuaded to practice law full time and get out of politics. I said politely that simply did not fall under my jurisdiction. I had told the widow of legendary Marine 'Chesty Puller', who lived in Saluda, the same thing in 1982 when she called and asked me to help dissuade her son, Lewis Jr., who had lost a leg in Vietnam, from running for Congress in Virginia's 1st District as a Democrat. I had once done a story about Mrs. Puller and she was a very kindly person, but I told her from what I had observed nothing would stop her son into getting into what she felt was the unseemly profession of politics.

Little Big Horn

The state Democratic convention held at Salem, Virginia in June, 1969 was a circus. I can't recall all the details but there was a big flap within the 8th Congressional District about credentials and the district chairman, State Senator John Gallaher of Prince William, was fighting the liberal element led by Rawlings tooth and nail.

Gallaher was a man known for his fondness for strong drink. Once he had stood up in the Senate while tipsy and asked that a bill he had sponsored be withdrawn. When asked why he wanted to strike the measure, Gallaher responded, "If I had known what was in that damn bill, I never would have signed it."

Now as he presided over the district caucus, Gallaher's rulings were being challenged loudly by Rawlings and company. Twice Gallaher recessed the meetings until order could be restored. But when the bickering continued, he angrily adjourned the meeting and stalked out. Spying me in the back of the room he said, "You got any whiskey in your car. I need a drink?" I did, indeed, happen to have some bourbon in the car and I walked with Gallaher to the vehicle and gave him a drink while he called Rawlings and the liberals every bad name he could think of. I recall him saying in a voice filled with disgust, "We're like Custer at Little Big Horn. All we can do is slow the bastard's down. But we can't stop them."

He was right. By 1970 the liberal element of the party with Rawlings and Henry Howell of Norfolk as its leaders, had effectively taken over and the purge was on.

I felt then, and still feel, if the liberals had showed some magnanimity in triumph they could have kept the Democratic Party at least partially a big tent and in position to win elections while at the same time assuring themselves a major voice in its affairs.

Instead—thirsting for revenge on the conservatives who had dominated the party for many years and ignored their views—the liberals were in no mood to tolerate anyone who would not accept all of their agenda. In locality after locality liberals took over Democratic organizations and threw out conservatives. They felt with their fanatical ways they could somehow impose on the people of Virginia a philosophy the people were not prepared to accept. They were doomed from the start.

As ultra-liberals in Virginia and in other states took over the

Democratic Party, the ultimate idiocy occurred in 1972 when the party nominated Senator George McGovern as its candidate for President. Even McGovern admitted years later that many of his policies were misguided and too radical for the American people to accept.

Hippies in Miami

In 1972 I went to my first national political convention and would go to six more.

The Virginia Democratic delegation to that Miami Beach convention was one the likes of which had never been seen before in the Old Dominion. Instead of a delegation of conservative middle-aged men in pin striped suits and matronly women in fashionable dress, it was a rag-tag bunch of hippies and near hippies. There were more than 70 people in the delegation and I believe at least a third of them were smoking marijuana on several bus rides we took together. There were feminists of all ages, union people who wanted to boycott lettuce and table grapes, bearded anti-Vietnam war protesters clad in scruffy clothes, egghead type liberal idealists who thought capitalistic pigs should be ostracized and that socialism was the wave of America's future.

Most of the people who came to that convention were just like their Virginia brethren. It seemed as if I was in the middle of a convention on some other planet than Earth—perhaps Jupiter or Mars.

The Virginia delegation was housed at a garish motel, The Castaways. The rooms were decorated in bright pink and orange and there was a huge bar where you could sit and look through glass at people swimming in a pool outside. Since many of the people did not know they were being observed, sometimes you could observe some fondling and petting when couples swam under the water. Hanging around the place were provocatively dressed women who, unless I miss my guess were ladies of ill repute.

The motel was allegedly owned by folks with shady reputations. Among reporters, I hung with were Mel Carrico of The Roanoke Times, Ozzie Osborn of The Roanoke News, Carl Shires of the Richmond News-Leader and George Kelly of the Norfolk Virginian-Pilot. Ozzie Osborn, a quiet spoken man, remarked when he saw a couple of raggedly dressed delegates lighting up joints, "I don't think this is what Thomas Jefferson had in mind."

Because of hassling over trivial matters, McGovern did not give his acceptance speech until about 3 a.m. He was already a dead duck since television was showing ordinary people images of these strange creatures who were parading around the convention hall. I talked to many of them and they weren't bad people, but they were so politically naive it boggled the imagination. I even met Dr. Hunter Thompson who had become a darling of the left with his Gonzo Journalism. McGovern went down in flames but the liberals who had taken over the Virginia Democratic Party remained in control until the late 1970s when more moderate leaders, tired of losing elections, emerged and changed the leftward direction of the state party.

That same summer, two weeks after the Democratic convention, I returned to Miami Beach for the Republican National Convention. The contrast between the two could not have been more stark. The state GOP delegation was well dressed and well heeled. We stayed at Bar Harbor in a plush first-class hotel with all the amenities. Every evening there would be a post-convention party in a room looking out on the Atlantic Ocean and I had a good time socializing and conversing with such stalwarts as Governor Linwood Holton, 4th District Chairman Dortch Warriner (later to become a federal judge), Congressman Joel Broyhill and others. Holton had been elected in 1969 as the first Virginia Republican Governor in modern times and was under fire from some elements for supposedly not being partisan enough in his dealings with the state legislature and in his dispensation of patronage.

Though Holton deserved some of the fire aimed at him, he initiated a long overdue reorganization of state government and needed help from Democrats in the Democratic controlled General Assembly to get his programs enacted. His message of racial understanding in his inauguration speech was timely in a state that had too long been marked by racial divisions.

For the first time I got tear-gassed, albeit accidentally. Carl Shires, Mel Carrico and myself were leaving the convention hall late one night when police moved in on a group of boisterous anti-war demonstrators who had been shouting obscenities at them and had begun to hurl objects. The cops used tear gas and as the crowd surged past, we were swept along with them. I felt my eyes stinging badly and my throat burning. There was nothing to do but move along with the crowd until we were safely out of range, but the experience is one I would never want to repeat.

I had a chance to see up close many of the folks who would later be identified with the Watergate scandal, including President Richard Nixon himself. He seemed to have not a worry in the world as he made his acceptance speech surrounded by Bob Haldeman, John Ehrlichman, Attorney General John Mitchell and others. Mitchell came to address the Virginia delegation one afternoon and I had a chance to ask him a few questions. He seemed supremely confident of victory and predicted that Congressman Bill Scott of Virginia would take the U.S. Senate seat then held by Democrat Bill Spong of Virginia. (It would have been astounding if I had realized at the time within a few years Mitchell would be in prison). As it turned out, it wasn't even close and Scott won in a landslide, beating a man who was a highly respected moderate and possessed a brilliant mind. I was with other reporters late in the campaign in southwest Virginia with Spong when he told us off the record his chances looked bleak. Like many other centrist Democrats, he was a victim of the takeover of his party by radicals and the ability of Republicans to brand all Democrats as ultra-liberals.

The 1970s were a turbulent time in state politics. In 1973 Mills Godwin, who has served as Governor as a Democrat from 1966 to 1970, made it official and became a Republican. He was handed the GOP nomination for Governor and won, narrowly defeating Henry Howell, the Democratic nominee.

Mills Godwin was the finest orator of his time and, though a product of the Byrd Machine, recognized during his first term that the state had been mired at the bottom in education of its young people far too long. Courageously, he campaigned for a state sales tax to improve education and saw it enacted. He should be credited with leading Virginia from near the bottom of the education barrel to a place much farther up the ladder.

Godwin, too, was the leader who deserves the major credit for originating Virginia's fine system of community colleges. When I saw Frank Turnage, president of Germanna Community College not long ago, I thought of the reason the main campus was originally located at Locust Grove in Orange County. Del. George Rawlings Jr. wanted it in Spotsylvania County, a locality he represented, by Del. French Slaughter, of Culpeper, wanted it located in his district and Slaughter prevailed. Later Del. Earl Dickinson pushed through another Germanna location in Spotsylvania and now a third campus will be opened in

Culpeper.

Henry Howell of Norfolk was a colorful character who could always be relied on to provide good copy for reporters who followed him on the campaign trail. He was invariably exuberant and irrepressible. He would stride into a country store, have his photo taken with a Polaroid with the owner and ask the owner to post it in the window as a conversation piece. He would decry the policies of the Virginia Electric and Power Company, or VEPCO (Howell liked to call it the 'Very Expensive Power Company') contending that "the big boys" kept electricity rates high at the expense of little people. He would ride through the state in a recreational vehicle equipped with a PA system and going down the streets of Harrisonburg or Grundy or some other place he would proclaim for passerby to hear, "This is Henry Howell, running for Governor of Virginia. There's more going around in the dark in Virginia than Santa Claus. Keep the big boys honest. Vote Henry Howell for Governor."

Howell had a knack for recalling people's name that bordered on the incredible. If he had met someone before, he knew their name even if a couple of years had lapsed since he'd last seen them. I was flattered when Howell said that the Fredericksburg paper had the finest political coverage in Virginia since I did most of that coverage. I liked Henry personally. He was someone you couldn't help but like, always friendly, always smiling.

And therein lies the rub. I have liked most of the politicians I have met, Democrats and Republicans, conservatives, moderates and liberals. George Rawlings and I were on good terms just as I stayed on good terms with Bill Scott and Harry Byrd Jr. There is much truth to the assumption that people who go into politics are largely ego-driven, but that is also the case in many other professions, including the media. In politics I have found that those who seek public office genuinely want to get things accomplished that they feel will be best for those they serve. The agendas may vary widely, but most politicians, believe it or not, do have core beliefs that keep them going.

Perhaps Plutarch said i best when he referred to public service. "They are wrong who think that politics is like an ocean voyage or a military campaign, something to be done with some particular end in view, something which leaves off as soon as that end is reached. It is not a public chore to be got over with. It is a way of life."

One example. I heard in the year 2002 that a young man who lived in Fredericksburg and worked in the office of the House of Representatives Majority Leader Richard Gephardt, a very liberal Democrat, was involving himself in local politics. I assumed the young man, Tom Byrnes, shared the political views of his employer. But when I finally got to know him I realized he was a moderate Democrat whose main job with Gephardt involved graphic design. I consider Tom a friend and a talented individual. He left the Majority Leader's office when Gephardt gave it up to run for President. Tom has now turned to consulting, hoping to make a go of it in the Fredericksburg area where candidates historically have tended to run their own campaigns and not pay for advice and guidance.

In 1976 I attended the Democratic National Convention where Jimmy Carter, an obscure former Governor of Georgia, was nominated for President. A year earlier when Henry Howell invited me to a campaign rally in Norfolk for Carter he introduced me to him and said with a straight face, "This man is going to be the next President of the United States," I had to control myself from laughing. By the time I got the convention at Madison Square Garden the laughter was gone.

The Republicans met in Kansas City and Ronald Reagan was challenging the incumbent President Gerald Ford for the nomination. It was a close contest with just a handful of uncommitted delegates left. Among them was a woman from southwest Virginia in her 80s whose name I cannot recall. I do remember that I wrote several stories about her demand that Reagan and Ford come to personally see her before she would decide which to vote for. And both did pay her a visit, thus rewarding her lifelong Republicanism. Ford squeaked by (she voted for him) but lost the election and the presidency. I think many who heard Reagan's powerful post nomination speech regretted that he had not been the nominee.

Ford had come a long way. In the late 1960s I had been at a meeting of the Virginia Press Association in Williamsburg when someone asked me if I would mind picking up the guest speaker at a nearby airport. I went to the airport and when I learned the plane had landed but could not find the speaker, I had him paged. A few minutes later Gerald Ford, then the Minority Leader of the House of Representatives, appeared. We had a pleasant conversation though I certainly could not have imagined, and I'm sure he could not either, that in five years time he would become President of the United States upon the resignation of Richard M. Nixon.

If you never heard Ronald Reagan speak in person then you cannot fully grasp why he has been called 'The Great Communicator.' Other than Franklin Roosevelt and John Kennedy, no other speaker in this century who became President has been his equal. He was absolutely spellbinding as he talked of "the shining city on a hill" that America could become, how the nation's greatest days were ahead of it. I was present in 1980 when he was nominated for President in Detroit and I had no doubt he would be elected because the electorate could not resist falling under the spell of his stirring oratory. One of Reagan's speechwriters, Landon Parvin, and his wife, Alice, live in Fredericksburg. Landon, who still does speeches for major American figures, was the genius behind Nancy Reagan's famous 'Second Hand Rose' skit at the Gridiron Dinner in Washington early in Reagan's first term. Landon and Alice are great down to earth people.

In my adult lifetime I have had the opportunity to know all the men who became Governor of Virginia, including Lindsay Almond, Albertis Harrison, Mills Godwin, Linwood Holton, John Dalton, Charles Robb, Gerald Baliles, Doug Wilder, George Allen, Jim Gilmore and Mark Warner Wilder hung a portrait of my ancestor George Mason in his office because he was the grandson of a slave and Mason had refused to sign the Constitution because it did not provide for the abolition of slavery over a period of time. I think they all performed well in their roles as chief executive. I will leave it to scholars and historians to decide which belong in the top ranks.

CHAPTER SIXTEEN

To The Egress

As the summer of 1987 ended I was looking around for a new career. I'd been a news reporter nearly thirty years and had the opportunity to meet many people and observe many significant events, but there were other considerations.

Foremost was there were no new worlds to conquer. I had been voted by legislators the most respected print journalist covering the General Assembly and felt that an honor, particularly considering that I worked for a paper, though its circulation was growing, that was not considered among the state's major publications.

I'd written hundreds of thousands of words about politicians and legislative actions and now it seemed that I was writing stories almost by rote. Maybe one could call it 'Groundhog Day' syndrome. There is an age-old journalistic question. Is it best to leave someone on a particular beat for many years so the person has a chance to become a respected authority on the subject, or is it preferable to have someone cover one beat, such as politics, for just a few years, give it all they have and then put someone else on that beat for the sake of a fresh perspective? I don't have the answer because there are benefits in both approaches. But my long tenure as the paper's political and legislative reporter enabled me to build up an increasing network of sources with a vast knowledge of state politics. Such people can be cultivated only if they find over time that you can be trusted with their confidence. The Washington Post rotated its reporters regularly. At any given time I knew more about what was going on in Virginia politics than any of the hot shot investigative reporters they sent down.

One such reporter in the early 1970s was a flaky guy named Carl Bernstein who was second string to Helen Dewar, a class act. Bernstein filed little of significance and was recalled to Washington where he was put on the police beat. The night of the Watergate burglary in June, 1972 he was working the beat and the rest is history. I have to credit him for persistence in demanding that he be kept on the story when some of his editors at The Post, who were not particularly fond of him, tried to freeze him out. I enjoyed talking with Bernstein and he had a nice sense of humor. But he seemed lazy and lacking ambition. Little did I know that he and Bob Woodward would make history through Watergate and become the inspiration for thousands of wannabee investigative reporters who started to flood into the nation's schools of journalism. And I would have been astounded if someone had predicted Dustin Hoffman would be playing the role of Carl Bernstein in a major movie within a few years.

Another reason I was seeking a new career was that the paper was starting to change dramatically from what it had once been. Newspaper publishers were increasingly worried about the future impact of television 'news' on their fortunes. TV news is all about folks with blow dried hair and acting ability providing information about the news, sports, weather, etc. in a format that entertains viewers. Reading detailed news stories is informative but is seldom entertaining. And we had reached—and the trend is even more marked these days—an age when people wanted to be entertained more than they wanted to be informed.

Therefore the people who ran the newspaper commissioned surveys to find out, not surprisingly, that the favorite reading of their subscribers was Ann Landers and the comic strips. Though to me the cartoon 'Crock' is must reading every day, the only cartoon I really look at regularly. Cartoonist Bill Rechin, who lives in Spotsylvania and does the drawing, is talented and a nice guy.

The decree came down that more photos would be used, all stories would be shorter no matter what the subject. Thus an analytical piece on the election of a new Governor, something that actually mattered, could be no longer than a feel-good piece about some senior citizen in his 80s who still bowled two nights a week. The paper de-emphasized hard news at the expense of entertainment, just as many other papers were doing. Nowadays I can flip through many papers in a couple of minutes by avoiding the fluff.

Congress

D. French Slaughter Jr. of Culpeper was a member of the U.S. House of Representatives and had been since his election in 1984. I had known Slaughter during his long years of service in the Virginia General Assembly and greatly respected him. He had been part of the Byrd Organization and was a quiet soft-spoken lawyer with a down to earth manner and a quick incisive mind.

He was the most uncharismatic of men, and yet that was part of his charm. People who met French Slaughter instinctively liked him even if they disagreed with his conservative political philosophy. He had gone unchallenged for re-election and he won fairly easily when he ran for Congress the first time.

When French Slaughter left the legislature, I had visited him and written a story for the paper on his retirement. He told me later how much he had appreciated it. In early October, 1987 I got word that the person who ran Slaughter's Fredericksburg office was leaving. I was asked if I was interested.

Some brief negotiations followed about salary but there was little doubt in my mind I would accept. Once the deal was made, I let the managing editor of the paper know of my decision. His name was Robert E. Lee Baker who had once been a Washington Post editor and who soon planned to retire from the local paper. We had a pleasant conversation filled with mutual memories of Virginia politics and political figures.

The newsroom folks gave me a going away party and presented me a few gifts. I have the print of the Virginia Capitol depicted around the turn of the century.

I quickly discovered that the Congress, fifty miles to the north, was a different ball game from the state legislature fifty miles south. In Richmond things actually got done. Legislators were given 60 or 45 days to complete action on hundreds of bills and did. Sometimes it resembled a three-ring circus, and sometimes members of the Assembly were able to give only cursory attention to important matters, but at least decisions were made, action was taken.

By contrast, Congress moved at a glacial pace. When someone called to inquire about the status of a particular bill, more often than not I found any action on the legislation was still months off, perhaps a year or more away. A bill would go to committee, be put in subcommittee, be rewritten, rewritten again and then for the sake of exercise rewritten some more. Lobbyists for special interests were well paid to examine every phrase and every clause in any bills that applied to their interest groups. If they found something they did not like, or if there was something they wanted to add, the lobbying wheels were set in motion. The appropriate legislators were contacted, greased, wined and dined. And why? Because often on just a phrase in a bill that might sound innocuous to anyone else, to some millions of dollars would be at stake, turf wars would be settled, the keys to the pharmaceutical or mining or agriculture kingdom would be bestowed.

My job was to hold the fort in Fredericksburg and that mainly involved dealing with people who had become frustrated with the federal government and sought the Congressman's help.

The work done by a congressional field office is varied in scope and ours was a busy office. Day in and day out came people with problems with Social Security, the Internal Revenue Service, the Postal Service, Army, Navy, Air Force, Marines, Coast Guard, Department of Agriculture, Office of Personnel Management, Office of Workers Compensation Claims, the Environmental Protection Agency, the Geologic Survey, the Library of Congress, the National Archives, the Department of Veterans Affairs and many others. Our job was to give constituents whatever help we could. Some had legitimate grievances and our assistance left them grateful. Others either had no case or were at the mercy of capricious federal regulations that were nearly impossible to change.

I could write a separate book about the ignorance of many people about governments that control much of their lives, the folks who call a Congressional office to complain about potholes or state taxes. Are they teaching government in public schools anymore?

There are many dedicated federal workers who do outstanding jobs. And there are federal workers who are arrogant, stupid, lazy and think they should be paid for not serving the public that pays them. Philosophically I believe that the federal government has grown far too big and needs downsizing. Yet I realize that many people who say they share that belief are the first to protest when it is suggested that any federal programs be cut that might affect them. One fellow said he felt the federal government ought to give him the money to start a gas station. Not loan him the money, but give it.

French Slaughter was not only my employer but a friend. He had no opposition for re-election in 1988 to speak of but then came 1990. A young challenger named David Smith (he was from Winchester and the son of powerful Democratic Del. Al Smith who had gone from rags to riches by placing various Tastee Freeze franchises around the state) was put up by the Democrats and I was asked by Chief of Staff Rick Holcomb to take a leave of absence from the federal job to go over to Culpeper for three months as campaign press secretary. I dutifully accepted and began the Culpeper commute.

French Slaughter was never in trouble, though his young opponent David Smith, did mount a vigorous challenge. But not long after I joined the campaign I detected something troublesome. It had also been spotted by the campaign manager, Tony Likins, and by Rick Holcomb.

French Slaughter seemed to have lost some of the sharpness that had always marked his political career. While traveling with him in the past we had often discussed history, particularly World War II and Winston Churchill, our favorite subjects. He was a remarkable student of history and seemed to never forget anything he had read. French had been seriously wounded in the leg during the World War II European campaign and walked thereafter with a limp.

But now it was different. As I traveled with him to various campaign events he talked little. He was always friendly and polite, but I sensed something amiss.

The media was constantly asking (particularly reporter Scott Rafshoon of The Free Lance-Star, son of one of Jimmy Carter's chief political gurus) why the Congressman did not meet his opponent in debate and I had an answer. The Persian Gulf War was looming, Congress was in session practically every day and the Congressman had been elected to go to Washington and represent the people. He was on the job where he belonged. I must say that I felt it was just as well because of my concern about his well-being.

My worst fears were realized on July 1, 1991 when Rick Holcomb called the staff together and said that Congressman Slaughter would resign his office effective that fall because of a series of slight strokes that had taken place. After he stepped down he lived in a home in Charlottesville until his death nearly ten years later. My belief is that the Alzheimer's that befell him was starting to take hold during that campaign in the fall of 1990. Rick Holcomb, his chief of staff later became Commissioner of the Virginia Department of Motor Vehicles during the administration of Governors George Allen and Jim Gilmore and in his usual efficient style turned it from one of the most inept state agencies to one of the best.

French Slaughter will be remembered as a dedicated public servant. Beyond that he was a splendid human being who was liked even by those who did not share his political philosophy. He was a southern gentleman to the core and I was honored to be a member of his staff.

Lemonade From Lemons

When George Allen won the Republican nomination for the seat to be vacated by Slaughter, I became one of his supporters. I had known him when he first came to the General Assembly as a member of the House of Delegates and was impressed immediately by what seemed his boundless enthusiasm for the principles of limited government. While other legislators made the party rounds in the evening, Allen studied dozens of bills looking for nuances in them. His hero was Thomas Jefferson and he was proud that he represented Mr. Jefferson's district. His father, also named George, had been the hard charging coach of the Washington Redskins who sought victory at all costs and it was obvious that the son had inherited his father's combative streak.

Once George won, he asked me to stay on in the Fredericksburg office and I accepted. But no sooner had he been sworn into office, than Democrats in the legislature set out to teach the young whippersnapper with his highly partisan ways a lesson. During the redistricting process following the 1990 census, they carved up the 7th district so that George's home was in the same district as the far more senior Republican Congressman Tom Bliley of Richmond. As all avenues closed, it became obvious that Allen's term would last only through 1992.

It must be said for George Allen that, like his father, when given lemons, he makes lemonade. While enunciating conservative principles in Washington, he began to explore the possibility of running for Governor in 1993. By the middle of 1992 his campaign for the GOP nomination was hitting its stride and it was sometimes hard to tell where the congressional office left off and the gubernatorial campaign began. There was criticism that he used the congressional office to run for governor but please don't be too "shocked, shocked . . ." (as they said in Casablanca) that this might have happened. It has before and it will again.

The bottom line is that George Allen is one of the most effective and charismatic political campaigners ever to hit Virginia. He had a special Reaganesque quality about him and when I traveled with him to town meetings during his congressional term and, wearing his cowboy boots, he invariably charmed the audiences, even those who had come to give him hell. Though many said he could not get the nomination, I knew better. He was folksy, he was caring, he was sincere and he had about him a boyish quality that was infectious and could not be resisted.

He was also one of the biggest cheapskates I have ever met and he was proud of it. His wife's brother told a story of when they first got married Susan, who is equally charming, asked him to bring home some toothpaste and instead he brought home a can of baking soda, saying it was cheaper and just as good. There were dozens of stories about his cheapness and he didn't mind telling many of them on himself.

Once while he was in Congress I drove him to several Spotsylvania County stops until early afternoon. He suggested we get lunch and I had visions of a nice restaurant. But he asked me to pull up to a 7-11 where hotdogs were advertised for two for 99 cents and we I stood outside munching on hotdogs while people came up and introduced themselves. "Man," said the Congressman, "you can't beat this. Where else could you get such a great meal for a buck fifty?" I could have told him what I thought of the meal, but resisted the temptation.

Among those seeking the GOP gubernatorial nomination was my long time friend, Clinton Miller of Woodstock, a former professional country music singer and state prosecutor (we had once collaborated on a song called, 'Electric Lady,' performed at a General Assembly party in Richmond) and I had mixed emotions. But Allen won the nomination and Clint Miller was later put on the State Corporation Commission and is now Judge Miller.

George Allen was easily elected Governor. I think he did a commendable job, particularly in economic development where his record is one that will be hard to match by any future chief executive. He also articulated his belief that the government is best which governs least. His administration was marked by much partisan bickering with the legislature that was probably unavoidable with a bitter struggle going on for control of the General Assembly.

I was more than happy to climb back aboard the train when George Allen ran for U.S. Senate in 2000 and defeated Chuck Robb. George would be a great Republican candidate for President in 2008, particularly if Democrats nominate BroomHillary.

Governor George Allen appointed me to the Virginia Board of Historic Resources and later the Virginia Military Advisory Council, but I later resigned as a member of the Historic Resources Board because it was taking an inordinate amount of time. Governor Mark Warner appointed me first to the Virginia Charitable Gaming Commission and then the Virginia Charitable Gaming Board.

A Man of Conviction

Herbert Bateman of Newport News had been a member of the

Virginia State Senate since the mid 1960s when he was elected to the U.S. House of Representatives in 1982. A moderate-conservative, Bateman rose to become an influential Senator and was a Democrat until ultra-liberal Democrats who did not like his conservatism made it clear they were out to get him.

He became an independent and then a Republican and maintained his popularity in his home region by winning re-election easily. I know of no public servant who made policy decisions based on his own conscience and convictions more than Herb Bateman and I had years of opportunity to watch him in the Senate of Virginia. He never caved in to expediency. He could have spared himself grief by voting against the Brady Bill and not incurring the enmity of the National Rifle Association, but did not because states such as Virginia with instant background checks were exempt from the bill's provisions. Although I might not have voted the same way, I thought the NRA overreacted by putting him on its top ten hit list.

I worked for the Congressman in his Fredericksburg office (most of the Fredericksburg area had been put in the 1st Congressional District as a result of 1991 redistricting) starting in 1993. For about six years my co-worker was Ruth Jessie, who had previously worked for Paul Trible when he was in the House and had worked in a Tappahannock office for Herb Bateman since his election. She left the Fredericksburg office when redistricting was changed and the Congressman opened an office in Warsaw, Ruth's hometown. Ruth's husband, Lewis, a prominent Northern Neck realtor, had died of cancer during the time she was in the Fredericksburg office.

At the beginning of the year 2000, Herb Bateman announced he would not seek re-election. The decision, I believe, was a good one since he had suffered a number of health problems and longed to spend more time on the golf links and with his wife and grandchildren. Unfortunately, in September of that year while still in office the Congressman suffered a heart attack and died. The office came under the supervision of the Clerk of the House until Jo Ann Davis of Gloucester, the winner of an election to be the successor in the district, took office in January 2001. I have been working for her since and she has been a worthy successor. But more about that later. I keep in touch with Dan Scandling, who was Bateman's Chief of Staff and is now Chief of Staff to Representative Frank Wolf, a powerful member of the Virginia delegation.

Travels with Politicians

Since leaving the newspaper business in the fall of 1987, I have kept my hand in journalism by writing a weekly column, 'Old Dominion Politics,' that appears in more than 20 Virginia papers—most of them weeklies, though the column is occasionally used by the Norfolk and Roanoke papers. It gives me a reason to drop by the General Assembly and keep in touch with state politicians.

The thing I miss most about being a political reporter is that I no longer get to travel with various candidates of both parties in October.

October in Virginia is glorious, particularly on mornings when there is a nip in the air, plenty of sunshine and the trees are laden with golden leaves.

In those final weeks before the general election, the campaigns moved into high gear and the adrenalin was pumping at full force. One could feel the electricity as crowds greeted the aspirants at rallies in various towns and cities.

I can still see John Warner walking down the streets of Farmville and stopping to advise a motorist looking forlornly at his engine on possible remedies for his car troubles. (And John Warner is a great campaigner as well as a great statesman). Or Henry Howell picking up a bottle of milk of magnesia in a drug store in Montross and decrying the cruelty of a state that imposed a sales tax on such patent medicines.

Often candidates would swing from euphoric moods to testiness in those final days of an effort to which they had devoted so much of the time and energy and other people's money. In 1978, locked in a race with Warner for U.S. Senate that all the polls said would be extremely close, former Attorney General Andrew Miller snapped at me and some other reporters for what he felt was unfair reporting of his campaign. He thought we had implied that his speaking style was dull and pedantic compared to Warner's folksy manner. But Miller quickly recovered his composure and lost the election by an eyelash. He had every right to demand a recount which would have prolonged the outcome, but didn't. That same gracious attitude prevailed in 1989 when Marshall Coleman didn't ask for a recount though he lost to L. Douglas Wilder in the closest gubernatorial match-up of the century. Miller and Coleman both did outstanding jobs as attorney generals of the state.

L. Douglas Wilder

When Doug Wilder came to the Senate in the early 1970's as its first black member he sported a full-blown Afro and was articulate, combative and eager to serve his mostly black constituency. As time passed and he saw the possibility of seeking statewide office, Wilder began to broaden his outlook and his interests. When I interviewed him he seldom mentioned racial matters. After he was nominated for Lieutenant Governor in 1985, the pundits gave him practically no chance but he embarked on a masterful campaign. Wilder traveled across the state in a modest caravan, relentlessly campaigning fourteen hours a day. He quietly solicited and got the support of old time conservative Democrats like Speaker of the House A.L. Philpott who had once been leaders in the battle to retain racial desegregation.

Some thought it was cynical of Wilder to seek such support and for Philpott and others of his stripe to give it, but I don't. I believe it represented a coming to terms of men who shared many of the same basic beliefs except that Wilder was the grandson of slaves and the others—some of them at least-the grandsons of slave-holders. Wilder recognized it was pointless and self-defeating to brood longer about the past and the others realized that the time had long passed when blacks could be denied political leadership roles in Virginia.

I was present in a small restaurant near Philpott's hometown of Bassett when he officially endorsed Wilder. I recall Wilder's gracious speech, praising Philpott and the other conservatives assembled for the occasion. Outside the restaurant a Confederate flag waved, but Wilder ignored it. I think this particular event was the spark that ignited the Wilder campaign and eventually propelled him to become Lieutenant Governor and then Governor. But it should be noted that flooding rains in parts of Virginia where the Republican vote is strongest contributed to the defeat of GOP nominee John Chichester.

Let me add that I have little doubt that Wilder's efforts to establish a National Slavery Museum in Fredericksburg will succeed. He has already shown his great determination to win no matter what the odds may be against him.

B-A-L-I-L-E-S

The most unassuming governor of those I have known—and in many respects the brightest—was Gerald Baliles. As a member of the House of Delegates, he kept a low profile, becoming best known for his law to allow right turns on red. But he had a shrewd mind and an uncanny ability to remember people's faces and names. Sometimes he would go into a room with as many as a hundred people, introduce himself to each and then before his speech say, "My name is Baliles, rhymes with smiles, and if you know my name, I should know yours," and then call everyone in the room by their names. It was an impressive gimmick. In 1981 he was elected Virginia Attorney General.

I don't know how Baliles managed to win so easily in 1985 and sweep with him into office the Democratic candidates for lieutenant governor and attorney general. The Republicans had what most thought was the dream ticket of Wyatt Durrette for Governor, John Chichester for Lieutenant Governor, and Buster O'Brien for Attorney General, all young, vigorous and popular.

But Durrette's campaign seemed uninspired and listless. Perhaps it was due to overconfidence as he lost several debates with Baliles until the realization finally hit panicky GOP state leaders that the dream was turning into a nightmare. Being too cocksure has led to the defeat of many candidates who thought they were surefire winners. If you are going to run for political office, you have to run hard and run long and ardently court every possible vote. If you have no stomach for such things, then it is best not to enter the arena.

No-one has ever been able to give me a convincing reason about what makes the electorate in Virginia and the country so volatile. Why do politicians whose poll numbers look great in July end up being beaten by landslides in November? Because I have been around politicians so long and have what I consider a more or less fixed political philosophy, it doesn't take me long to make up my mind. But the public in general cares little about politics, is often largely tuned out to politicians, has less of philosophy than what it considers enlightened self interest, and people can be converted in large numbers to change their minds.

A good case in point was 1993's gubernatorial election. When Republicans nominated George Allen, Democrats were gleeful. He was barely known outside his home area and his Democratic opponent Mary Sue Terry had widespread name recognition and had been elected Attorney General twice at the top of the ticket.

But Allen sensed her support was a mile wide and an inch deep and launched a campaign blitz that gave him a huge victory after the early polls in June showed him virtually dead in the water. Ms. Terry's campaign was among the worst I ever observed by a statewide contender, although I liked her personally and considered her someone of great ability.

Another example of perfect political timing was Republican Jim Gilmore's adoption of a 'No Car Tax' slogan in the 1997 gubernatorial race. Ironically, his Democratic opponent, Don Beyer, had the opportunity earlier on to call for repeal of the state's dreaded car tax, but declined to do so because he is a car dealer. Although Beyer is very personable, his campaign was a shambles from beginning to end.

CHAPTER SEVENTEEN

The Lottery

I've never held public office so I've never gotten a law enacted, though I have observed laws being made at the local, state and federal levels for a long time.

I think I can take at least a small piece of credit for one law that has had an enormous impact on Virginia.

Back in the 1970s Billy O'Brien, a member of the House of Delegates from Virginia Beach, started trying to pass a bill that would give Virginians an opportunity to vote on the creation of a state lottery.

O'Brien was a coach and teacher and a man of great charm, but the cause he espoused seemed absolutely hopeless. He was practically the only supporter of a state lottery and it had opposition from some of the most powerful people in Virginia, including Speaker of the House John Warren Cooke and A.L. Philpott, the majority leader, both of O'Brien's own Democratic Party.

I saw O'Brien frequently, particularly in evenings when we would gather at Garry DeBruhl's hospitality suite.

I felt Virginia should adopt a lottery. Why let other states such as Maryland make all that money from a lottery? I was a frequent purchaser of Maryland lottery tickets as were thousands of others who lived in the Northern Virginia area. People who worked in that region were frequently enlisted by others to purchase lottery tickets for them as I often did.

A Voluntary Tax

O'Brien asked if I might help him write some press releases and speeches concerning the justification for a lottery. My thought was that the best way to sell the lottery was to depict it as a voluntary tax that people were eager to pay and one that would bring in many millions in new tax revenues to the state.

With that money, releases and speeches should suggest, such

things as education, senior citizens, mental health, public transportation and the like could be given significant economic boosts. I felt it important that O'Brien make the lottery appeal to the widest spectrum of interest groups.

And that's what he did. News releases were issued at intervals favoring a state lottery. He made speeches all over the state. He began to convert people and groups to his cause and those people and groups put pressure on their elected representatives to back a lottery. Within six years of the adoption of the strategy to sell the lottery by giving it broad appeal, the General Assembly was ready to go along. O'Brien wanted lottery funds earmarked to specific groups, but the legislature balked at that, saying it might be done later. A lottery referendum passed and today the lottery is the third largest generator of funds in Virginia. Revenues were first put into the general fund where they were often gobbled up by legislators who for years resisted the idea of supporting a lottery. Now they are mainly used for public education. And what about Billy O'Brien, the man who made the lottery possible in Virginia, the man responsible for the fact that today the lottery generates about $400 million in revenues annually for the state?

The answer is he wasn't given the time of day. Though he quit the legislature they wouldn't consider putting him on the Lottery Commission. Not only that, but when he got paid a little to go around the state campaigning for passage of the lottery the media howled, contending he was using his office to benefit the groups paying him.

If you ever feel that perseverance and sticking to your guns in politics will result in victory, then I suppose you are right when you consider O'Brien's case. Yet it is also instructive that the bottom line of politics is if you are successful someone will come along and try to steal your ideas and take credit for them. That is what happened to Billy O'Brien who was simply pushed out into the cold while others remained behind to divvy up the spoils.

Mr. Speaker

When Tom Moss of Norfolk, who has one of the quickest wits I have ever known, was elected to the House of Delegates in the late 1960s as a Democrat, his future in that chamber did not appear very bright.

Moss, along with others, had run on a platform whose slogan was, 'Get Virginia Out Of The Byrd Cage', an allusion to the long control of state politics by the Byrd Organization..

The Speaker of the House at the time was W. Blackburn 'Blackie' Moore of Berryville, a Byrd Democrat to the core. And Moore wasn't prepared to give Moss or any of his ilk the time of day.

But after Moore left, John Warren Cooke of Mathews County became Speaker and not only put anti-Byrd Democrats on important committees, but also for the first time gave some choice committee assignments to Republicans. He could afford to be magnanimous since conservative Democrats were in a big majority. (It was a time when tobacco was still king, rural elements dominated the legislature and some did not consider the northern part of Virginia worthy of any attention).

Cooke was a man of integrity and judgment who will go down as one of the best House Speakers in Virginia history. He still publishes a newspaper and, though in his 80s, remains active.

Later, as Moss became more influential and conservative, he joked about those early days when he and others who had run against the Byrd Organization were regarded as lepers.

When A.L. Philpott, a man of iron discipline who liked to drink bourbon and apple juice, became Speaker, Moss became Majority Leader. Philpott held the job for years and Moss, who aspired to become Speaker, doubted if he would ever reach that pinnacle. But after Philpott developed a terminal illness and stepped down, Moss took over the role of Speaker, something that would have seemed the longest of shots when he first came to the House.

The philosophy Moss espoused initially that was regarded as liberalism when he first ran and won, became moderate conservatism as time passed. Yet today in a new century the Virginia House of Delegates is controlled for the most part by conservative Republicans who are pro-life, pro-gun and fiscal conservatives. Thus by some sort of reverse osmosis, one chamber of the state legislature is again in control of a political philosophy that the late Harry Byrd Sr. might well have approved. Moss is currently Treasurer of the City of Norfolk.

CHAPTER EIGHTEEN

Travels

If I had saved all the money I've spent on travel I probably could have retired long ago. But I don't regret it because going to places where the way of life is different from the familiar one of Fredericksburg and surroundings has always been a priority for me.

I haven't traveled as much as some, although I undoubtedly would have if I'd had the means to take extended trips around the world. But I've probably traveled more than most.

Growing up, I recall hearing the voice of Edward R. Murrow on radio as he reported from London during The Blitz. To a boy, London seemed as remote and far away as the Moon or Mars, as did Germany and France and other places where war was being waged. Now people travel to London for weekend getaways. I've been to Europe many times and I've been in England at least 30 times, maybe more. I had a great trip to London and Paris in February of 2003 with Heather Young, my co-worker, and her mother Joanne Young, although heavy snows at home delayed our arrival back in the States.

Another memorable trip was with buddies Willie Mills, Pete Marshall, Doug Derieux and John Edwards in 1981. We covered an incredible amount of ground, going to Ireland, England, Germany and Austria. Derieux, who died young, was a close friend. One of the highlights of our trip was when Doug was allowed to drive the rental car in Malton, England and the young lady with him reported to us that 'he was driving on the footpaths' (sidewalks).

London is among my favorite cities, one that is always an adventure in the exploration. Since I have tried to develop cheap travel to a science, I may write a pamphlet on the subject. A few years ago I spent ten days in the United Kingdom. I flew Icelandic Airways from BWI to London at a round-trip cost of $349 plus tax, half the fare being asked by most airlines. True, you have to go by way of Reykjavik Airport in Iceland and the trip takes a couple of hours longer but is cheaper. Landing in Iceland is a weird experience since as the plane approaches the Keflavik airport and you look out the window, it seems you are about to land on the moon. The times I have been there it has always been late fall and there is only a brief period of daylight. It seemed strange to look out of the restaurant window at 9:30 a.m. while eating breakfast and see only darkness. But in summer it stays light practically around the clock. In my hotel room there was a sulfuric smell because underground semi-volcanic hot springs are used to provide heat.

In London, I stayed at the Victory Services Club, a place that is semi-subsidized by the British government and whose sponsor is the Duke of Edinburgh. It is operated for the benefit mainly of British veterans who can go there and enjoy cheap rooms, food and drink. It is located in the heart of London near Marble Arch and being an American veteran for just fifteen bucks a year dues I can belong. I paid about twenty-five dollars a night for a room and could get a full English breakfast for three dollars and dinner for four dollars. Of course, English dinner consists of something that is going to be boiled, bland and tasteless, but that's the case no matter if you eat at the Victory Services Club or Claridge's.

There used to be a bar in the club called 'The El Alamein Room' where crusty old British vets gathered to talk about the past. I was thrilled to meet men who served in North Africa under the command of General Bernard Law Montgomery or 'Monty' as they called him. They had fascinating stories to tell about those long ago days when they were fighting the legendary German General Erwin Rommel in North Africa. Some of them went on to take part in the invasion of Europe. Sadly, nearly all of Monty's boys are gone now as is the El Alamein room.

I have witnessed House of Commons in session and was struck by how extraordinarily small the chamber is. Yet I could imagine Winston Churchill, whose statue stands across the street within sight of Westminster Abbey, rallying members of Parliament and all of Britain to the cause during the bleak days of 1940 when all appeared lost.

Paris is more architecturally impressive than London and the food is better. I have been there a number of times and it has great charm and history, though some Parisians seem to care little for American tourists.

But to see the real France, as to see the real America, one must go out into the beautiful provinces. Nothing has ever impressed me more than visits to the beaches of Normandy. Looking out at the English Channel one can appreciate even more the incredible bravery of the troops who waded ashore on June 6, 1944 and thereafter. Thousands were killed, even more were wounded. Row upon row of crosses in the American Cemetery represent a grim story. Just being there provides an insight into what it must have been like on that day to come ashore with the murderous fire of German soldiers raining down. It is an awesome sight and the artificial Mulberry ports put in to allow supplies to be shipped ashore can still be seen underwater for they were sunk by a storm that came several weeks after the invasion.

(Incidentally, I first went to England in 1974 along with about 20 others, including my wife and daughter, for the wedding of Russ Yinger, owner of Metro Drug Store, to Liz Bowers, an English lady, in the small town of Malton near the Scottish border. The wedding took place in a church dating back to the 13th century. When I went back to Malton a few years ago, I was dismayed to find that it had grown tremendously and no longer had that small town atmosphere.)

George Smith Patton Jr.

There is an American Cemetery at Hamm just outside Luxembourg City. There under a small cross that says PATTON, GEORGE S. JR, GENERAL, THIRD ARMY, is buried one of the greatest military leaders who ever lived—a man who is one of my heroes. Next to him are the graves of several enlisted men. While some have opined that Patton's remains should be brought home, I think it is fitting that he is buried in the soil of a land he helped liberate. Patton was a great-great grandson of Hugh Mercer of Fredericksburg and his grandfather, the first George Patton and among a number of Patton kin who served in the Civil War, was killed in action

I was in Geneva in Switzerland in 1984 when President Ronald Reagan met Soviet premier Gorbachev in a summit meeting. It was one of the coldest Novembers in European history and I stood shivering as Reagan and his entourage drove up in limousines and entered the place where the first session was to be held. It was a historic moment and we had a President whose firm determination would eventually lead to the demise of the tyrannical Soviet Union. The Reverend Jesse Jackson was also there for some reason. He had about as much to do with the meeting as I did. My friend, Willie Mills, found a warm pub and stayed there while I visited the summit site and stood freezing outside. He was much smarter than me for though I had on heavy clothing, I had to remain outside in the intense cold while reporters with press credentials found warm places inside the meeting place. Reagan held several more summits with Gorbachev, including one in Iceland in a small cottage that I saw later. His firm determination to oppose totalitarian government made him one of the great presidents of the century.

Deutschland

Germany is among my favorite countries and I have spent considerable time there. The Germans are friendly to Americans though we fought against them in two wars. They are also a very neat and precise people. You see them sweeping their sidewalks at nights and in the mornings and the only litter you ever spot along German roads or streets is that thrown by American troops stationed in the country. Driving on the autobahn where there are no speed limits is a bit harrowing. And if you go into a restaurant at an autobahn interchange you may see dogs sitting by tables as their masters eat. Germans love dogs.

I have walked the streets of Berlin a number of times and stood near the place where Hitler lived in his Bunker until the Russians entered the city and he committed suicide, ending the so-called Thousand Year Reich. Though I am a World War II buff, you meet very few Germans who want to discuss that war. They prefer to forget it. The late Bobby Heflin and I used to take about the years he and his wife, Alice, spent in Germany while he was on military duty. It was a perilous time and the Berlin Wall marked the chief emblem of The Cold War. Thanks to a great president, Ronald Reagan, it came down.

The Wall

The Berlin Wall was still there when I visited the first few times. I spent a few days in West Berlin which was prosperous and glittering. When I passed a checkpoint to board a train in East Germany, the contrast was stark. East Berlin was dimly lighted and gloomy. Instead of Mercedes, the people drove beat-up old cars and the infrastructure was crumbling. The train I took to Warsaw was frayed and deteriorating. All those who criticize free enterprise should have witnessed the contrast between a socialistic society and a society that rewards hard work. It was startling. Even more incredible is the number of American liberals who were taken in by the communist system. It is still fashionable to talk of the witch hunts of the Joe McCarthy era, and certainly McCarthy brought his fate on himself, but evidence has since demonstrated that there were many communists and fellow travelers in various branches of government, including the State Department. Two of Franklin Roosevelt's top aides, Alger Hiss and Harry Dexter White, were traitors who passed along highly classified information to the Soviet Union.

Many Others

I have probably not mentioned a number of people who have had some impact on my life. C.M. "Pete" Hearn was a political confidante and a personal friend until his untimely death.

State Senator Edd Houck, though a member of the opposite political party, has been a genuine friend as has Pete Poulos, a man that I have long admired. Pete came to his country from his native Greece and worked hard to learn the English language (and I think all who come here should learn to speak our country's language).

I've already mentioned Bill and Cessie Howell and they are two of the nicest people I know. Bill is now Speaker of the House of Delegates and a finer choice could not have been made. Del. Bobby Orrock of Caroline has been in office a long time and makes major contributions. Del. Mark Cole, a Republican, is a relative newcomer, but a person of rock solid integrity.

Wes Hall and I grew up together and he came from a proud but non-affluent family. Wes made it big time when he got in on the new era of credit cards and his name is on a gymnasium at Fork Union Military Academy built with his donations. In the old days Wes used to come by my house to read my comic books, since his folks frowned on that kind of entertainment. The Halls lived in a small house, still standing, on lower Charles Street near the railroad overpass. Wes was an outstanding basketball player in high school and remains a great friend to this day. Though he has been supremely successful financially, he has never forgotten where he came from.

Another boyhood friend who has done well is Bill Clift. I have only a hazy recollection of it, but Chip Houston is amused by a Clift anecdote (they were roommates at Randolph Macon Academy in Front Royal) concerning my brother and me.

According to this version, my brother Bob and I had a paper route and we partnered with Bill and split the proceeds three ways. He says I delivered five papers, Bob 10 and that he carried 65 papers. However, when Christmas came and Bill got a ton of dollars from rich folks when he gave out calendars, he took his mother's advice not to split the money with the Goolrick brothers. Thus he may well owe a debt of gratitude to his mother for starting him on the path to business success.

Both Wes Hall and Chip Houston carried the long defunct Washington Star newspaper as I did. I signed up just 12 subscribers and won a free trip to New York City. It was difficult to get anyone to take a Washington paper since the area was so Richmond oriented and people often went to the state capital to shop at the big stores on Broad Street.

It was my pleasure to work with Dan Scandling, Chief of Staff to Congressman Herbert Bateman, and despite our age difference, I think we've been very much on the same wavelength. The same is true for Chris Connelly, Chief of Staff to Representative Jo Ann Davis (he's from Buffalo) and Tim Baroody, her Legislative Director (and a good southerner) Their respective wives and daughters are Jennifer and Reagan and Kristin and Eden. Jennifer, who is also from Buffalo, gave up her job on the staff of House Speaker Denny Hastert to marry Chris, and Kristin Baroody helps with much of the political fund raising for the Congresswoman. Tim's father and grandfather were both prominent lobbyists on Capitol Hill. Another Davis staff member is Joe Schumacher who lives in Williamsburg and he and his wife, Karen, have a daughter, Madison. Joe and I enjoy frequent chats about baseball and books. And at the Congresswoman's Fredericksburg office are the indispensable Heather Young and Jenny Stein who manage to find all the things I regularly lose. (Ruth Jessie, who runs the Congresswoman's Tappahannock office, and I were co-workers for years, and Angela Welch of the Yorktown office was on Mr. Bateman's staff at the same time Ruth and I were. Angela's husband, Bill, has a terrific sense of humor and seems to be wired in to all significant political developments in the state).

Someone I admire is the Rev Don Forrester, blind pastor of Faith Baptist Church. He has a gift for inspiring people to do their best.

Coach John Fenlon and Coach Jake Maynard were inspirations for me as was General John Castles, the finest military leader I have ever known. Ray and Patsy Glazebrook have been good friends and I have long felt that my friend, Hugh Cosner has never gotten the recognition he deserves as one whose foresight helped lead to the economic boom that this region saw in the 1970s and 1980s.

Steve Ravinsky, Melvin Rhea, Harry Fleming Jr., Leon Mills, Dick Smith, Harold Boutchyard, Joe Beasley, Bob and Bobi Hamner, Robert, Lorraine and Gary James, Jim and Myrtis Carver, Dick and Peggy Johnson, Joe and Mary Wilson, Bill and Alma Withers, Bill and Betty Poole, Maj. Gen. Carroll Childers, Chief Jim Powers and his wife, Sheila, have been close friends as have many others, including my long time buddy Charlie Jones who has done me many favors. You can often see Charlie driving around town in his Green Monster. I recall an incident at the old Elks Lodge when Charlie ordered a cheeseburger with lettuce and tomato. When he bit into the burger he exclaimed to the cook, a grumpy sort who could do only one thing at a time, "Mr. Shelton, this cheeseburger has no meat on it." And the cook replied, "Can't you see I'm busy?" My current neighbor, Fitzhugh Pates, and I often talk about those days when you dared not interrupt the cook while he was hovering over the one hamburger on the grill.

As a dog lover, I will always recall Blackie, the dog of my youth as well as Chester, the Chesapeake retriever, Foster Grant, the Old English Sheepdog, and Sandy, Sammy and Sandra, and now Samuel, the Pembroke Welsh Corgis. One of the hardest things for humans to accept is that the life spans of their animal companions are much shorter than theirs. My first three Corgis are gone but today Samuel is a faithful companion who lives for affection.

And speaking of dogs, I well remember the Chesapeake Bay retrievers owned at various times by my Aunt Bessie (my grandmother's sister) and Uncle Ben. They were Tilly, Tiny and Tots and I can recall frolicking with Tilly in days when they lived in Maryland near the Potomac River. I spent some time there with them and they had no lights in the house but it was lighted by kerosene lamps. Aunt Bessie was a superstitious woman who thought it bad luck to let any woman, including her own sisters, visit her house on New Year's Day and she never did.

Once Around

People sometimes pose the question to others of what they would do with their lives if they had it to live over again. I can't really say if I had known then what I know now what I would have done. But I do know that such questions are pointless because sometimes we are able to chart our own destiny and sometimes unforeseen events chart it for us. That is why so called long range planning oft goes awry. Life guarantees us only one free trip around the sun a year.

I am naturally curious about what kind of world my grandsons will inhabit. I hope it will be one in which they will have the same opportunities as I have been fortunate to have, but one that will eliminate much of the strife and violence of the last century, the bloodiest century in history. But events of September 11, 2001 and thereafter do not augur well for that.

When my grandsons reach my age and have children and grandchildren of their own, maybe they will pick up this book and compare their own lives in whatever burgs they settle in to the life their grandfather lived in Fredericksburg. That is one of the reasons I have recorded these thoughts on an average life because I have enjoyed reading the memoirs of men and women whose own lives preceded mine. Doing so makes history real and history, after all, is nothing more than the day-to day actions of men and women, most of them average people. The difference between America and most other nations is that you are judged not on your ancestry or social standing, but on your performance.

Miscellany

A few things come to mind worth noting.

--Though this books touches on Virginia politics and government, it merely scratches the surface. Anyone who wants to learn more about Virginia politics in the last century and the first few years of the new century should read, 'The New Dominion' by the late Virginius Dabney and 'The Dynamic Dominion' by Frank Atkinson. I'm happy to report that Frank, who is head of the McGuire Woods Consulting group in Richmond, is presently working on a second edition of the book to add coverage of the dozen years since its publication. Frank's father was once school superintendent in Caroline County and I met Frank in 1972 when he was in high school and active in several Republican campaigns. I did not realize until recently that he had also been a page for the late Democratic State Sen. Paul Manns of Caroline in 1972, a page/messenger in the office of Attorney General Andrew Miller in 1973 and an intern for

Congressman Ken Robinson, a Republican, in 1974. When he went to college and law school, he fell under the influence of Dick Obenshain and other conservative Republicans and joined their ranks. He was chief legal counsel to Gov. George Allen during his term in office from 1994-98.

—A major local social event occurred in 1994 when Elizabeth McDaniel, the daughter of Charles and Mary Wynn McDaniel, got married. For a full description of the lavish reception held at The Sentry Box, the McDaniel home on lower Caroline Street, you can consult the files of either The Free Lance-Star or The Richmond Times. Charles McDaniel, the chairman of Hilldrup Transfer and Storage, has been a long time friend and a political activist. We often talk politics and find ourselves in agreement nearly all the time. He has been active in many civic and charitable causes and has worked tirelessly to promote Fredericksburg. Charles is a descendant of General George Weedon of Revolutionary War fame and lives in the historic Sentry Box house that was once the home of both Weedon and Hugh Mercer. And like me, he also had a grandfather who served in the Civil War and was at Appomattox when the surrender took place. There is no one whose advice I value more than his. Charles served on City Council as did his father before him. His son, Charles Jr., was an outstanding football player at the University of Virginia and might have made it in professional football but opted to join his father in business.

—As noted previously, I knew Carl Bernstein in Richmond when he was a second string reporter. In the early 1970s there was a young TV reporter from Roanoke named Ann Compton who was working as the Richmond correspondent. She went on to become a national correspondent for ABC, often covering White House events. In 1972 her station would not send her to the national political conventions in Miami Beach so she paid her own way. Mel Carrico and I bought her a few meals. These days she travels and reports from nearly everywhere the President goes.

--Alice Rabson, a former Mary Washington College teacher, and I have nothing philosophically in common. She is an ultra liberal who believes in all the causes I opposed. But when late in life she joined the Peace Corps and went to the Marshall Islands, we struck up a correspondence and I printed some of her observations. Though we will never think alike, she is a kind and caring person and very smart, even if she is politically misguided.

—It is amazing how certain silly things stick in your mind like glue while you forget more important happenings.

When television first came out, I went to Charlie Este's place to watch televised home games of the Washington Senators along with Charlie's regular customers such as Spike Howard, William McGhee, Doodle Brown and many others. The play by play on radio and TV was done by Arch McDonald and Bob Wolf and the games were sponsored by National Bohemian Beer, then a popular regional brand made in Baltimore. Only the home games were broadcast live since the team owner was too cheap to send a broadcaster to away games. They were done by McDonald from play by play telegraph reports. A jingle was repeated over and over during the commercial breaks.

It went:

Drink National Bohemian beer
It is your better buy in beer
So pale, so light and so full-bodied too
It's the better beer for you

It's the beer that three ways better
Satisfaction to the letter
If you want a better buy in beer do this
Drink National Bohemian beer
(and so on)

I can also remember some of the jingles I heard on the radio in the 1940s.

Pepsi Cola
Hits the spot
Two for a nickel
That's a lot

Super suds
Super Suds
Wash lot more duds
With Super Suds

I GO FOR THE MAN
WHO WEARS
AN ARROW SHIRT

TO FEEL SHARP
EVERY TIME YOU SHAVE
TO LOOK SHARP
EVERY TIME YOU SHAVE
TO BE SHARP
EVERY TIME YOU SHAVE
USE GILLETTE BLUE BLADES
THE SHARPEST BLADES
EVER HONED

HALO EVERYBODY, HALO
HALO IS THE SHAMPOO
THAT GLORIFIES YOUR HAIR

    AS I GREW UP, THE BIG RADIO STARS WERE BOB HOPE, BING CROSBY, JACK BENNY, FRED ALLEN AND OTHERS WHO ALL HAD THEIR FAITHFUL SPONSORS. AS I RECALL, PEPSODENT TOOTHPASTE SPONSORED BOB HOPE'S PROGRAM FOR YEARS AND I THINK MAXWELL HOUSE COFFEE WAS THE PRIME SPONSOR OF JACK BENNY.
    COMMERCIALS ON THE RADIO IN THOSE DAYS WERE STRAIGHTFORWARD AND SIMPLE AND EVEN I, AS A 12 YEAR OLD, COULD EASILY UNDERSTAND THEM. THESE DAYS SOME OF THE TELEVISION COMMERCIALS I SEE FOR SUCH PRODUCTS AS NIKE SNEAKERS ARE SIMPLY INCOMPREHENSIBLE TO ME. I'M SURE THEY MEAN SOMETHING TO THE YOUNGER GENERATION BUT IN MANY CASES AFTER I HAVE WATCHED A MODERN DAY COMMERCIAL COSTING THE SPONSORS HUNDREDS OF THOUSANDS OF DOLLARS I HAVEN'T A CLUE AS TO THEIR MARKETING TECHNIQUES.
    ANOTHER PRODUCT I RECALL, AND ONE I SOMETIMES USED, WAS WILDROOT CREAM OIL, A WHITISH HAIR TONIC THAT STUCK LIKE GLUE TO THE HAIR. I DON'T KNOW WHY BUT THE YOUNG MEN OF THAT GENERATION THOUGHT SLICKED DOWN HAIR WAS FASHIONABLE AND WOULD ATTRACT YOUNG LADIES. ANOTHER HAIR TONIC WIDELY USED WAS VITALIS THAT LOOKED SOMEWHAT LIKE THE MOUTHWASH LISTERINE. I HAVE NO IDEA IF YOUNG MEN OF TODAY'S GENERATION USE ANY SUCH CONCOCTIONS ON THEIR HAIR, ALTHOUGH I DO THINK THE PRACTICE IN MY DAY WAS FAR LESS HARMLESS THAN THE TATTOOS AND BODY RINGS OF THE PRESENT GENERATION. I

cannot believe it when I see some young women walking around with tattoos on their skin. I predict that when their hair turns gray they will be rather embarrassed when they have to explain why grandma has a tattoo on her forearm.

But by that time it may well be that most young people will consider tattoos socially necessary. Unfortunately, the California culture seems to be spreading more and more to our region and state and people with orange hair are considered normal.

Roads

There was a time it used to be a pleasure to drive area roads with the possible exception of U.S. Route 1 that was heavily traveled and extremely dangerous since it was four lanes undivided. But other area raods were relatively uncluttered.

In those days we had so called 'Sunday drivers' who would take the family for a spin on Sunday afternoons. One of my uncles who had a car would sometimes take us to the Fredericksburg battlefield park for a picnic at their facilities.

Travel by greyhound of trailways bus was a common way of getting places. I can recall a long trip from Fredericksburg to upstate new york with frequent stops along the way. There were not rest rooms aboard the buses so sometimes there was a mad dash when the bus pulled into the state. As I also recall, the worst tasting sandwiches ever made wee sold at such station.

It may have been on this trip when I was about 10 years old that I first saw burma shave signs dotting the highway. I later learned that such signs were commonplace on the nation's major roads and were a huge advertising tool. The signs were spaced about 20 yards apart and featured often silly rhymes ending with a punch line and plug for the product.

Burma-Shave, incidentally, was a soapy substance that came in sticks in those days before shaving cream was put in cans. There were literally hundreds of different poems but here are a couple that I can remember.

    Don't lose you head
To gain a minute
You need your head
Your brains are in it
Burma Shave

Driver in ditch
Car in tree
The moon was full
And so was he
Burma-Shave

- In 1984 in San Francisco I briefly met O.J. Simpson. The Democratic National Convention was being held there to nominate Walter Mondale for President, an exercise in futility, and Willie Brown, Speaker of the California House, was holding a waterfront reception for invited guests, including the freeloading media. Simpson, who lived in Los Angeles but came from the Bay area, was among the guests and I recall speaking very briefly with him. Anyone who doesn't think he killed Nicole Brown Simpson and Ron Goldman has sawdust for brains. The not guilty verdict practically guarantees that I will never serve on another jury since if Simpson could get off, I would be reluctant to convict anyone.

—While I never met Lyndon B. Johnson personally, I saw him and his wife on a number of occasions and got to know their daughter, Lynda Bird, who married Chuck Robb and was First Lady of Virginia for four years.

I was in Culpeper in 1960 when Johnson came on the LBJ special when he was running for vice president on a ticket headed by John Kennedy.

A famous episode occurred when Johnson, as the train was pulling off, shouted, "Remember folks, what has Dick Nixon ever done for Culpeper." The press corps picked up on it and poked fun at it relentlessly. It was vintage LBJ. I was also at the Fredericksburg train station in 1964 when Lady Bird Johnson's special train came through. She was campaigning for her husband who had become President after Kennedy's assassination and was now seeking election to the office. She was accompanied by Mills Godwin who was then the state's lieutenant governor. The next time I saw her in person was when she came to the State Capital to see her daughter, Lynda Bird, and son in law, then Gov. Charles Robb. Lyndon Johnson had a good knowledge of Culpeper since in his early days in the Senate he clandestinely visited a rich married women there at one of the estates she and her husband owned. The husband, a major contributor to Johnson campaigns, did not know of the liaison.

Adlai Stevenson came to Fredericksburg for a visit in 1956 when he unsuccessfully ran against Eisenhower a second time. George Bush came in 1992 when he was seeking re-election and made a campaign stop at Goolrick's Drug Store. While President, Eisenhower was due to make a speech at Kenmore but it was canceled when the Secret Service got wind of an assassination threat. (I saw Ike close up when he was President and he came to the Dahlgren Navy facility and boarded the Presidential yacht for a trip up the Potomac). Before he was President, Gerald Ford gave a talk one night at a banquet at the Princess Anne Hotel honoring Congressman Bill Scott.

–The first city manager of Fredericksburg was L.J. Houston but that was before my time. When I covered City Council the manager was Freeman Funk who later became a member of council. Funk is probably the best modern day manager the city has had but Marvin Bolinger would be a close second.

Lawrence Davies, Mayor of the city for many years, left office and I can't add anything new to the accolades he received. He is as fine a person as I have ever known.

--Donald Crowder is younger, but I knew him well in his boyhood days. Donald lost his right eye while splitting wood when he was 42. He decided that on his 62nd birthday, July 27, 2003, he would skydive from a plane, something he had yearned to do for years. And he did exactly as he said he would, saying he had been inspired by former President George Herbert Walker Bush who had done his one and only skydive in his 70s.

It proves that you can do just about anything if you set your mind to it. My close friend, Joe Synan, and I were in the National Guard together. He became a juvenile probation officer but decided he wanted to go to law school, got loans, worked hard and became an attorney.

I wish I could write nearly as well as Florence King, who lives in Fredericksburg, or Dino Brugioni, who lives near Berea in Stafford. Both have written many books and articles and are nationally recognized. When Florence stopped writing his column in National Review, I did not renew my subscription to the magazine.

Another inspiring success story is that of Carroll Childers. When he came into our National Guard unit under command of Capt. Alvin Bandy, he was a private first class. He went to Officers Candidate School and in time became a Major General in command of the famed 29th Infantry Division that stormed Omaha Beach.

Anyone who says America is not a land of great opportunity, simply ignores the truth.

–There was a Pope of the Roman Catholic Church who died after being Pope only about a month. I was in Germany on National Guard duty and that weekend a group of us rented a car and drove to Switzerland, Austria and from there into Italy by way of the Brenner Pass. When we got to the customs booth at the Italian line and tried to exchange some money, I noticed that some of the customs officials were crying. I told one companion, 'I've always heard the Italians are very emotional but I wasn't prepared for this.' As it turned out that they had just received word of the Pope's death which made the episode much more understandable.

–I have attended four presidential inaugurations going back to Dwight Eisenhower in 1952. I have also attended the inauguration of every Virginia governor since J. Lindsay Almond. It was bitterly cold during the inauguration of Charles S. Robb in 1982 and even colder during the inauguration of George Allen in 1994. It was also extremely cold with snow on the ground during the inauguration of John F. Kennedy in 1961.

I've met six presidents, including Eisenhower, Nixon, Jimmy Carter, Gerald Ford, Ronald Reagan and George Bush (but lest it sound like bragging I was just among hundreds of thousands they met, another face in the crowd). I was introduced to Reagan before he was President when he visited Richmond. My good friend, Mel Carrico of The Roanoke Times, had been Reagan's First Sergeant in a California propaganda unit during World War II, and Carrico made the introduction. I met Jimmy Carter through Henry Howell in 1975 when Howell was touting him for the presidential nomination and I thought Henry had lost his marbles. I had no desire whatsoever to meet Bill Clinton who I consider a disgrace to the presidency. And if BroomHillary ever becomes President, I may be forced to leave the country.

—I mentioned earlier such dedicated physicians in my youth as John Eugene Cole, Earl Ware, Frank Pratt, William Butzner, Philip Cox and others. I did not mean to imply that we don't have physicians today that are just as dedicated. Some years ago Bob Vranian probably saved my life when he discovered a large aortic aneurysm in me that required immediate attention. He is a man who is praised by all who know him as are many others in the medical profession here. One great surgeon was Lou Massad who is now retired. Stewart Kohler has also been a friend over the years. People endlessly complain about the high cost of medicine, but forget the exorbitant malpractice fees physicians must pay in this litigious society.

Hugh Cosner

I first met Hugh Cosner when he ran a general merchandise store at Snell in Spotsylvania. He frequently attended meetings of the Board of Supervisors. Years later he would become a member of the supervisors. He was controversial but I think he did as much or more to transform Spotsylvania from an agricultural society to a fast growing suburban county. I know some are not happy that our region has changed so dramatically, but even they should recognize that the leadership of people such as Hugh Cosner helped usher in an era of unprecedented prosperity. Spotsyvlania was fortunate to have the services of Steve Foster and Kim Payne as county administrators and Stafford got their money's worth and more from Chuck Sharp and C.M. Williams.

—As I write this in late June of 2003, Bill Howell is Speaker of the Virginia House of Delegates succeeding Del Vance Wilkins who had to resign because of a sexual harassment scandal.

While that is regrettable, particularly since Vance did so much to build the Republican Party of Virginia, there could be no better choice to succeed him than Bill Howell. When Bill first decided to run for the House in 1987, a rumor somehow made the rounds that I was thinking of becoming a candidate. Bill, a friend, asked me about it and I assured him it was totally unfounded and that I would gladly support him. He is one of the most honest and devoted public servants I've known and I cannot say enough in praise of his wife Cessie who is always upbeat and cheerful and liked by everyone who knows her. Bill, Tom Bricken, Tom Moncure (or a combination thereof) and I have breakfast occasionally at the fabulous Paradise Diner in Stafford, although in his new role scheduling such breakfasts is immensely more difficult. Bricken and fellow attorney Walter Jervis Sheffield were instrumental in getting a referendum passed back in the mid 1980s to reduce the size of City Council from 11 to 7.

-Gordon Shelton has left the City Council after years of distinguished service. Gordon always did his homework and was one of the prime architects of the annexation agreement that restored Fredericksburg to fiscal prosperity. He began as an outsider looking in and was regarded as a renegade by some fellow council members. But his contributions to the city and region were enormous. Though no longer on Council, Gordon, unlike MacArthur, is not inclined to just fade away. He is a frequent critic of the present Council and took them to court for a violation of the state's Freedom of Information Act.

Kids Today

It seems to me from observing my grandsons and others that kids today are turning into couch potatoes.

When I was a boy we used to make our own entertainment. We'd have pick up games of baseball and football and marbles. We could always find things to do.

Nowadays there doesn't seem to be any such thing as pick up games. Kids take part only in organized events. There have to be adults running the show, uniforms, professional playing fields. The corner lot isn't good enough. Video games are the unfortunate substitutes.

But when I think about it, the reason kids don't do the same things is that this is a different era entirely. During my boyhood, my pals and I could walk from one end of the city to the other without difficulty and there wasn't much traffic except on Princess Anne Street. Now there are few vacant lots left anywhere that could be used for a pickup ball game. Not to mention the fact that young children are no longer safe in the region as evidenced by the brutal Silva-Lisk kidnappings and murders by an evil man named Evonitz who, thankfully, committed suicide before the American Criminal Liberties Union could spring to his defense. But they have plenty of other pedophiles and serial killers to defend.

-Do children read the newspaper comic pages anymore or is it just adults? From the time I was six I read the comics every day. The Free Lance-Star carried some that have long ago vanished, comics like Oakey Doakey, Big Sister, Smilin' Jack, Terry and the Pirates, Mickey Finn, Bringin' Up Father. Not all of them may have been in the local paper but they could have been in Richmond or Washington papers.

Among my comic favorites was the Katzenjammer Kids, young boys in Germany who were always tormenting the Inspecktor and speaking in broken English. As I recall (and I may be wrong) when World War II broke out and Germany became a hated enemy, it spelled the demise of that strip.

Of all the comics I read then, only a few have survived, among them Snuffy Smith (originally Barney Google and Snuffy Smith) and Blondie. Some papers still carry The Phantom but I don't get any of them.

Comic books these days cost an astronomical $2.50, or more. In my day they were a dime each and I remember John Wesley Hall reading such comic books at my home since his parents did not want him being corrupted by Batman, Superman, Captain Marvel or Plastic Man. Wes Hall, who came from a poor but proud family, was one of the bank credit card pioneers in Virginia and did well for himself.

I recall Charles Rowe telling me that he tried for years to get rid of the comic strip Big Sister that was pretty hokey but every time he did a bunch of little old ladies would call to protest and he was forced to reinstate it.

--Warren Barry and I go back to Hotel Raleigh days. In the 1970s Warren started a tradition of making a farewell address to the House of Delegates. That year and succeeding years I helped him write the material. He got his picture in the paper when, after jokingly remarking that his home territory of Northern Virginia was treated like a stepchild by the legislature, he threatened to lead a movement for that region to secede from the rest of Virginia. He put on a white hat, pulled out a paper sword and proclaimed, 'North, By God, Virginia.' After Warren left the House to became Circuit Court clerk in Fairfax, Buster O'Brien did the speech one year, Del. George Beard of Culpeper gave it a couple of times and then the torch was passed to Vince Callahan. I helped all of them write some of their material, although as time passed I did less and less. The farewell address stopped when some female legislator without a sense of humor called Callahan's material offensive to women. Vince, another friend from Raleigh days, has done an admirable job as chairman of the House Appropriations Committee, succeeding Earl Dickinson.

Cemeteries

Cemeteries are one measure of the history of any region. In them are buried the men, women and children who lived the history from the time of the first settlements to the present.

The national military cemeteries in Fredericksburg and Spotsylvania are grim reminders of great battles fought during the American Civil War. Many young men from northern states are buried in the soil of a southern state that saw much of the hardest fighting of that conflict. The Confederate Cemetery in Fredericksburg is the last resting place for some of the southerners who took part in that war, including my grandfather, John T. Goolrick Sr. and grandmother, Frances Goolrick.

I often go to Oak Hill Cemetery where are buried my parents and my maternal grandparents. It is instructive to walk its paths and note the names on the tombstones. I am always amazed at how many of the people who are there that I knew when they were living. Fifty years ago I would have known few of those buried.

Here under a large marble monument inscribed with the words, Engineer, Executive, Philanthropist, lies John Lee Pratt, once among the wealthiest men in the nation. Born in King George County, he became a vice president of General Motors while a young man and at a time that great corporation was just beginning to grow. He gave away millions of dollars to good causes and spent the last years of his life at Chatham Manor in Stafford that had been headquarters for several union generals during the Civil War.

Mr. Pratt once told me a story about Freon and the refrigerator. When General Motors produced a refrigerator to take the place of iceboxes (just what the name implies), housewives were skeptical about the newfangled devices and Pratt had to go door-to-door convincing some to try them out. In his later years Pratt, who wore wrinkled clothes, would take walks across the Chatham Bridge and more than once be taken for some old person down on his luck by strangers who stopped and asked if he needed a ride.

Buried not far from my parents is Marbury Fagan—Al Fagan as we all knew him. Al was a good-hearted man who ran for many political offices, though he seldom won. We spent many hours talking and he sincerely loved his community.

so many others. Andrew Ross Jones, Elizabeth Sisson Jones, my grandparents. Nunra Ferrara, Paul Ventura, Israel Silver, Arthur Smith, Walter Lowry, all good friends, all good citizens.

And there are all the church cemeteries and the other resting places of people who made the history of this very historic region whether they lived ordinary or extraordinary lives. The only thing that separates us from the those buried in such cemeteries is not even a millisecond in time.

Big Apple

—New York City was a relatively safe place to visit in former days. We took subways to the stadiums with no problem. We walked the streets of Brooklyn and the Bronx and never felt threatened. We went out to Coney Island and rode the world's tallest Ferris wheel, ate foot-long hotdogs and enjoyed ourselves. Similarly, we could visit Washington, D.C., walk around and never feel in danger of being mugged or robbed. Sad to say, not only cannot that be done anymore in New York, Washington or other big cities, it cannot be done once darkness falls in the city of Fredericksburg. Though we have grown more prosperous, we have been robbed of the feeling of personal security that once existed. It is hard to imagine there was a time when some people left their doors unlocked and thought nothing about it and would not hesitate to walk along the streets in the midnight darkness.

--Few could grow up in Virginia without acquiring a taste for southern fried chicken. It was, and maybe to a lesser extent, still is something that appeared frequently on the dinner table. In those days Sunday dinner was a big event with the family gathering for it. Now it is more a time when you grab a sandwich while watching the NFL pre-game shows.

My maternal grandmother was an expert in the fine art of cooking southern fried chicken. She could have made a fortune if she had someone sponsor her before Colonel Sanders came out with his insipid Kentucky fried chicken. Another great practitioner of chicken cooking was Mrs. Julia Payne, wife of Slickpot Payne who was known for his friendliness, his years of living by the river in Falmouth and for his excellent homemade wine.

I was a dinner guest at the Payne's often and Mrs. Payne knew how fond I was of her fried chicken. Somewhere I suppose you can still get fried chicken like she cooked, but I have no idea where it would be. Her meals were some of the finest I've ever had and I think of them often as I am sitting down to eat yet another frozen dinner thawed out in a microwave.

    Among the Payne children were Mennis, Tom and Togie, the first two now dead. They were close friends. Ivan, the oldest, lives in Florida. When he was a babe in arms, famed artist Gari Melchers, who lived in Falmouth, painted a picture of his mother holding him. Slickpot and Julia were flooded out of their Falmouth home a number of times, but with indomitable spirit always returned when the waters receded. A granddaughter, Julia Payne, (daughter of Togie and Janet Payne) later served on the staff of Vice President Gore and was Bill Clinton's press secretary for several years following his presidency. She is a charming and talented young lady and will undoubtedly be a future force in national politics.

  --Dick Obenshain was a friend and a man of unflinching integrity. With his owlish glasses, he looked more like a college professor than a politician and he was more than a little bookish in nature. Yet he had the convictions of a true believer in conservative causes and the fervor he exhibited attracted to him many people of a conservative nature who had never before been active in politics. Obenshain did more to shape the present conservative Virginia Republican Party than any other person.

    I once asked Obenshain if he sometimes felt he would have a wider appeal if he would moderate some of his views since there were those who considered him an extremist. Obenshain answered, "The day you start altering for expediency what you feel in your heart is right is the day you have no right to ask people to put their trust in you." Obenshain went to his untimely death adhering closely to his conservative convictions and presenting himself to people not through a lens of clever spin doctors, but just as he really was.

    —The highlight of any of the small charity carnivals that came to Fredericksburg was the drawing of the winning ticket for the new car that was invariably the prize. The drawing would take place at the carnival late on a Saturday night and by Monday morning everyone in town knew who had won the automobile. Whoever it was would be the envy of all who knew him or her.

    —We talk frequently now of the -gay community'. When I came along so far as I know the gay community in Fredericksburg was limited to Keith, Eddie and Tilly. Bu to be homosexual in those days wasn't socially acceptable so undoubtedly many who were did kept their secret. Tilly was one exception. He was a brilliant man who dealt in genealogy and knew the ancestry of most of Fredericksburg's citizens. I suspect everyone treated him well since he could probably find a horse thief or two in their backgrounds if he tried.

—Though my name has appeared in the local paper thousands of times, it has not led to any great amount of recognition. Often than when I give my name to anyone in the Fredericksburg area they will inquire if I have anything to do with Goolrick's Drug Store. The store was apparently started by Dr. William Barber Goolrick some time in the mid-1880s. He died in 1909 and I think the business was sold out of the family in 1921 or thereabouts.

—There was a black gentleman named Lewis who shined shoes at a barbershop Lewis would make several trips to the liquor store each day. And he had good reason since when the store closed for business at 6 p.m., Lewis opened up his own shop.

When I was a young man needing some bourbon late at night. I went to his home and knocked on the door. He recognized me, let me in and showed me his selection. He had literally cabinet after cabinet overflowing with pints that he sold a dollar above his actual cost. I went there several times and I cast no moral judgments, but appreciated his entrepreneurial spirit. I often saw Lewis walking up William Street happily whistling while making a run to the liquor store.

—On several occasions I covered re-unions of Spanish American War veterans held at the Princess Anne Hotel in Fredericksburg. And I also attended a number of meetings of veterans of World War I. I used to enjoy Harry Fleming Sr.'s tales of serving in the Army in Europe in the so-called Great War. Unfortunately, a war of much greater scope came along. But traveling throughout France, one cannot help but encounter countless memorials laid to the memory of those two wars and the people who fought them.

—I don't know how it is today, but for my generation no matter how old we get, we never forget the names of the people who were our teachers in school long years ago.

The names still spring to my mind. Ethel and Virginia Nash at Lafayette Elementary. Mrs. Scott, the cafeteria superintendent, who once in a while would give me the end unit of the cake with a lot more frosting than an ordinary slice. At James Monroe (Intermediate) such dedicated teachers as Mrs. Keel and Mrs. McGhee. And at James Monroe High superb teachers such as Frances Armstrong, Mrs. Allison, Mildred Chick, Mrs. Hester, Emmeline Sterns, Emma Euliss, Bruce Neal, Mrs.

Pappandreou and many many more. And a few of them are still living. I guess when I was fifteen or sixteen, someone ten years or so older seemed ancient. Now they are almost like contemporaries. (Once I showed up in Mrs. Euliss' class in a T-shirt and she told me, 'Young man, you do not come to class in your underwear.' I was sent home to get a shirt).

—When I see the thoroughly obnoxious Democratic political consultant James Carville on television my mind goes back to 1982.

I was still in the political reporting business and chairman of a small committee of the Virginia Capital Correspondents Association that was sponsoring a debate between U.S. Senate candidates Paul Trible, a Republican, and Richard Davis, a Democrat. (Along with George Wilbur of the Associated Press, I was a co-founder of the Association).

Carville, known as The Raging Cajun, was not well known then but was managing the campaign of Dick Davis. We had to deal with him on debate arrangements and that was frustrating because he was ill tempered and wanted everything his own way. Nothing we suggested suited him. The debate was finally held, Davis lost the election and I heard no more of Carville until he emerged as one of Bill Clinton's top consultants in the presidential campaign of 1992. Both of those bozos deserved each other.

Incidentally, the press secretary for Davis that year was a nice guy named Joe Lockhart. During the closing years of the Clinton Administration he was the presidential press secretary.

I also met another former presidential press secretary while working for Congressman Slaughter in the 1980s. At that time developer Til Hazel wanted to acquire land near the Manassas battlefield to build a shopping center. A nationwide furor resulted and the opposition was led by Jody Powell, former press secretary to President Jimmy Carter. I met Powell several times. He was a nice guy but determined that Hazel would not get the property. And he didn't. The government paid a big price for the land and Hazel came out the real winner since a recession ensued and he probably could not have proceeded with his plans.

People You Meet

If you're a news reporter or involved in politics, you are probably destined to meet characters that are unforgettable.

I don't recall how I came to meet Buddy (last name withheld but it was most likely when he joined the Elks. Buddy was a great guy and could tell stories with the best of them, but had a serious drinking problem. He had once done well for himself in business as the part owner of a warehouse in Prince William County that distributed frozen meats.

Buddy loved country music and in the 1950s often went to Washington nightclubs featuring that kind of music. Along the way he met two young men who were little known outside their own limited circles. Their names were Roy Clark and Jimmy Dean.

Clark, a native Virginian, was singing and playing with a small group and Buddy took a shine to him. He bought Clark a new guitar and gave him money to help promote his career. When Clark got married, Buddy was the best man at his wedding. Buddy also got on friendly terms with Dean who had his own group called the Texas Wildcats.

As Buddy said later after he had become sober, if he'd had any real business sense he would have become the agent for both entertainers who would go on to have fabulous careers. But he was too busy having a good time.

By the time I met Buddy, Clark had become a major country music star and lived in Davidsonville, Maryland. One day Buddy, Jerry Leonard and I went over to Roy Clark's house in Leonard's Mercedes. When we got there, Buddy, who had been drinking all the way, strode into the house unannounced. Roy had gone out for a haircut but his wife, Barbara was there. It became immediately apparent to Leonard and me that this lady had little uses for Buddy, would probably have preferred to have a rattlesnake slither into the house. But Buddy paid that no attention. He simply opened the refrigerator, took out food and made sandwiches for us to eat.

When Roy returned he treated Buddy with affection and took us down to his basement to show some old kinescopes of his TV appearances in the Washington area. I think Clark's wife resented Buddy's frequent late night calls to their house and that he went around with Roy Clark photographs in his briefcase and autographed them himself for anyone who wanted one, claiming Roy had authorized him to sign on his behalf. I never ceased to be amazed when people thanked him for signing Roy's name to a picture for them.

In gratitude for what Buddy had done for him in leaner days, Roy offered to let him promote an appearance at the Richmond Coliseum. Buddy wanted me to act as publicist for the show and both of us could undoubtedly have made money except that Buddy by then was so controlled by alcohol that he managed to screw everything up and the project never went any further.

Buddy was full of surprises and always loved performing card tricks for an audience. One day while voluntarily helping tend bar at the Elks, a customer ordered a Bloody Mary. When Buddy could find no tomato juice, he opened a can of tomato soup, put it in a blender and poured vodka into it. The customer was not pleased with the result.

While I liked Buddy, after a while I could no longer stand his constant drinking and his boisterous ways and tried to avoid him, though that was difficult. Others were doing the same thing and relations between Buddy and his long-suffering wife were increasingly stormy.

One evening in spring I walked into the Elks around seven and the bartender told me Sheriff B.W. Davis of Spotsylvania wanted me to call him right away. I went to a pay phone and called the number the Sheriff had left.

When the Sheriff came on the line he said, "Boy, we have a Mr. _____ out here (at certain apartments) holding a gun to his wife's head and he wants to talk to you or Ben Woodbridge (a Fredericksburg attorney) and Ben ain't available."

My reaction was 'Please Mr. Custer, I don't want to go,' but I had no choice so I fortified myself with a drink before I drove to the apartments. There were four or five sheriff's cars parked there. I got behind a tree and called "Buddy." Soon I heard his voice, "That you, John?"

"Yeah," I answered, "it's me."

"Come on in here," he said "but don't bring none of those cops with you or I'll have to shoot."

"All right, Buddy," I said, "I'm coming alone."

I opened the front door of the apartment with a very queasy feeling in the pit of my stomach. It was pitch dark as I entered the living room and I could barely see the outline of Buddy with a pistol held to his wife's head.

"Hey, pal," said Buddy, "go in the kitchen and fix me a drink. I'm tied up right now."

I did as he asked and fixed him several more drinks over the next hour while trying to persuade him to put down the gun and give himself up. All that time his wife said not a word.

Finally I succeeded and he let me bring in a family doctor who had been summoned to the scene. He gave the gun to the doctor and the sheriff took him into custody.

Buddy was given a stiff fine and a suspended sentence, but after that night never again took a drink of alcohol until his death ten years later. He became a drug and alcohol rehabilitation counselor and was widely praised for his work. He and his wife divorced, but Buddy later remarried a widow who was affluent and he lived in homes in Virginia and North Carolina. He still kept in touch, but it was like talking to a completely different person since, though I had known him four or five years, I had never really seen him when he was sober.

I met only one person that I felt could function as well when he was drinking alcohol as when he was sober. I'll simply call him Ed. He was a successful businessman who drank day and night and managed to pull off sharp deals even when he was intoxicated. Ed was sitting at the Elks bar one night when he ordered a steak to go with his bourbon. When the steak was put before him, he stuck a fork into it but jerked his hand and the steak went flying over his shoulder and landed on the floor behind him. Without missing a beat, Ed looked at the cook and said, "Gimmee another

One friend and a real character was Tommy Gayle of Stafford County. Tommy was a free spirit and a man of independent mind. His father, T.Benton Gayle was superintendent of schools both in Stafford and King George and a nephew of John Lee Pratt, one of the nation's richest men. Tommy Gayle might have come into a fortune since Pratt liked him. But Pratt wanted Tommy to do things his way and Tommy was a person who was going to do things his own way come hell or high water. He wouldn't kowtow to anyone no matter if they had all the money in the world.

I could tell a thousand tales about Tommy Gayle. He once opened a restaurant on State Route 3 in Stafford called the Hoof'n Claw. I went there with my wife one February evening and we ordered the crab cake dinner. When it came, the crab cakes had a different texture and taste to them.

When Tommy came over, I said "Tommy, these crab cakes taste different. It tastes more like bluefish cakes."

"That's because they are bluefish cakes. You can't get crab meat this time of year."

"Then why do you advertise crab cakes on the menu?" I asked, and he answered, "Are you goofy? Nobody's going to buy bluefish cakes."

I laughed and finished my meal. Tommy always had a way of getting away with the most outrageous things. It was part of his charm.

On another occasion at the Elks the conversation between Tommy and I turned to dog racing. One of the more gullible people at the table asked how dogs were made to run around a track.

Tommy answered, without missing a beat, "They have jockeys.

The man looked at him and said, "But how can you find anybody to be a dog jockey."

And Tommy replied, "They have to get Pygmies and pay them a lot because dogs don't like saddles on them and sometimes throw them off."

Billy Reamy was another person who was colorful and intelligent. When I first met him he had been elected president of the National Livestock Association and was riding high. He was an expert in cattle futures, as well as other commodities, and made lots of money. He also lost lots of money and was up and down for years. But rich or poor, he was always cocky and confident and had a mind like a steel trap.

Tommy Gayle and Billy often traveled together and Tommy had many stories about him. He told of the time Billy wanted to order breakfast. When the waitress told him it was too late, Billy called for the manager and said he would like to order two dozen eggs, two dozen strips of bacon and twenty pieces of toast. The manager took the order and it was brought back to Billy's table.

According to Tommy, Billy got up and went to pay the bill without eating a mouthful. Billy's son, Chip, a lawyer is a close friend.

Newton Bourne who had grown up poor near Quantico on the Potomac recalled days when a bushel of crabs could be purchased for a dollar. He worked for the RF&P Railroad for years and through thrift and hard work managed to accumulate a good amount of money.

In the 1960s, convinced that the Salem Dam would be built, Bourne built a home on Sophia Street in Fredericksburg within sight of the Rappahannock River. It was a lovely view, but as time went by and it became obvious the dam was not going to be built, Newton became increasingly concerned about floods.

Whenever there was a heavy rain, Newton would either call or come to see me so that I could contact the river service in Maryland to find out how high the water would rise.

He had several narrow escapes when the water slowly came up the length of his backyard and almost spilled into his basement. His luck ran out in 1972 when Hurricane Agnes came along. I had called the river service all day and then in early evening got unwelcome news. The water was going to rise to between 33 to 35 feet above normal, meaning that it was going to spill over into Sophia Street and beyond, giving the area its worst flooding since 1942.

I went to Newton's home to tell him and his wife they had to evacuate the home since the water would be in the living room by the next day. They went reluctantly and we got a group of Elks (the Lodge was just across the street) to load the furniture on a big truck to put it in storage for them. I will never forget standing out in the driving rain all that night while the moving took place. I've never experienced any harder downpour. After the moving was complete, we went back to the Elks at 4 a.m. to have a drink to warm up and dry out. I got to bed around 5 a.m. and had barely put my head on the pillow when the phone rang. I answered it and it was Conrad 'Jiggs' Brennan, the First Sergeant of our National Guard Company, telling me to report to the Armory right away since the unit had been activated for flood duty.

It was my job to put into effect an alert plan using the chain of command to reach members and tell them to report for duty immediately. The flooding was extensive and in mid-morning I got a jeep and driver and drove around the area to get a first hand look at what was going on. As I had feared, Newton Bourne's home was practically underwater and Sophia Street was now an extension of the river. Even worse scenes met my eyes in surrounding counties. Our Guard unit did itself proud over the course of its three-day duty, rescuing many stranded people and animals. The same was true with other units activated in various flooded regions of the state.

Hurricane Camille, in 1969, devastated other parts of Virginia but caused only mild flooding in the Fredericksburg region. Coming in from Mississippi, where it wreaked havoc, it stalled over Nelson County near Charlottesville and the hardest rain ever recorded in North America took place during the next eight hours. I had occasion to fly over Nelson County a few weeks later and the tops of some mountains had been literally chopped off by the downpour.

'Jiggs' Brennan, someone for whom I had great affection, came to Fredericksburg in the 1930s at the height of the Great Depression as a member of the Civilian Conservation Corps. He was from Hazleton, Pennsylvania in the heart of the coal mining country and came from a large family. He fell in love with the Fredericksburg area after being stationed at the CCC's Berea campsite in Stafford and marrying a local woman. After Army service during World War II, he returned to the Fredericksburg police force and remained a member for many years until his retirement. (Three CCC camps in Spotsylvania were run by the National Park Service and the one in Stafford by the Department of Agriculture).

He was an outgoing man with a loud voice and a tough manner that belied the fact he had a very soft heart. I have heard him threatening members of the Guard unit with severe punishment on many occasions, but seldom did he follow through and actually punish them. Everybody in town knew Jiggs and more than one person has told me that he stopped them while they were driving with too much to drink and instead of locking them up, made them park their cars while he summoned a cab.

There was an old retired Marine Colonel that we simply called "The Colonel" and whose last name I won't use here. The Colonel had been a member of the old Army Air Corps originally and had been stationed at Kessler Field at the time in the 1940s it had been commanded by my uncle Colonel Robert Emmett Mason Goolrick. (Another person under command of my uncle at one time was Jack Rubinstein, or Jack Ruby as he was known at the time he shot and killed Lee Harvey Oswald in Dallas).

The Colonel had crash-landed a few planes in World War II and again in Korea and was tough as nails, but yet softhearted. He was in charge of the Christmas toys project for the Elks Lodge and labored all year to collect used toys and fix them up for distribution to needy children when Christmas came around.

Sometimes The Colonel would have flashbacks. I learned this one evening when I was sitting at the Elks bar and he was there and suddenly I heard a loud voice crying out, "Fighter pilots man your planes! Japs at eleven o'clock." The bartender explained to me that once in a while when The Colonel had a few drinks he vocally re-fought some of the aerial battles in which he participated in World War II.

The Colonel had a sharp mind and all of his children went into lucrative professions and were successful.

H. Wilmer "Bouncer" Heflin was another unforgettable character who spent time at the Elks. Bouncer told the story that one time in the

1930s he and Bob Cowie were driving toward the Sylvania Plant to apply for work when they reached the entrance. Suddenly, Bouncer said to Cowie, "You better turn this car around?"

"Why should I do that?" Cowie responded.

"Because," said Bouncer, "if we go in there, they might hire us."

Thinking about it, Cowie said, "You've got a good point," and turned the car around.

Brewer Beckwith, a retired fireman, was another enjoyable character. Once he and a man named Red Fletcher went into the business of putting up television antennas in those pre-cable days when an antenna was needed for reception. They had installed an antenna on a home when suddenly Fletcher looked at the order form and told Brewer, "I hate to say this, but we've put this damn thing on the wrong house. It should be on the house next door."

Brewer looked at him and said, "Well, that's no problem at all." Then Brewer ran the antenna wire from the house on which the antenna had been installed to the house next door. He told Fletcher, "Now if we can talk the guy who lives in this house into an antenna, we'll get paid twice."

CHAPTER TWENTY ONE

Eureka

America is the greatest land of all and I have been to every state but Alaska. I particularly love San Francisco and the parts of California north of it. If I were much younger I might be tempted to move to Eureka that has one of the most ideal climates in the nation, according to weatherman Willard Scott who lives in nearby Fauquier County and grew up in Alexandria. I've driven the coast highway from Seattle to San Diego and it is breathtakingly gorgeous. The same is true of the drive through the Big Sky country of Montana and other parts of the American west as well as visits in autumn to Maine, Vermont, and New Hampshire.

I know people who hate to travel. They are perfectly content to stay in Fredericksburg or wherever they live and that's fine. But I believe that by seeing other parts of the world, one is able to appreciate even more their own little corner of the earth. The late Key Howard, a friendly man who in the 1930s and 40s sold ten cents a week insurance to my maternal grandparents, would invite me to his Cornell Street home and we would have mint juleps in his backyard which he described as his 'little corner of the world.' I just wish that other places would resist the temptation to further Americanize their own cultures. It is unsettling to see a McDonald's on Baker Street in the very neighborhood where fictional detective Sherlock Holmes was said to live at 221B. I cannot think of anything this world needs less than another McDonald's, the symptom of our cultural malaise.

Given thechoice of one place in the world I could visit and one place only, it would be a difficult decision but I would choose to return to Brecon, a small town in southern Wales. I spent time there on military duty and made a number of friends and I have been back a half dozen times since. What I like most about Brecon is that it reminds me of what Fredericksburg was like fifty or sixty years ago. It is a town of several thousand people, a market town, where folks from rural areas that surround it come to shop on market days. Milk is still delivered door-to-door, there is one bank, several nice restaurants and a hotel reminiscent of the old Princess Anne Hotel in downtown Fredericksburg that played host to the likes of David Lloyd George and Winston Churchill. (And I hope my friends Tommy Mitchell and Van Peroy succeed in bringing one or more quality hotel backs to downtown). When I saw children playing soccer contentedly in the fields around Brecon, it brought back memories of the pickup baseball games of my own childhood days. For the sake of its people, I hope it stays the same for while I would be the first to acknowledge that the changes that have taken place in my area during my lifetime were inevitable, yet we have still lost the simple life that once suited us so well.

—When I was there in 1988 Poland was still behind the Iron Curtain and it was even worse than East Germany. Warsaw was a gray drab city without an ounce of charm since it had been bombed into near oblivion in World War II and rebuilt by Russians with no sense of architectural beauty but only interested in boxlike utilitarian buildings. I visited the place where the Jewish ghetto had stood and where hundreds of thousands of Jews had been taken to their deaths in extermination camps before the final heroic Jewish uprising in the spring of 1943. I walked along Mila Street, the site of Leon Uris' famous novel, Mila 18.

Such scenes and my visit to Auschwitz-Birkenau, the terrible death camp near Krakow, made it clear to me why Germans prefer not to talk about the events of World War II. I had been to Dachau earlier, the world's first concentration camp located not far from Munich, but Auschwitz is the most infamous symbol of the Nazi degeneracy. Here as they came off of boxcars, Dr. Josef Mengele pointed left or right and determined in an instant whether particular Jews would die that day in gas chambers or be made slave laborers and allowed to live a while longer.

Anyone who is not troubled by a visit to this hideous place must lack human feelings. It is an overwhelming experience as you walk past the gas chambers and crematoria and the barracks where hundreds were packed under the most filthy and depraved of conditions. Auschwitz is visible proof that the Holocaust was one of the most terrible events in human history, and here was its epicenter.

Riding trains in Eastern Europe in such countries as Poland, Czechoslovakia and Hungary were not what I would describe as particularly pleasant experiences, though I hear they have improved somewhat since the downfall of Communism.

One painful experience came at the Central Rail Station in Warsaw in the fall of 1988. I was traveling alone and put my luggage in a locker while I went to visit the Jewish Memorial. When I returned, my locker was empty. I had the police summon a lady from the American Embassy who told me I had been spotted as an American mark the moment I got off the train. Luckily I had my passport and money with me, but had been robbed of all my heavy clothing and the temperature plummeted during the next few days. The problem was it was nearly impossible to buy clothing in Poland without a long wait so I was not able to get a sweater and coat until I reached Vienna, Austria. Since the train station was owned by the Polish puppet government, I put in a claim for the loss and got a document in Polish that said, when translated, the government was prepared to offer me 500,000 zlotys for my loss. Only trouble was that money from Iron Curtain countries was no good elsewhere and what they offered would not have nearly covered even the cost of a one-way plane fare.

But as one who loves traveling by train, I recommend the British Rail system and trains in France, Italy Germany, Sweden, Denmark, Norway and most other parts of Western Europe. I buy BritRail passes and EurRail passes and they are among the world's best bargains for first class travel. The trains are always clean and on time in stark contrast to Amtrak in the United States that pales by comparison. Even sleeping accommodations are fairly cheap on European trains and the train is a great way to go overnight from London to Inverness Scotland, or from Frankfurt to Oslo.

Everywhere you go in Europe there are reminders of the greatest war in history. If you walk along the streets of Dresden, you cannot help but think of the firebombing that destroyed it in February, 1945 and was among the worst bombings in history in terms of the death toll. If you stop in Bastogne in Belgium, a town much the same now as it was then, the brutal Battle of the Bulge comes to mind, particularly if you visit the American museum. Even in Rome, the ancient cradle of civilization, you can imagine Benito Mussolini speaking from a balcony as he prepared to enter his country into a war its people most surely did not want.

Time Warp

In these days of fast food stores on every corner, many can't grasp the concept of a time when if you needed gas, a pack of cigarettes or a loaf of bread you'd better buy it by five o'clock in the afternoon or possibly be out of luck.

It was a 9 to 5 world. The corner grocery store opened at 9 a.m. and closed at 5, although it might stay open a couple hours later on a Friday or Saturday night. And there was hardly anything you could buy on a Sunday unless one of the drugstores that stayed open to fill prescriptions sold it. By Virginia law the wheels of commerce nearly totally ground to a halt on Sunday, the Sabbath. It didn't make any difference that other religions might have had their Sabbath on a different day, the Baptists who controlled the legislature would dictate to merchants when the Sabbath would be observed.

Drive-in banks were not even on the horizon and banks operated from 9 a.m. to 2 p.m. which is where the term 'Bankers Hours' come from.'

Not being able to buy things on Sunday was no great hardship. People knew to fill up the tank before Sunday or make sure there was enough bread in the house. I often went around to Johnson's Grocery at the corner of Princess Anne and Dixon streets to fetch groceries for my grandmother. There were no shopping carts or self-service at Johnson's. You went in, waited your turn and then gave the clerk behind a counter your list. The clerk then got the groceries, sometimes using a long stick with pincers on the end to get a box of oatmeal or soap located on the top shelf. It was an inefficient system it disappeared in the 1950s. I had just about forgotten it until I went to Poland in the mid-1980s and was amazed to find they were still doing it this way. I had been in Poland only a few hours when I figured that someone could make a fortune bringing in goods from the United States and selling them Western style. But the more I thought about it, the worse an idea it seemed. I had already been repelled by the sight of a McDonald's restaurant just a few doors down from 221B Baker Street in London where the mythical Sherlock Holmes and Dr. John Watson rented lodging from Mrs. Hudson.

The Memorial Day parade was a major event. It was called Confederate Memorial Day and the parade always ended at the Confederate Cemetery where formal ceremonies followed. There were lots of parades, including a parade to the Fredericksburg Agricultural Fair that was always eagerly awaited by young people starved for excitement in a town that had little to offer the young except hanging around the parking lots of the Hot Shoppes or R&S or stopping by Carl's for frozen custard.

There were two yearly events that were big deals, the dollar throw on the Rappahannock held at City Dock and the Fredericksburg Dog

Mart held at what is now Maury Field.

Both events attracted widespread publicity and participation. Contestants gathered at the Dock and tried to throw metal washers across the river to emulate the legendary feat of George Washington in tossing a coin across the river. Once in the 1930s famous baseball pitcher Walter Johnson had tossed a coin across and when I was coming along the event always attracted lots of interest. Why it was stopped I don't know. Seems to me it reaped the city much favorable publicity.

The Dog Mart is also a curious story. It once attracted national attention as one of the oldest such events in the country. It has never been the same since it was taken from the city's Maury Field and held somewhere out in the boondocks.

—Since I can appreciate the skill of people who occasionally bend the truth in the interest of good PR, two of my favorite folks were the late Jimmy Karn of Colonial Beach and Judge Nelson Waller of Spotsylvania.

Karn was connected with the Colonial Beach Chamber of Commerce and every year after the town's Potomac River Festival was held a reporter would call him and ask for an estimate of how many people had attended and the answer was always so outrageously padded that it became a standing joke in the newsroom. I think we went ahead and printed it anyway, carefully attributing the estimate to Karn. If his figures were correct, more people would have attended the obscure beach festival than went to the baseball's World Series.

Waller's seemed to want to put Partlow, where he lived in Spotsylvania, on the map. The Judge had weather equipment and was one of the semi-official people the state used to collect weather data. When reporters doing weather stories called Waller, the readings at Partlow were nearly always lower than anywhere else in the area and often anywhere else in the state. If the low temperature was 35 at Corbin, it would be 29 at Partlow. If the high were 96 at Spotsylvania Courthouse, it would be 89 at Partlow. The Judge attributed it to geographic eccentricities that kept the readings down, but I never had an earthly idea what he was talking about or whether it had any scientific basis. I know that after he died, temperatures at Partlow became more nearly equal to those in other area locations. (Nelson Waller was descended from the owners of some of the slaves in the famous novel, "Roots," written by Alex Hailey. Much of that story takes place in a county which, though fictional, is obviously Spotsylvania and some of the story is true).

Greta the Great

The first name Greta is a household word these days. Greta Van Susteren, noted TV personality on the Fox News Channel.

Back in the 1970s a young man named Wayne Eastridge of Stafford County, a Vietnam veteran, joined up with a motorcycle gang called 'The Pagans.' He went along to Alexandria to celebrate a birthday of one of the members and from there the party moved to a Washington nightclub.

Six members of the gang got into an altercation with a young black man inside the club. When they came outside, the man fired a shot at them, some of the gang pursued him, caught him and slashed him to death with knives, an incident that made big headlines in Washington and Virginia newspapers.

Two Fredericksburg area men, Eastridge and Nick Sousa, were charged with murder. Wayne Eastridge was given a court appointed defense counsel who was a habitual drunk and whose defense was minimal.

Wayne Eastridge was sentenced to 20 years to life. His father, Earl Eastridge has spent many years and much of his money trying to prove that his son was not involved in the stabbing of the young man. I got involved after reading the transcripts and hearing other evidence that convinced me Wayne was innocent of the charge. I went to Washington a couple of times to visit Wayne's attorney, Greta Van Susteren, who was confident that she could persuade federal prosecutors to grant him parole. But that never happened and eventually Earl Eastridge pursued other avenues that were just as unsuccessful, spending a fortune in the process. Greta Van Susteren was diminutive but full of self confidence and regarded as one of the top criminal lawyers in the Washington area. Her father had been a judge in some mid-western state and was involved in some action to remove him from the bench. I was not particularly impressed with Ms. Van Susteren then and do not watch her on television now, though she apparently has a vast audience. (She gained fame as one of the commentators on the endless and farcical televised court trial of O.J. Simpson). Wayne Eastridge is still a federal prisoner, having failed to this point to achieve parole. The best years of his life are now far behind him and he has spent at least 25 years behind bars for something I am convinced he did not do. In fact, some other members of the gang stated later that he had nothing to do with the slaying of the young man. Our justice system is good to an extent, but certainly failed in the case of Wayne Eastridge. I write this as I read the morning paper and note that a Judge in Westmoreland County has dismissed a murder charge against a man who clearly was involved in the murder of a prominent banker.

High profile murder cases have always been a part of American life. Growing up, I can heard the story of a Massachusetts spinster who had allegedly gone off the deep end and committed atrocious acts that resulted in a famous trial in its day.

> Lizzie Borden
> Took an ax
> And gave her mother forty whacks
> And when she saw what she had done
> She gave her father forty-one

Although all the evidence pointed to her Lizzie, like O.J., was acquitted.

In Fredericksburg I vaguely recall the trial of a man accused of poisoning his wife who was found not guilty and it was alleged that notorious broadcaster Walter Winchell proclaimed that if you wanted to get away with murder, go to Fredericksburg, Virginia. But I am not certain if I have the story straight. My maternal grandparents never failed to listen to Winchell's broadcasts as well as those of Drew Pearson and Gabriel Heater who were all great admirers of Roosevelt.

CHAPTER TWENTY TWO

JUST MESSING AROUND

I've had a propensity for practical jokes since I was a young man. Not mean-spirited practical jokes, but just those to stir things up a bit.

One of my best friends is Chip Houston who lives in Richmond witgh his wife Susan who manages to put up some of his antics. Chip is the son of a Fredericksburg legend, Lem Houston, who for many years was the city postmaster and before that was city editor of the local paper. He served as a Marine officer in the Pacific during World War II and was recalled to active duty during the Korean Conflict, rising to the rank of Colonel. Chip Houston, too, became a Colonel in the Marines Reserves.

Lem Houston loved practical jokes. When he was editor of the paper people could walk by the office on William Street and look through the window into what was the newsroom.

The desk of the paper's managing editor, Josiah P. Rowe Jr., was in a corner of the room. One evening Lem, according to the story, got a department store mannequin, put a suit on the dummy and leaned the dummy over on Rowe's desk. Beside the dummy he put a bottle of whisky with the top off and a cup next to Rowe's head.

When people came by they got the distinct impression the managing editor had over imbibed and passed out at his desk. Lem stood outside and heard comments of passerby, including that of an elderly lady walking with a lady friend. She said, "Oh dear, look at that disgraceful spectacle. Somebody is going to have to talk to Mr. Rowe about his disgusting habits."

When the Japanese bombed Pearl Harbor on December 7, 1941, the local paper printed an extra edition. There were no photos available to such a small paper so Lem allegedly pulled out a file picture of the Lusitania sinking and used it on the front page, saying it was one of the battleships going down in Hawaii. I could go back and check it out but it's too good a story to ruin.

Chip Houston is aptly named. There was a reporter who worked at the local paper and had a famous father. He lived in King George County and one morning when high winds came, the reporter stopped and took pictures of a big tree that had been felled by the storm. The paper printed the picture with an accompanying story.

The next day I got Chip to call the reporter to berate him. Chip said, "Mr. ____, this is 'Dick' McGhee of Chancellor and I saw your picture of a tree that got blowed down in King George. How come we had lots of trees blowed down out here in Spotsylvania but you didn't take any pictures of them?"

The reporter explained that he lived in King George and that he had been en route to work when he saw the tree, but the fictitious McGhee was not satisfied, replying, "I think you're prejudiced against the people of Chancellor and Spotsylvania and I'm going to organize a boycott of the paper if you don't give Spotsylvania as good a treatment as you give King George."

Thereafter Dick McGhee was a frequent caller to the reporter with complaints about practically anything he wrote. I tried to suppress laughter as I heard the reporter, his face growing red, saying loudly, "Mr. McGhee, I'm tired of your insults and I'm not going to put up with it any longer. You are simply not a gentleman."

Not long thereafter the reporter left and I've wondered ever since if Dick McGhee had anything to do with it.

Chip and I decided to launch a write-in candidacy in a City Council election for L.M. "Dick" Jones who put out campaign literature pledging to dump money into the Rappahannock River rather than spending to improve the waterfront since it would only flood again and the taxpayers money would be wasted. Several days before the election we posted 'Jones for Council' signs on telephone poles around the city. Jones may have gotten twenty or so write-in votes. What had me worried was that the reporter covering the Council election for the paper kept complaining that he had searched unsuccessfully for Dick Jones but nobody knew who he was.

There was a weekly paper in Spotsylvania County and a few of us decided to amuse ourselves by sending out frequent press releases to the paper. The releases were entirely fabricated. One announced the appointment of a man named Sam Sausalita as coordinator in the Partlow area of Spotsylvania for the statewide re-election campaign of Senator John Warner. Another said that a South African mining company had found promising underground gold deposits in Spotsylvania at an undisclosed location and might eventually employ hundreds of people in its operation. Other releases announced the pending entry into Spotsylvania County of an abortion clinic as well as a professional jai alai team. Amazingly the newspaper printed all these releases, dozens of them, until they finally caught on and let my managing editor know I was on of the prime suspects. Actually half the newsroom was in on it.

About the same time I dug up an old photograph of some geezer who appeared to be in his mid 60s. He wore a strange suit and a wide tie. I dreamed up a press release about a fellow named Frank Scorontino (or something to that effect) who was retired as police chief of Scottsdale, Arizona and was now living in the Northern Neck. The release said that Mr. Scorontino would run against incumbent Senator John Chichester for the Virginia State Senate on a law and order platform. Unless stern measures were taken, said Scorontino, violent criminals would soon be running loose in the once tranquil Northern Neck. I sent the release to one of the Neck papers and they promptly ran it on the front page along with the photo of the fake Scorontino.

When the paper came out, I got a call from John Chichester who wanted to know if I had heard of this this person. I told him innocently I knew nothing at all. Chichester said, "I've called every voter registrar in the Neck and he's not registered to vote in any of the counties." I told Chichester if I heard anything from the guy, I would let him know. Of course, I never heard another word.

I had absolutely nothing to do, however, with one of the best scams I ever heard. Charlie Unglebower lived in Fredericksburg and was a very friendly and outgoing fellow. He liked to see his name in the paper and, as told to me later by the late Judge Francis Gouldman, he found a dead black snake in the woods and put it in his car. Then he drove halfway across the 14th Street Bridge leading into Washington, got out of the car, flung the snake onto the bridge and started hitting it with a stick as amazed drivers of cars passing by looked at him. Finally a police patrol came by and stopped and Unglebower said he had seen the snake slithering across the bridge and, as a public service, jumped out to kill him. The next day a photo of Unglebower with the snake was in The Washington Post.

Charlie Unglebower was, in his own way, a visionary. He predicted that the time would when everybody would be drinking bottled water and that he was going to start a bottled water business. He died before that happened and we skeptics have to admit he had great foresight as we watch nearly every college kid walking around with a bottle of Dasani or Evian.

Once when a fellow we knew wrote a letter to the editor praising President Truman's decision to drop the atomic bomb on Japan, Chip sent the man a personal letter supposedly from the grand nephew of Admiral Yammato who had planned the attack on Pearl Harbor. Chip said that he was attending school at Virginia Commonwealth University and that Japan had attacked us only because of American aggression, including using Pan Am Airlines flights to the South Pacific for spy purposes. The man who got the letter was so livid with anger that he showed it to a number of friends at the Elks. One of them Sam Branscome, who had served in the Marines, told me about it, saying the grand nephew should be kicked out of the country.

On another occasion a mutual friend of ours was exploring the possibility of getting appointed to the Virginia Racing Commission by Governor George Allen. Chip printed a fictitious letterhead saying, 'Committee on Gubernatorial Selection,' and wrote the man that the committee had discovered his relatives in the Lynchburg area had been staunch Democrats so therefore he was disqualified from the Racing Commission but might be offered a spot on the Virginia Egg Commission. The enraged friend called Senator John Chichester who was about to call the Governor's office to protest but called me first to see if I knew anything about it. I advised him not to contact the Governor's office.

Prohibition

By the time I was born the great misguided national experiment called Prohibition designed to stop the use of alcoholic beverages had proved a total failure and had been repealed. People consumed more alcohol per capita during Prohibition than at any time in the nation's history. Prior to the enactment of Prohibition, there had been numerous taverns and saloons in Fredericksburg dating back to Colonial days.

The legendary Sam Perry, a member of City Council and vice mayor for many years, had a father named Silas Perry who was police chief during part of the Prohibition era. Sam also told me there was a police officer named Sergeant Chichester (I am going strictly from recollection here) who specialized in arresting Southern moonshiners who were trying to take their illegal liquor north. The Sergeant gained quite a reputation and was the Eliot Ness of the Fredericksburg region. I recall Sam telling me that Chichester once traded gunfire with moonshiners on the run.

Sam Perry was a dedicated man who lived in Fredericksburg all his life, was a pillar of the church, was a volunteer fireman and even into his 70s ran Rescue Squad calls. Sam Perry Boulevard now runs from the Bypass to Mary Washington Hospital and the late Rep. Herb Bateman had the Fredericksburg Post Office named in his honor since Perry was a postal employee at least 40 years.

TWENTY THREE

Egos

I'm not bashing Marshall Coleman. If he had a large ego that is the norm for people in political life and, frankly, also the norm for the media types who report on people in public life. Coleman narrowly lost in his second bid for the governorship in 1989 to L. Douglas Wilder. I think he would have made a brilliant chief executive.

I was present during an episode in 1989 involving Coleman that was to become legendary in the inner circles of state politics.

Coleman was seeking the Republican nomination in a three-way race that also included former U.S. Senator Paul Trible and Congressman Stan Parris.

A Spotsylvania County church that each Memorial Day has what is called "God and Country" services had invited all the candidates to attend and Coleman and Trible showed up. The Reverend Don Forrester is pastor of Faith Baptist Church

Many public office holders attended the service. When Trible had run for Senate in 1982 he had been questioned about the 4F draft status he had received during the Vietnam War. The criticism irritated him immensely since the status was legitimate.

On this particular Sunday, only about a week before the primary election, both Coleman and Trible were given opportunities to say a few words. When Coleman got up he noted the next day would be Memorial Day and added, "You know, it's only fitting on Memorial Day that we pay tribute to all the men and women who have served in the Armed Forces of their country. I'd like to ask everyone in this room who's ever served in the military and our country to stand up right now."

Nearly all the men in the room stood up with the exception of Trible whose face I could see turning beet red. The episode was widely reported in the next day's papers.

—No matter how big you are or how much money you have, death is still the great leveler. J.Sargent Reynolds was a man who had everything to live for. He was part of the Reynolds Metals empire in Richmond, he was bright with an ability to closely connect with people.

He got elected Lieutenant Governor in 1969 as a Democrat and was considered a shoo-in for Governor four years hence. He was immensely popular and I found his company enjoyable and stimulating.

He was a young man who had it all until they found a tumor in his brain. Not all his fortune could save him from a premature death.

At various times I met important people including Dwight Eisenhower, Richard Nixon, Jimmy Carter, Ronald Regan, Robert F. Kennedy, John Warner, Harry Byrd Sr. and Harry Byrd Jr., John Connolly of Texas, John Glenn, the astronaut turned politician, and others. Lest I be accused of trying to pad my resume, these were brief and fleeting meetings and I do not claim to have had any close relationship with most of the above, though I do correspond from time to time with former Senator Byrd Jr. who still goes to his Winchester office nearly every day. The point is that the historic figures we read about who seem to tower above all the rest of us are flesh and blood, mortals with the same feelings and passions we have. Most succeed because of ambition, intelligence and perseverance combined with luck. In politics, as in other fields, timing is everything.

Of all the famous people I've met there is one that gave me the greatest satisfaction. In 1984 when a national political convention was held in San Francisco I ducked out to visit the famous DiMaggio's Restaurant on the pier. It was afternoon. I ordered a beer and then I saw the tall gray-haired man coming out of a room at the rear.

Joe DiMaggio had been my boyhood hero, 'The Yankee Clipper.' I had seen him play in many baseball games and pestered him for autographs and he was certainly among the immortals. I hesitated at first to approach him, but finally did and he asked if I was in town for the convention. I told him I was and added that I had been a lifelong Yankee fan because of him. He was very pleasant and the conversation lasted only a couple of minutes but I couldn't have been happier if someone had given me a million dollars.

—I have never gone to extremes but I've enjoyed occasionally betting on horse races.

I had little money to spare in my younger days as a reporter but once in a while would scrape together a couple of bucks and visit Temple Allen, a paralyzed man who ostensibly ran a newsstand on Lower William Street near the Chatham Bridge.

Temple was a cheerful outgoing fellow, despite the bad hand life had dealt him, and was the best bookie in town due to his backing by an affluent prominent businessman. Unlike many bookies (who shall go nameless and the town had its fair share) Temple would take such bets as round robins and parlays at a time exotic bets had not become fashionable and were considered dangerous by most bookies who recoiled at the thought any of their customers might actually win money at any time.

Though his customers occasionally hit it big on a round robin or parlay, Temple paid them off with a smile, knowing he had the money to hold out and in the long run would come out on top if they kept betting.

I was a piker, but I enjoyed reading the Washington Post racing page and dashing the few blocks to Temple's newsstand to get in a bet.

I,ve studied the art of betting thoroughbred racing and used every imaginable system. I consider myself a pretty good handicapper, particularly for shorter races where speed counts most, but I'm convinced the average horse player can never beat the races in the long run due to a variety of reasons, not the least of which is the exorbitant amounts taken from each wager by the state and track. At one time I was a regular customer at such Maryland tracks as Bowie, Pimlico, Laurel, Hagerstown and Marlborough and the West Virginia tracks Charles Town and Shenandoah Downs. These days while I watch the big races on television and can bet nearly any track via internet, the urge to bet horses is largely gone. That's because horses racing seems to be a dying sport, though once it was the largest spectator sport in the country. NASCAR now has that distinction).

Though Virginia has a track of its own, younger people show little enthusiasm for horse racing.

In 1972, probably in summer, Sonny Ludlam and I visited The Meadow Stud at Doswell, Virginia in Caroline County and talked with the manager, Howard Gentry, a kindly man who knew nearly everything there was to know about horses. He received us graciously and gave a tour of the place. The Meadow Stud was owned by a Penny Tweedy, a Chenery by birth,and that year she had a horse named Riva Ridge who had won two of the three triple crown races.

When I told Gentry what a thrill it must be to have such a horse, he allowed that it was but added, "And the best part is that we've got one coming along even better next year."

I didn't understand how it would be possible to be much better than Riva Ridge, but he said they had a chestnut colored horse with what I thought one of the weirdest names for a racehorse I had ever heard.

Secretariat.

He said the name had been suggested by Mrs. Tweedy's aunt and was taken from the Secretariat at the United Nations.

It was a name destined to live forever in thoroughbred racing history. Secretariat became the greatest horse that ever raced. I have on my wall at home a framed photograph of him winning the Kentucky Derby easily in May 1973. And he went on to win the Triple Crown. Secretariat ran faster over a distance greater than a mile than any horse that came before him or after him.

A friend named Ace Lawson and I often went to racetracks, sometimes as many as three nights a week to Charles Town, West Virginia where at the time there were two tracks, Charles Town and Shenandoah Downs. If we had a day off, we might go to Bowie, Pimlico or Laurel in Maryland and then that night drive to Charles Town, something called going around the horn.

At Charles Town we often saw a Fredericksburg man we thought was making a living playing horses. He always went to the $50 window and occasionally would give us a tip on a horse. I thought if anyone could make a living betting horses he could. Later I learned this gambler had lost everything. He was to become a prominent member of the Gamblers Anonymous organization in Virginia.

Though you can't beat the races, I like them and have visited racetracks in many places, including Churchill Downs and Keeneland in Kentucky and Saratoga in upstate New York, the most beautiful track of them all though I have never been to Santa Anita.

Some years ago there was a referendum in Fredericksburg about whether to allow an off track betting facility. Though I favored it, it failed because of opposition that maintained it would attract organized crime. Actually it would have generated a considerable amount of revenue both to the city and state. You can go to off track betting parlors anywhere, here, in London, the rest of England, Germany, or wherever and you will see that the patrons are much too busy figuring out which horses to bet to engage in any kind of crime unless drinking a few beers and losing your money is a crime.

No matter. Through the magic of the Internet I am now able to bet nearly every track in the United States and some in foreign countries. I can watch the races being run on my screen and pull up in an instant my account balance and I don't have to leave home. And the state of Virginia seldom gets any of my betting dollar so the last laugh is on those who persuaded the voters of Fredericksburg to turn down an off track betting facility.

Horse racing finally came to Virginia but there are several flies in the ointment. Colonial Downs, a beautiful track, is simply in the wrong location. The track should have been put in Northern Virginia. And no locality north of Richmond has approved off track betting which was foreseen as a major source of its revenue so it will likely continue to struggle.

--Since dropping out of political reporting, I have worked for four members of Congress, all of them with different styles but all outstanding public servants.

Being a member of Congress is no easy task. Each member represents about 660,000 persons and is in constant demand. Thousands of letters pour in each week and any constituent who doesn't receive a speedy reply is offended. Congressional staff is perpetually overworked and underpaid, but for young people being a staff member is an experience that will prove valuable.

Most members of Congress, except those who represent districts bordering Washington, have to maintain two residences, an expensive proposition. Will Rogers once quipped that Congress is America's only native criminal class and it is far from being anywhere near perfect. But democracy, as Winston Churchill pointed out, remains the worst form of government except for all others.

I work now for Congresswoman Jo Ann Davis and she is remarkable in that she proudly says she is not a politician. And that is true. She carries a peanut butter and jelly sandwich in her purse to eat between stops and always finds time for constituents no matter how busy. In a short period she has become a major player in the U.S. House of Representatives but, unlike many, does not let the trappings of office go to her head. Her husband, Chuck Davis, is a retired firefighter and a nice guy who enjoys life on their Gloucester County Farm where horses and dogs roam freely. I have no doubt Mrs. Davis will be in Congress as long as she wants the job because she is people oriented.

One of my duties in the past was to help politicians extract themselves from a room after a meeting or dinner. I quickly learned that Mrs. Davis did not want me to continue in that role since she always sticks around to speak to everybody until it is time to turn out the lights.

--Donald Crowder is six years younger than me, but he grew up around the corner from my grandparents. When Donald was 42, he lost an eye while chopping wood. Inspired by President George Herbert Walker Bush, he decided that to celebrate his 62nd birthday he would skydive. And he did from the Orange County airport. He described to me the fearful sensation of falling a mile in 30 seconds until the parachute finally opened. During the process, his false eye popped out but was retained in his goggles. Donald said afterward the experience was a great thrill but he would not care to try it again.

—Two of my favorite people are Tom and M.C. Moncure. Tom, whose grandfather Frank Moncure served in the Virginia House of Delegates, was elected to that position and was succeeded in office by Bill Howell who became Speaker of the House. Subsequently, Tom was elected to two terms as clerk of the Stafford County Circuit Court and is now on the staff of Virginia Attorney General Jerry Kilgore, someone that I think will be the next Governor of Virginia. I first met M.C. Moncure, Tom's future wife, when she was a student at Mary Washington College and involved in Young Republican activities.

I speak with Tom frequently, though his present job keeps him very busy. He has a vast knowledge of American history and can expound for hours on various theories about the Revolutionary and Civil Wars. His father Thomas (Mac) Moncure Sr., a Stafford lawyer, jokes that his son sometimes uses words he does not think are in the dictionary. I have never met a brighter or more pleasant person.

—In the early 1970s Sonny Ludlam and I conceived the idea of the Greater Fredericksburg Sports Club and began to schedule events and take in members. Incredible as it seems in this day and age of inflated prices for athletes, our first guest speaker was baseball star Pete Rose, then in his second year with the Cincinnati Reds, and we paid him just $750 plus his airfare. Rose was a great guy and deserves to be in the Hall of Fame. We had at least 125 people at that first dinner meeting at the Sheraton.

Later we'd have such guests as Johnny Bench, Bill Kilmer, Mickey Mantle, Gail Sayers, Bobby Richardson, Tommy Bell, Lefty Drisell, Mrs. Penny Tweedy, owner of Secretariat and Riva Ridge, Shirley Povich and many more.

The membership was confined to men and I recall reporter Gwen Woolf writing a story decrying the all-male policy. My philosophy has changed since I was the proposer in 1995 of the first woman to join the Elks in Fredericksburg. I still find it hard to agree with the ruling to allow women in VMI. Tom Moncure, a VMI graduate, was on the school's board of visitors at the time of the court ruling and resigned from the board when the first woman gained admission. Dabney Oakley, another friend and VMI graduate who lives in Caroline County, shares the Moncure opinion. Dabney is someone who seems to know everybody worth knowing in the state.

The sports club disbanded because the charge by athletes for appearances steadily escalated. Joe Namath wanted $10,000. There are few athletes around these days who deserve to be anybody's hero (Cal Ripken and Darrel Green excepted). The first president of the Sports Club was Jack Elwell, an FBI agent, and Ollie Stephens, a former vice president of the National Bank of Fredericksburg was treasurer.

Mickey Mantle was a great baseball player and I loved to watch him play. I was a bit disillusioned the night he came to talk to the sports club because he said he had to get away early by plane to meet Billy Martin in New York City at a party. And then when we went to a room at the Sheraton afterward where he could change clothes, he was asked what he wanted to drink and said a Tru Ade grape and vodka. That did not seem a very sophisticated drink for a famous person, but we got it for him anyway. In his memoirs Mantle admitted t his years as a ballplayer were shortened by his hard drinking. Even so, he remains one of the greatest players in the game's history.

CHAPTER TWENTY FOUR

Here Comes the Judge

Circuit Judge Leon Bazile was unusual. He came to court wearing cowboy boots and never wore a black gown. And he did not run a tight ship. Often shouting matches would erupt between Fredericksburg Commonwealth's Attorney Billy Cole and defense attorney Francis Gouldman (who was also a very colorful character). Bazile would let them go at it without maintaining order. Fredericksburg lawyer Billy Gibson tried to get the legislature to impeach Bazile but his effort failed.

I was in court one day when Bazile was reading a newspaper while a defense lawyer was arguing some point. On another occasion, Bazile fell asleep on the bench and City Sergeant T. Frank Fines ordered the proceedings halted until he woke up.

Someone I got to know was Harry Berry, a King George farmer who talked long and loud. His neighbor a mile away was King George Commonwealth's Attorney Horace Morrison, and Morrison was so offended by Berry's loud calling for his sheep in the evening that he hauled Berry before Bazile. But the case was dismissed.

Berry put numerous claims before the county board of supervisors for alleged destruction of his sheep by stray dogs. Under a state law, such compensation was mandatory if loss could be proven.

When the supervisors finally balked at paying Berry, the farmer brought a flock of sheep to the Courthouse and posted them at the door while the supervisors were meeting inside. A photo made the front page of the Free Lance-Star and was also carried on the Associated Press wire.

-In the late 1990s while working for Congressman Herbert Bateman in his Fredericksburg District Office I had two interns who were students at Mary Washington College.

One, Heather Young, is now associated with me in the Fredericksburg District office of Congresswoman Jo Ann Davis. Heather is one of the smartest and nicest persons I have ever known. She is just the greatest and that sums it up. She grew up in Texas and Louisiana.

The other intern the second part of that semester was Erika Grace from Altoona, Pennsylvania who in her tomboyish way was the All American kid. She had been a basketball star in high school played on the women's basketball team at Mary Washington before abruptly giving it up. Erika graduated with honors.

She interned with us about three months and was pleasant and bright. A few years after her internship I learned that a young lady named Erika Sifrit had been arrested along with her husband in Ocean City, Maryland for allegedly killing a man and woman, chopping up their bodies and disposing of them in various places.

Sifrit turned out to be the married name of Erika Grace. I was stunned and told that to a number of media people who had learned of her internship. She has been convicted of first-degree murder of the male victim and second-degree murder of the female victim, meaning she could get life in prison. Her husband, incredibly, was acquitted of one of the murders and convicted only of second-degree murder for the other offense. I believe Benjamin Sifrit, who was kicked out of the Navy Seals, had a Svengali-like hold and was the evil force behind what happened.

The Computer Age

I was a late getting into computers and my grandsons, Corey now 17, and Cody, 14, know much more about them I do. Practically everything I know about computer technology, and that is limited, was taught me by Heather Young.

The instant communication allowed by e-mail is great but also a mixed blessing. In the heat of the moment we sometimes express thoughts via e-mail we might have otherwise put in a traditional letter and then torn up when we cooled down. And e-mail leaves a record of what is said. I think the e-mails of public persons should not be subject to Freedom of Information laws because such laws have already gone too far and are often intimidating to elected officials in the necessary give and take of the political arena.

Nearly every day I receive e-mails from Dabney Oakley and Chip Houston. Dabney, a VMI graduate, is attuned to just about everything that goes on in Virginia and has a vast network to which his e-mails are directed. He lives in Caroline County with his adorable Beagle and, like me, thinks Secretariat was the greatest racehorse of all time. Other frequent e-mail friends are David Kerr and Ferris Belman of Stafford and Netta

Glover who lives just outside London, England and is a remarkable person with a keen sense of humor. I met Netta and her husband Ray when I stopped by the small village of Wing, Leighton-Buzzard, to visit the former Sandra Walker of Fredericksburg who married Bob Walker, a former star photographer for The Free Lance-Star. Sandra is now a nationally known artist in England and once did a portrait of Margaret Thatcher. She also formerly worked for Senator Ted Kennedy who was in the same UVA law school class as my brother and was far from being the best and brightest in his class. But though Sandra is a flaming liberal she has great talent and I like her despite her leftist ways. Sandra, who has lived in England 14 years, was elected President of the Royal Institute of Painters in Watercolour, a huge honor since she is an American and a woman. I have a couple of her paintings at my home.

Greased Lightning

Apollo XXIII was a terrific movie and brought to public attention the high risks involved in space travel.

I was present at one space launch where the astronauts were almost killed shortly after liftoff but no great fuss was made about it.

It must have been Apollo XI. I know that it was the first launch after the moon flight and the astronauts were going to the moon again.

I persuaded the managing editor of the paper to let me fly over to Cake Kennedy (now Cape Canaveral again) on my way back from a seminar for political reporters held at the University of Mississippi in Jackson, Mississippi.

I obtained Press credentials, spent the night at a hotel near the base and drove my rental car to the base long before the sun arose. The launch was scheduled for 9 a.m.

The rocket, bathed in light, looked enormous even from the media area several miles away. The skies were overcast and it rained intermittently from time to time. I hoped the launch would not be postponed by the weather since it might be my last chance to see something as dramatic.

The weather wasn't getting better by the time President Richard M. Nixon and Vice President Spiro Agnew arrived about forty-five minutes before the scheduled liftoff. Sitting with Nixon and Agnew in the covered VIP section were assorted military brass, the President's chief of staff Bob Haldeman and his close friend Bebe Rebozo.

It rained harder and since I didn't bring a raincoat, I was getting drenched. Then there were rumblings of thunder and I could clearly see flashes of lightning. I figured there was practically no chance the launch would go ahead as scheduled. The best I could hope for would be a delay of several hours.

But as the minutes ticked away, the countdown continued. I saw more flashes of lightning about two minutes before the launch. Then at the appointed hour came the ignition of the fuel followed by a tremendous noise. As the rocket lifted into the air I could feel the earth shake beneath me so great was its force. It was an awe inspiring sight as the huge rocket went up into the clouds, albeit one I saw only about fifteen seconds until the clouds swallowed it up and it was gone from view.

I hurried away as the rain came down harder and by the time I got to my car I was soaked to until I reached the airport and had time to change.

It wasn't until the next morning that I read with surprise that the rocket had been hit by a bolt of lightning shortly after it got into the clouds and for a moment had lost its power systems. It was a crucial time and if the power had not snapped back on instantly the whole thing might have come tumbling down.

I couldn't believe the AP story said there had not been any sightings of lightning in the area before the launch. I had not wanted the launch postponed, but wondered if NASA had gone ahead because the President and Vice President were there.

—I met Paul Howard in basic training at Fort Knox, Kentucky in 1958. He was a quiet guy who wasn't enamored of the rigors of military service, but did what he had to do.

We learned that Paul's father was Moe Howard, chief stooge of The Three Stooges, but in those days he didn't want to talk about it.

In later years I made contact again with Paul who now lives in New York and we e-mail each other from time to time. He calls me Private Goolrick and I refer to him as Private Howard. It was not until he was in his 30s that he came to realize that his father and the other Stooges had become American icons still seen on television around the world. Paul is a frequent guest at Three Stooges Fan Club events and I am a member in good standing of that group since some of my most cherished boyhood memories are laughing at the antics of the Stooges at the Colonial Theater. Even today, my grandsons avidly watch the Stooges on TV.

At Christmas of 2002 I was given a set of old Stooges comedies and enjoyed viewing them as much as I did 60 years ago.

Paul told me that his father in real life was a good dad and shrewd businessman. He also said he had come to realize over a period of time how much laughter and entertainment his father and the others had brought to the nation. I could not agree more. Neither Paul or his sister get a nickel from any of the modern day revenues generated by The Stooges since in those days movie studios insisted on absolute rights to all marketing. But they plan to write a book about the years spent with their mother and father.

-I still have a photo I took during high school days when I occasionally worked for the paper. It was one of two small kids dressed in cowboy outfits who had won the annual Kiwanis Club talent show. Their names were Jerry and Wayne Newton who had grown up in White Oak. Some years later when a group of us from the area saw Wayne Newton at the MGM Grand in Las Vegas he spoke about his White Oak Newton relatives. One of my close Elks friend is Glenn Newton, Wayne's first cousin.

-While in the National Guard at A.P. Hill I met a soldier from Philadelphia whose last name was Ridarelli. He was personable and while we were not close friends, I enjoyed his company and easy going ways. The entertainment world knew him as Bobby Rydell, a teenage singer idol. I took him to several area radio stations for interviews. That was a long time ago but Rydell is still appearing in Vegas lounge acts and one day I hope to see him perform again.

Reflections

Not long ago I was leaving the Pratt Medical Center where I had picked up some pills. As I did, a young woman came by pushing a small thin boy of about four in a wheelchair. The youngster had obviously been born crippled but had a smile on his face as his mother talked to him in soothing tones.

I hoped, despite the cruel hand he had been dealt, he would with the help of that loving mother be able to deal with his handicap and grow up to be someone who succeeded. I am amazed how so many people who suffer such ill luck get on with their lives and not only cope with ill fortune but conquer it. Two great examples are Franklin D. Roosevelt and former Virginia Lt. Gov. John Hager, both struck by polio in adulthood, but both strong and courageous enough to move ahead. And there is Rex

Holland who lives in Fredericksburg and lost his sight some years ago. Rex, a native of England, was an RAF pilot during World War II and has an absolutely indomitable spirit.

I've have lived a fortunate life. I wasn't ambitious enough to become rich and most of the money I made I spent on travel and other pursuits. Yet without being affluent, I somehow managed to visit many different parts of the world and to meet people who were wealthy, famous or both, as well as many who were not wealthy or famous but interesting people with a wealth of knowledge.

In my childhood automobiles weren't the prevalent force of today and one saw few planes passing overhead. Fredericksburg was a sleepy town surrounded by bucolic counties where the pace of living was slow and easy. Farming was the major way of life and you could not drive a few miles without seeing dairy barns or cows grazing peacefully in meadows.

The prime means of entertainment were radio and movies. I tuned in eagerly to my favorite programs and the whole family often sat around listening to a radio program. Among those I never missed were The Shadow, Mr. District Attorney, The Lone Ranger Jack Benny, Fred Allen, Fibber McGhee and Molly, Amos n' Andy, and the Friday Night Fights from Madison Square Garden. The Amos and Andy shows were done by two white men from Virginia using Negro dialect. They were never mean spirited, but still demeaning to blacks, something I did not realize at the time.

For the past few years members of the Jones family—my Jones family—have been holding reunions. My mother was a Jones, Olive Elizabeth Jones, daughter of Elizabeth and Andrew Ross Jones. They had ten children who survived, six girls and four boys. Four others died in infancy. Only four of them are still living today. My mother died in 1990.

I have Jones relations I have never met since with such a large family there is a multiplier effect. And though so far as I know every Goolrick in this country is descended from Peter or John Goolrick who came from Sligo in Ireland, there are also Goolricks I have never met since Peter and Jane Goolrick had a large family.

In the case of Goolricks, there is no doubt they came from Ireland. But I can't determine where my branch of Jones' came from. It was probably Scotland, but trying to trace a family of Jones' is the worst nightmare of any genealogist.

--On Friday, Sept. 7, 2001 I took a train to New York City and saw a game at Yankee Stadium on Saturday afternoon. As the train starts to pull into New York City one can see the skyline. It was a bright day and the skyline was dominated by the Twin Towers of the World Trade Center. I returned by train on Sunday, Sept. 9 but did not look at the skyline as we departed. It would have been inconceivable to think that just two days later those twin towers would stand no more.

--I got to know Hugh Doggett Scott Jr. when he was a member of the U.S. Senate from Pennsylvania and Senate majority leader. Scott was a native of Fredericksburg whose father was president of the National Bank of Fredericksburg for years. Scott Jr. recalled that my grandfather, Judge Goolrick, had given him the oath for some minor local office after he had graduated from law school. Scott introduced me to a number of colleagues, including legendary Speaker of the House John McCormack who was then quite elderly and seemed senile. McCormack was a product of Boston politics, a cutthroat arena totally unlike Virginia politics. One only has to remember Mayor Curley (The Last Hurrah) who was sent to jail for accepting bribes, served part of his term and then returned to his job as Mayor as if nothing had happened.

--I became a friend of Matt Willis on his return to Fredericksburg in the 1980s. Willis had been a character actor in many Hollywood movies and on Broadway, most often as the 'heavy.' In one movie he played The Wolf Man. Willis told me he had abandoned the Hollywood scene in favor of real estate because whether a person could afford it or not, they had to put on a good front and often live beyond their means. Though never a well-known actor, he had hobnobbed with some of the biggest names in movies. I also met actress Illona Massey when her career was finished. She had married Army Gen. Robert Stack who in World War II accepted the surrender of Hermann Goering. The couple was living in King George County at the time.

I think, to paraphrase Winston Churchill, I have lived a not uneventful life and don't have any particular regrets. Life is basically a trip of whatever duration from the starting pole to the finish line. The great novelist Thomas Wolfe said you can't go home again, and that's probably true, but you can remember how it was and the simple pleasure of growing up in a small city such as Fredericksburg.

APPENDIX I

Though the method by which Virginia selects its judges is often criticized as a political process more than a merit process, somehow it works.

A prime example occurred in the 1970s when a Circuit Court Judgeship in the Fredericksburg area was vacant.

State Senator Paul Manns of Bowling Green had promised Horace Revercomb, King George commonwealth's attorney, to back him for the position. But A.L. Philpott, Speaker of the House of Delegates, was backing his brother-in-law former Delegate Walther Fidler of Warsaw.

Fidler had left the General Assembly with the full expectation of getting a Judgeship. Manns was a close friend of both Philpott and Fidler but refused to go back on his word that he would back Revercomb.

The battle over the judgeship between the Senate and House was fierce since Democrats with a majority in both branches were divided.

Then in the final hours of the session, when it appeared the judgeship would go unfilled, Delegate Lewis Fickett of Fredericksburg produced a compromise candidate in Jere M.H. Willis Jr. Fredericksburg's commonwealth attorney.

At the 11th hour, the names of Revercomb and Fidler were withdrawn and Willis was selected. It was an excellent choice and he later was named to the Virginia Intermediate Court of Appeals. And in time both Revercomb and Fidler were rewarded with lesser judgeships. I had contacts in both camps and wrote a lengthy piece on the judicial battle that won a number of awards. During my lifetime I have known colorful judges such as Leon Bazile and Francis Gouldman and judges of good temperament and wisdom such as Mac Willis, Bernard Coleman, Joseph Savage, John Butzner, Bill Ledbetter, Horace Revercomb, Peyton Farmer (a fellow Yankee fan), Ann Hunter Simpson, Dean Lewis, John Scott and many others.

I had had a long friendship with Jud Honaker, vice president of Silver Companies. His dad, Ben, was also a great friend and I gave the eulogy at his funeral. Jud has done wonders for his company and the community and is one of the hardest working individuals I know.

Another close friend is John W. Edwards, who not only is a sign painter but an artist and genealogist. I own several of his paintings and particularly cherish one of the old Eddie Mack's Grill where I spent much time in my youth. He did the cover of this book. John's hometown art show was a tremendous success and evoked nostalgic feelings in those who attended.

As I write this, Fredericksburg's political scene is in its usual turmoil but I'm sure the city will muddle through as it has in the past.

Two close friends on Council are Joe Wilson and Bill Withers. I have known Mayor Bill Beck for some time and though we have differences of opinion on the direction the city should take, still commend him for all he has done to help preserve the history of the city and the region and his continuing work in that field.

Our principal differences come on such things as Silver Companies and the Central Park and Celebrate Virginia projects (the latter I think can help make our area a tourist destination instead of a stopover.) I also think an Outer Connector road serving the area is badly needed while Bill seems to be against it (Paul Akers of The Free Lance-Star notes that most of the opponents are people who don't have to hit the congested roads every day). Waldo Beck, Bill's dad, is one of the nicest people I've ever known and his mother fell into the same category. Bill has done a superb ceremonial job as Mayor and keeps his cool when presiding over Council even when during public comment periods some folks are saying bad things about his performance.

Certainly, Bill, Cessie Howell and Vernon Edenfield were the key players in saving Ferry Farm from a Wal-Mart development and that accomplishment alone should earn them enduring gratitude. Now I want Edenfield's plans for Ferry Farm to become a major tourist attraction to work out. And I'm positive it will for Vernon is a visionary who sees far ahead of most of us.

As a footnote, I was talking with former Spotsylvania supervisor Jim Smith not long ago and he recalled that when the major stores and car dealerships left Fredericksburg, the city was in such bad financial shape that at one time it considered reverting to town status. He said he and other supervisors had discussed the possibility on several occasions with city officials. Those who do not recall those perilous financial times have short memories or have just arrived. Central Park enabled Fredericksburg to go from one of the most fiscally stressed cities in the state to one of the most fiscally prosperous. Citizens who make a career out of criticizing the Silvers and its alleged stranglehold on former Councils simply are badly misinformed and slanting the truth. I would be happy if not one more home were ever built in the region, but I know that is not going to be the case because of location, location, location.

--The thought occurs to me that I spent much of my young adulthood under the constant threat of nuclear warfare. The Cuban missile crisis in October,1962 scared the pants off the whole nation and much of the world when the threat of a nuclear holocaust seemed immensely real. Through a so called civil defense system advocating fallout shelters and stocking of large supplies of food and water, we fooled ourselves into believing that we could survival a nuclear war, but, of course, that would not have been the case. Even today a nuclear threat remains very real, but does not seem nearly as imminent as it did in the darkest days of the Cold War.

--One of my friends is Jeff Rouse of Stafford who won several Olympic goal medals for swimming and,now in his 30s, is aiming for the 2004 summer Olympics. I was saddened to learn of the death of his mother, Gail Rouse Presnell, a fine woman who had worked at Mary Washington College. She was just 56 at the time of her death. I hope Jeff is able to collect even more Olympic medals.

I know I have left out the names of many people and events that have been part of my life but at some point there must be an ending point. I learned very early in the newspaper game that the copy had to be in by deadline even if it did not include everything you would have liked to convey to the reader. And even in the work I have been doing for the past 17 years there are almost daily deadlines for action, meaning for nearly all my adult life I have lived by the clock.

APPENDIX II

My Dear Goolrick

The life of my great-grandfather by one of your ancestors just arrived and I cannot tell you how pleased I am to have it because, except for the statue at Fredericksburg and Princeton and a picture I have of him getting bayoneted, he is more or less an unknown character to me.

I trust that your wounds have healed and that you are in good shape again. If you want to get even for any nastiness I did to you go in the churchyard of the Episcopal Church and you can stomp on the tombstones of a number of Pattons, Mercers, Thompsons, etc.

      G.S. Patton Jr.
      General 15th U.S. Army

The letter was sent to Capt. Kinloch Goolrick, my second cousin, who then lived on Lewis Street in Fredericksburg. He is a retired editor of Time-Life books who now lives in New York City. The letter was dated October 24, 1945, less than two months before the famed General George S. Patton Jr. suffered a fatal injury in a traffic accident in Germany. The first Army MP to arrive on the scene was young Peter Babalas of Norfolk, Virginia who later became a Virginia State Senator. He told me the accident occurred at low impact and the General's fatal injury was a one in a thousand shot.

Kinloch had been on Pattons's staff in Morocco, Algeria, Sicily, England and France and then was severely wounded in the Battle of the Bulge. He recalls waking up in the hospital and seeing the General standing at his side.

The book he sent Patton was, 'The Life of General Hugh Mercer' written by my grandfather, John T. Goolrick Sr. and published in 1906. Mercer, who was killed in action during the Battle of Princeton during the Revolutionary War, was not Patton's great-grandfather but his great-great-great grandfather.

In a chapter called, 'The Confederate Pattons,' from a book Fredericksburg historian Bob Krick is writing he notes that the first George S. Patton, the grandfather of the World War II General, died at the head of his brigade at Winchester on September 19, 1864 in the first major battle of the 1864 Shenandoah Valley Campaign. A number of Patton brothers fought with the Army of Northern Virginia.

Although born in California, General Patton's roots were in Fredericksburg. Robert Patton, his great-great grandfather, came from Scotland to America around 1770. He settled in Fredericksburg, joined St. George's Episcopal Church, became a prominent merchant and finally married Anne Gordon Mercer, Hugh Mercer's daughter although by then Mercer had been killed. Many of Patton's ancestors were members of St. George's Episcopal and Fredericksburg Presbyterian Church.

With her husband dead and her state devastated, Patton's grandmother, Susan Patton, accepted an invitation from a brother to move to California. The famous future General was born there in 1885 into an affluent family since his father was an attorney. Patton grew up hearing stories about his Confederate ancestors and knowing he wanted to be a soldier. Among those who often visited the Patton home and told war stories was the famous Confederate 'Gray Ghost' Col. John Singleton Mosby who regaled young Patton for hours with tales of his Civil War adventures.

Patton returned to Virginia when he enrolled in Virginia Military Institute, but next year, 1904, got an appointment to West Point. He saw combat action both in 1916 in Mexico and in France in World War I.

Since the General, who loved cavalry, was stationed a number of times at Fort Myer, there is little doubt he visited the Fredericksburg region often where he saw the Washington Avenue statue of his ancestor and studied Civil War battlefields. After I sent a copy of the Krick chapter to Joanne Holbrook Patton of Massachusetts, daughter-in-law of the General, she wrote back in gratitude that, "Even our son, Bob, who wrote the family up in his book 'The Pattons', said he was reading about some of the Patton brothers in Mr. Krick's manuscript for the first time." Bob Krick coached Robert Duvall on the mannerisms of General Robert E. Lee for Duvall's role as Lee in 'Gods and Generals.'

Krick, knowing that Patton is one of my heroes, occasionally brings me brochures advertising authentic signed letters and photos from the General at prices far beyond my pocketbook. When I sent Mrs. Patton one of the brochures, she wrote, 'We are always amused — and sometimes shocked — by the outrageous prices people charge or pay for 'celebrity memorabilia,' such as the signed Patton parade photo. Imagine–$5,000"

Sadly, Patton's son, George Smith Patton who also followed in his father's footsteps and became a General with a distinguished record, is now, according his wife, no longer able to read or correspond. He is a person who had always been proud of his heritage and, though I never met him, had the pleasure of conversing by phone with him several times.

When I was a child in World War II days and began to adopt General Patton as a hero, I had no idea of his Fredericksburg connections since my grandfather wrote his Mercer biography in 1906 when young George Patton was just 21.

I haven't been to the Hugh Mercer Apothecary Shop in recent years but hope they tell visitors about the Patton connection. He was the greatest combat general of the 20th century and I think Mercer, his distinguished ancestor, would have been proud of him. I bought a bust of Patton from a downtown store and proudly display it in my office. Though he was called 'Old Blood and Guts' I think most of those who served under him were proud of the honor, including Bill Stern who for years operated a country store in Stafford.

APPENDIX THREE

The following is a brief account of his life written by my father, John T. Goolrick Jr., for a federal writers project in the 1930s. My father wrote several histories of Fredericksburg and while employed with the National Park Service a long biography of Union General George Gordon Meade, a strange endeavor for someone who was the son of a Civil War soldier who been present at the surrender at Appomattox. A major publishing company almost accepted the book but World War II was nearing and interest in the Civil War waning. A few years ago my brother and I donated the manuscript to The Meade Society of Philadelphia and I ended up becoming a member of that society. John C. Goolrick. (July 5, 2003).

By John T. Goolrick Jr.

Born in Fredericksburg, Virginia, I went at 11 years old to work as a page in the House of Representatives. The pages sat on the steps below the Speaker's desk and when a member clapped his hands ran to his desk and did what errand he required. Each was assigned several members to do special work for, such as filing the Congressional Records, etc. and among those I waited upon especially were William Jennings Bryan, then new in Congress, "Uncle Joe" Cannon, Bourke Cochrane, Charles O' Ferrell of Virginia. I asked Mr. Bryan for his autograph and he said, smiling, "That may be valuable when I am president."

At 15 pages were "over age", and relieved. I went to the pension bureau, as messenger in the office of the First Deputy Commissioner, and here I waited again upon Senators and Representatives, when they came to seek pensions for action on claims of constituents. My job was to go to the files and get the papers in the case. When I was 18 I tired of this and took a night train for Pittsburgh. Why Pittsburgh I do not recall.

The Pittsburgh Engineering and Construction Company employed me at $40 a month, so I learned not to overeat, and I learned drafting there. Later I became bookkeeper and later accountant with them, but at 20 I decided to go to Africa. I went second class to Liverpool, London and, in the Avondale Castle, first class to Capetown.

There were interesting passengers. Lord Menzies and I became friends. At Santa Cruz, Island of Tenerife, we passengers went ashore and having underrated the potency of the fine wine sold there for six pence a glass, some of them got into an argument with a pool room proprietor on this gala day—it was May 1st a Spanish holiday—and were put into cells. With others I went through a crowd that was starting a small riot and saw the Governor, who released them, but only after a payment of two pounds.

At Capetown I faced difficulties. The Boer War had just ended. Soldiers were coming from up-country in droves. The American consul was a red-headed, long mustached gentlemen from Kansas who was quite entertaining as he sat with his feet on the desk and told us jokes, but he got nowhere; so after 30 days we went to the British authorities and got a passport.

It's a thousand miles and more from Capetown to Johannesburg, and it takes three days to make it — or did in 1902. We had to carry water bags and get water as best we could at stations when, and if, the train stopped, and we had oil stoves to cook what food we carried, and slept at night on the benches on which we sat on by day. It was a tiresome trip across the Great Karoo and the Veldt. At stations we passengers had a little amusement when the train stopped for half an hour or an hour or an hour and a half, seemingly at the engineers whim, the fun being. We paid half—grown Kaffirs to fight, which they did with earnestness, sometimes with clubs.

In Johannesburg things were dull. I was selling for the Westinghouse and Carleton Chase companies, on commission. The British wanted at once fifty pounds yearly license. The mines were closed, because the owners wished to bring in Chinese labor and the Government forbade it.

There was nothing to do after a month of ill success but go down to Durban. Thinking to save money, which was now short, I took a third class passage on the train. I didn't know: the third was taken all by Zulus and Kaffirs, in an open coach. They ate honey and strange foods and gormed things up. Young women with cans of water they had put aboard at Johannesburg stripped and standing upon the seats bathed nonchalantly, no one paying the slightest attention, and a few men did the same. British trains did not have aisles and are locked, so I had to ride this for about 80 miles before I could see the conductor and change to second class, which was all white.

At Durban, a tropical sea coast town, I got a job as "Junior" on the Durban Chronicle. I had a little newspaper experience, gotten on the Washington Post as a semi-pro at night. A junior is what we call a cub reporter. I did not please the English editor much as I knew nothing of their style and customs in journalism, and I was made to know this by being kindly allowed to resign.

Finances reached the ebb of one shilling, enough to pay for coffee and two rolls. I bought these and the Greek proprietor told me he had worked in America and wanted to know how to make hot cakes. I showed him, and he gave me a meal ticket. That day I made a bluff and secured a job as house wire-man, working on a big building, where the labor was all Zulu. The pay was $12 a day, or two pound ten, and although it was a precarious job, I held it somehow, mainly by buying much beer for the Scotch foreman, got overtime work with him at a big hotel, because, I think, I bought beer at the bar often. The bubonic plague and cholera were raging and each day a scow took the dead to sea and dumped them. So when the foreman told me we were to wire a hospital, I told him I was a specialist at molding, but would not work in the hospital, and despite his protestations that the plague cases did not go to this hospital (I knew that) I quit, drew my pay and paid my passage on the Warragal to London.

We ran into a bad storm en route to Capetown. The cargo shifted. When we were about the Equator it got worse and we listed badly. A big ship headed near us but, seeing our plight, drew miles off and went by. The Warragal limped into London and began to sink at the docks in the Limehouse district. In London I idled about White Chapel and Cheapside and looked over the tough spots in the town, as well as Westminister and St Pauls and all that.

Back in Fredericksburg, I got a little money and bought the Fredericksburg Weekly Journal. At the end of a year I sold it and went to civil engineering with the R.F. and P.R.R. as a rodman. I learned the instruments, was in Florida with the Seaboard Air Line, and then in West Virginia, Western Virginia and Kentucky, in the mountains, in various capacities, always in tent-camps far back in the hills. Once the corps stopped a night at a mountain home, and we learned the owner was "Bad Dan" Wright. By the firelight he told us he had killed 24 men, which was well known to the mountain folk, and a few years ago was printed widely when Bad Dan died. He told us a story worth hearing, about "Devil Anse" Hatfield, whom I knew well.

Devil Anse lived on an island, in the Ohio River, and had for years defied capture, though a large reward was offered for him. Bad Dan went to get him (and the reward) "Dead or Alive". At the river edge Devil Anse hailed him, and when Bad Dan called to him "come fetch me over", Anse told him to lay his rifle down. When he did, Anse got him and took him to his island home. They drank sociably at the bar that Anse maintained in violation of the law, and retired to a room in which there were two beds. "Stranger" said Bad Dan "I sleep light. If you stir, raise some noise first, I might grab my pistol in my half sleep". Dan put his gun under his pillow. Anse did likewise. And each lay awake all night waiting for a move from the other. In the morning they had drinks and breakfast and then Devil Anse said. "You told me you was named Cary, but I knowed you from the time I seen you on shore for Bad Dan Wright. If you'd moved, I'd killed you". "He would'er, I knowed" said Bad Dan "And if he'd went asleep, I'd killt him".

I left here for the west; Texas coal mines at Thurber, City Engineers force. Guthrie Oklahoma, Great Northern Railroad, Farmington, Montana. Then to Seattle and to Los Angeles, where I went back to news papering with the Los Angeles Express. Hearing of a job in Porterville, California, I went there as reporter, and worked some months. The paper was an anti-saloon paper, in a tough town with 27 saloons, but the paper had a new plant and was backed, by a cooperative of good citizens. When the manager failed to make it go, I was made manager and worked 18 hours a day, including Sunday. The paper was getting ahead when Leslie McAuliff, of Iowa, came along and with almost nothing we bought the paper. McAuliff had some thousands, though, and from now on we sailed well. In two years, after three elections, we won the fight and the saloons were closed. From then on we were far ahead of our competition, another daily, and we made money. It happened, though, that McAuliff was in love with a young lady who became our bookkeeper, and while he was away she and I became engaged: so I sold out to McAuliff for $9,000.

I lived well in Los Angeles for a year and a half, and then, being a person who knew nothing about money, I woke up broke, and went away to the 300,000 acres cattle ranch of William Randolph Hearst, the Rancho Piedra Blanca, San Simeon, San Luis Obispo county, as a laborer. In three months I qualified to ride — partly because the manager, Bursell Lee of Virginia was a friend of mine — and became a cow-puncher. I was at roundups, drove beef cattle to the loading place forty miles away, and for six months at a time never slept in a bed or bunk, but on the ground. Once I spent three weeks alone, with my horse, in a Canyon far from the Rancho, with food and blankets, and a pretty wildcat for a companion. Though he never came very near, I could hear him walking about near me at nights, and he ate all the meat I left out for him. I was not a real cow puncher: no man ever uses a lariat or learns to lasso unless he begins as a kid. But I did the best I could.

There were a lot of in-between, after I left; riding on the Sisquoa ranch, and doing other things. After a time I landed back in the newspaper game as managing editor of the Santa Barbara Press. I was there a year. Later, I was managing editor of the Visalia Delta.

About this time—or perhaps it was before the last two newspaper jobs—I went down to Baja California, a part of Old Mexico, and joined the rebellion of Rhys Pryce. Pryce, an Englishman, ostensibly was fighting for Madero, then President. He was a former officer of the British army, said to have been cashiered, later was in moving pictures in Hollywood, and died bravely in the British army in the World War.

With him was an assorted collection of humans. His leading generals were General Longstreet and General Mosby, American army officers who had vamoosed for reasons known to themselves and their Government and who used the names of the confederate commanders to hide their own. In the army were about 450 men. Probably a hundred were American soldiers, officer or privates, deserters and absconders, and an additional eighty Negro American soldiers who were brave and efficient. About 270 or so Mexicans were with the army. At first our camp, 13 miles below Tijuana, was soaked with rain, mud tangled our feet, and food was scarce—it always was. The sun came out and we got a little more to eat and put the equipment in shape. Pryce had got somewhere enough rifles and ammunition, two one-pound field pieces and two machine guns — old "Gatling guns". With this, in the spring, after I had been about three weeks in "the army", Pryce assaulted Tijuana. We had to go up two small ravines. The field guns and gatlings were advanced and opened, and after a brief shelling, we advanced. The wild elements did not care what happened and the negroes and whites went into Tijuana on the run, firing as they moved, the Mexican regulars, who were barefoot, small, and ill equipped, giving way in half an hour and retreating back to the main part of Mexico. The army at once looted every store and liquor place, got drunk and smashed up fixtures and windows. A few corpses lay about. The postmaster was in front of the office, disemboweled by a shell. While the soldiers raised hell Pryce called an election, at which a few voted, and Baja California was created "The Republic of Lower California", with a Los Angeles actor and adventurer, who had aided Pryce, as President. The flag raised was a combination of the Mexican and American.

The Mexicans misunderstood. They believed Pryce had betrayed them and annexed the country to the United States and that the flag was the United States flag, so they withdrew and fired on it in volleys. The motley gang that made the army fired on them in return. A small battle began and in the end "the Army" chased the Mexicans back, driving them down the ravines, and killing a lot of them. Pillaging went on. By next day the Army had gone to pieces, and the Republic was virtually at an end. Soon Mexican regulars, given permission by the government to travel on United States soil, came by train part way, and marched the rest, and retook Tijuana. We got out the best way we could. I made it over the border, got to Yuma, Arizona, and to Los Angeles.

Here William M. Van Dyke, clerk of the United States Circuit Court, appointed me deputy. I served there for two years. Rhys Pryce, Gen. Longstreet, Gen. Mosby and a half score others were tried here on Mexico's request for extradition, the trial lasting a month and every day I was in court and every day we talked it over in the office, but I carefully refrained from mentioning that I had been with Pryce, and neither he nor the two Generals knew me, of course. Mr. Van Dyke refused to extradite them, and said to me and the other deputy, Mr. Charles Williams, "It was legally proper they should be extradited. But I did not propose to do so, they would have been shot against a wall as soon as they crossed the Mexican line."

I went back into the newspaper business, working in several California cities, the last at Modesto as City Editor. From here I went to Honolulu, on the Star Bulletin, as reporter. I covered police, which in a city with such a mixed population and where murders were frequent, was a lively assignment.

There are three incidents of my stay there that I remember as interesting—among others.

On Kamahameha day the Hawaiians sail small boats, made by themselves, in races—why I do not know, it is a custom. I was sent to the

Hawaii Nui Boat Club for a story, and was told Prince Kalianaole would be there. He was the once-heir to the throne, then the delegate to Congress. In the boat club were Hawaiians with boats, preparing. I talked with one or two, and a rather chubby man, with overalls rolled to his knees and a toy boat in his hands asked me over to the keg of beer in the corner for a mug of beer. We drank and I told him who I was. "I wanted to see Prince Kalianaole, if I could" I said quite humbly, seeking to interview a Prince. He smiled. "I'm the Prince," he said.

The command of the Militia here was under Samuel Johnson, who had landed here during the Rebellion, a sailor from a ship, and was now Brigadier General of Militia. All knew he was not "Samuel Johnson", but no one knew who he was. The city editor, Arben, said to me one day. "Goolrick, you see Sam Johnson every day. No one has ever gotten a story from him, or even a personal conversation. You won't succeed, but see what you can get".

I tried it. After an hour Gen Johnson decided he would tell me and I got a real "beat". He was the son of a Russian nobleman, cadet on a Russian Naval training ship, disobeyed orders and was arrested and probably would have been shot or sent to Siberia but at Philadelphia he jumped overboard, swam ashore, and then went again to sea on merchant ships, winding up in Hawaii. His story ran in 1917, continued, in Liberty magazine, he now being a U.S. Regular officer. That story swung the whole front page.

When the Army was reviewed and a fete held in February, 1916, I covered that, a big story. For the first time Queen Liliukolani came out in public, seated between General Carter and the Governor of the islands, on the grandstand. The Queen, since the American consul had betrayed her by concealing a stenographer when she thought she was talking privately with him, and the American Marines had blocked her forces and compelled them to give up to the rebels, and she had imprisoned in her erstwhile castle for a year, had spoken to very few "whites". She had remained in her beautiful home, or driven with her son and others, but never attended theaters or gone to public places. She was much aloof.

I had seen her when I was a page in Congress. She was there then to try to retain her Queenship. She was somewhat fat, young, brown, pretty, wearing a big picture hat and rather gaudy clothes, though costly and fashionable.

One the night of the review she was in her carriage in Kapaolani

Park, at a concert of the Royal Hawaii band. There were thousands there, but all respected the Queen and left a space about her car. I took a chance. Gen. Carter spoke to her, and knowing him, I asked him to introduce me. He hesitated, but he took me to her side. I said. "Your majesty, I saw you years ago, in Washington". She was interested and smiled, and asked "Where?" "In the gallery of Congress" I said and mentioned the two day debate. Surprised she almost beamed "You heard all that?" I talked for a minute or two and left. The Queen then was old, thin, wrinkled but immensely dignified, though not stiff, courteous and, after I had broken the ice, friendly. I wrote very briefly of the interview, — she had said I might use a "little" of it. It was the first and only interview with Hawaii's Queen since she lost her throne, in, I think, 1893.

I concluded my Hawaiian experience by trying to learn shallow diving, with a group of Hawaiian boys and girls, at Wakkiki, and at the end of three or four months, when I was getting proficient, I hit the bottom and broke two vertebrae of my neck. Followed 5 years in the hospital and five operations, three of them major. I lived, slightly handicapped.

Since then I have written three books, historical. and hundreds of Sunday Newspaper Magazine, and magazine articles, I edited the Fredericksburg Free Lance Star for 8 years. In Writer's Project Work, my line has been mainly in court houses, searching records, in looking over old books and documents, I have had a few interesting experiences, the present task, interviewing old people, being the nearest to Human Interest I have come.

But the other work has been of great value—mine and that of the others I know. We have proved facts that were disputed, shown some alleged history data to be baseless, discovered new things of interest: my research revealed that one Fredericksburg building was the "Old Theater", in Washington's day, that James Monroe lived in a certain house, that Hunter's Iron works were at a certain place and of vast import to the Revolution. That Gen Weedon, camped opposite the town and when Tarleton advanced toward Fredericksburg, occupied that city and turned Tarleton back to Charlottesville; the facts as to the Prisoners Hospital at Alum Spring near the city. The history of the mysterious "old warehouse" — all of these entirely unknown before. There were other things that I, and the associated workers found, too numerous to go into.

There is an incident possibly worth telling.

When I went down to Capetown on the Avondale Castle, among the passengers was a big, black, thin-shanked Zulu in golf trousers, golf stocking, and saffron silk shirt with embroidered initials, and a gaudy tie. He wore a coat only at meals. I learned he was an African Prince, the son of King Lobengula, who was one of the last Zulu chiefs to fight the British in the Zulu rebellion. The Prince was a ward of the British Government, well pensioned, and had been a student at Cambridge. He dined at our table, with about ten, and as British have no distinctions as to color, I had to forget my Southern ideas—and, anyhow, he was a Prince.

He became fond of me when he learned I was an American. He would not stay on the first class deck, but spent his day with the steerage people. However, I got to talk to him, and he spoke excellent British English. He liked me and told me of his adventures in America, which was the epic of his life.

The Prince had gotten some cash and by devious means gotten out of England and into America. Here he enjoyed himself for a time, and then he got a job as laborer on a railroad gang, with other colored men, in New York. He worked on the grade there, and then "shipped" from a labor agency to Omaha, and worked in Minnesota with a railroad gang. He bought a bicycle, and rode to Kansas City and again labored, and then to St. Louis and here and there, always working at intervals on the railroads. His speech and manner was a puzzle to fellow workers, but he told them—(he had studied geography at Cambridge)—he was brought up by an Englishman on a Virginia farm. When he was working back in Pennsylvania, after two years, the British found out where he was and coaxed him back to England. He was going back now to live in Africa, his school days done. "But", he said "I may run off to America again. I liked the work on the railroads". The Prince was not quite civilized, rather not civilized by a long way. He showed this one day soon after coming aboard when at dinner he pointed to a pretty Scotch girl and said to the steward, pointing directly at her, and aloud. "I want that one."

One of the things I discovered while working under the Writer's Project, was the original will of Gen. Hugh Mercer, in Spotsylvania courthouse. The clerk of the court knew it was there, but no one else did, and I had looked for it for a long time. Also, I found from records that Betty Lewis, widow of Col. Fielding Lewis, moved from Kenmore to Millbrook, not far from Spotsylvania Courthouse, and died there, something not known before to anyone. I also found other things, which it is not for me to relate here. I believe the work is of immense value, and as I have written and studied history hereabouts for twenty years, I know it is of great worth to find the truth, the facts, as opposed to tradition and rumor.

This touches the high spots of my life. I have worked in Canada and traveled to Mexico, and was at Mazatlan as a correspondent once when a naval battle—the whole Mexico ever had—was on between two ships. I and another man, Kelley of a New York syndicate, were put into jail and held for nine days, without charges, and then freed and told to take a ship back. We did. I have worked also on Canadian newspapers, and on about fifteen in various places which I have not mentioned here, among them recently some eastern and Virginia papers and the United Press.

REUNION

In June, 2003, we had a 50th reunion of the James Monroe High School senior class of 1953. I had not seen some of the classmates for a half century. We had 72 in the class, nine have died, several were in too frail health to attend. About 30 classmates attemded. one coming from Washington State and another from California. The planning committee consisted of Bev King, Tom Mann, Majory Gallahan, Betty Sullivan, Tom Higgins, Tom Mann, Anne Rowe and me.

I acted as master of ceremonies during a Saturday evening program and jokingly said that I knew some members who had come from metropolitan areas were happy that nothing much had changed in this area and that farming was still the principle industry.

We were the first class to graduate from the present James Monroe High School, although another may soon be built. I told classmates if that happened we would have lived through three Mary Washington Hospitals and three James Monroe High Schools. The thought occurred to me that in our class of 72 people many of us had grown up and attended school together all our lives. We knew each other's parents and relatives.

These days we have graduating classes with hundreds of people and there is not the same opportunity develop a rapport with classmates. So why should members of classes so large bother to hold reunions in the future since they did not know each other in the first place.

Our class of long ago did well. We had two West Point graduates, including one General, our class president Jack Apperson, and a number of successful doctors, businessmen and educators. Unlike today when some schools have huge graduating classes and there are often transient school populations, many of us grew up together and were in the same school classes from first grade to senior year. The various get togethers that weekend brought back many fond memories. We lighted nine candles in honor of the nine classmates who were no longer with us. Life is fleeting and new generations will always replace the old. We agreed to have another class reunion five years hence and I hope all of us who enjoyed the 50th will be around.

AFTERWORD

This work was never intended to be a 'tell all' book. I have deliberately left out many persons and events that might amuse readers but cause embarrassment to persons living or relatives of the deceased.

Fredericksburg was and is a wonderful place to live. But the changes have been tremendous.

Recently I walked along William Street and saw folks sitting outside a coffee shop housed in the old Cotton Lewis drug store that was adjacent to The Free Lance-Star building of my youth. After that it had been used by Jimmy Pates for his Pates Realty operation (Jimmy is a former Councilman whose son, Jim, is Fredericksburg's City Attorney).

Fredericksburg, now officially 275 years old, was a bustling seaport in Colonial times and a place where talk of revolution was common at Weedon's Tavern where strong ale was served. The city played an important part in the Revolution and the city and surrounding area saw more Civil War action than any other places in the nation. For many decades after the war, the economy of the area was stagnant and little growth occurred. Even by the time I was born in the mid 1930s, Fredericksburg was a place where traffic passed from north to south and south to north on U.S. Route 1 but life was mainly slow and easy. When Winston Churchill visited the area in 1929, my uncle, C.O'Conor Goolrick, was head of the host committee for his luncheon at the Princess Anne Inn. In dispatches home, Churchill described the area battlefields and his conversations with some people who had been very young at the time but had witnessed the Battle of Spotsylvania Courthouse.

A Yuppie element seems to have taken hold in the downtown area of the city that is now filled with antique and artsy shops. When I grew up the people who lived above the stores and shops of William (Commerce), Caroline (Main) and Sophia (Water) streets were anything but Yuppies. They were plain working folks living in the low rent district. I have nothing against Yuppies, they are pleasant people, but I find myself hoping Fredericksburg will not become The Peoples Republic of Alexandria South. (If you want a more complete story of things that happened in Fredericksburg before and after George Washington left town, I recommend that you read Paula Felder or the books written by my grandfather and father or other more serious histories). The Fredericksburg where I grew up can only be visioned in my mindseye now because it has been a half century since I graduated from high school and that era in our region was as different from that of today as the moon is to the sun.

We do need to preserve the many things that make Fredericksburg and surrounding areas the nation's most historic region. We particularly need to carry on the work my grandfather began 80 or more years ago to restore Ferry Farm, the place where Washington grew up. I am also grateful that the Central Virginia Battlefields Trust, brought into being by such people as John Mitchell, Mike Stevens, Eric Nelson, Jim Pates, Enos Richardson and others, has accomplished so much in its relatively brief history.

But I hope in the process of preserving sacred land such as that of the Chancellorsville battlefield, we won't forget the principles of property rights on which our nation were founded. I am always a bit amused and dismayed when people write letters to the editor telling how others should give up their property rights in the interest of the community. Such letters are usually from people who have done little or nothing for the community and have little or no property of their own. Many such people wrote letters when John Mullins, someone I knew when he first came to Fredericksburg, was trying to protect his investment in his land near the Chancellorsville battlefield. The Mullins family has done an enormous amount for the area in the way of good works, including large donations to churches and other organizations, and yet some who had done nothing chose to drag their names through the mud. If John Mullins and family had been treated with more respect, than they may well have done more in the way of historic preservation.

As of this writing, I am encouraged that the city may enter into a partnership with Mary Washington College to convert at least part of the Maury School into a James Monroe Presidential Library, a dream of John Pearce, director of the downtown James Monroe Museum. Certainly, Bill Anderson deserves much of the credit for making Mary Washington College (when I grew up it was part of the University of Virginia) into one of the best institutions of higher learning in the country.

A final thought. We have a rich heritage but we have not exploited it nearly enough and need a clearer focus on our future.

PARTIAL GOOLRICK FAMILY HISTORY

Peter Goolrick came from Sligo, Ireland married Jane Tackett

One child of the union was John Tackett Goolrick who married Frances Seymour White, a direct descendant of George Mason of Gunston Hall

They had four sons, C.O.'Conor Goolrick, John T. Goolrick, Jr., Chester Bernard Goolrick and Robert Emmett Mason Goolrick

O'Conor Goolrick had one daughter, Frances

John T. Goolrick Jr. had two sons, John C. and Robert Mason

Chester B. Goolrick had a son, Chester Jr. and two daughters Lindlay and Josephine

Robert Emmett Mason Goolrick married Majorie Craig

Frances Goolrick had two sons, James Ashby III, O'Conor Goolrick Ashby and two daughters, Virginia Turner and Nancy Ashby

Robert M. Goolrick had a son, Meade Allen, and a daughter, Stephanie

John C. Goolrick had a daughter, Lisa Cole

Chester B. Goolrick Jr. had two sons, Chester III,

and Robert Cooke, and a daughter, Lindlay

Lindlay Goolrick had a son, John Hinkle and a daughter, Maitland Goolrick

John C. Goolrick has two grandsons, Corey and Cody Martin

James Ashby III and his wife, Louise Rice Dickey Ashby, had three sons,
James IV, Turner Dickey and O'Conor Goolrick Ashby II

O'Conor Goolrick Ashby and his wife, Elizabeth Massad Ashby, had two girls, Elizabeth Claiborne Ashby, and Catherine O'Conor Ashby.

Virginia Turner Ashby did not marry.

Nancy Ashby McNeil had three children, Virginia McNeill Poindexter, Kimberly McNeil Thompson and Elizabeth McNeil Reed

PARTIAL HISTORY OF JONES FAMILY

Andrew Ross Jones married Elizabeth Ann Sisson

Their surviving children were Olive, Margaret, Othello, Bessie, June, Gloria, Robert Ross, Thomas, Benjamin and Richard. Four children died in infancy

Olive married John Goolrick Jr. and had two sons, Robert Mason Goolrick and John Cole Goolrick

Margaret married Jim Sisson but they had no children

Bessie did not marry.

Othello married Sam Hayden and had one child, Shelda Lane Hayden

June married Harold George and had two children, Wayne and Susan

Benjamin married Dorothy Whittaker and had two children, Wendy and Mitchell

Robert Ross did not marry.

Richard married Lucille Collins and had three children, Sonny, Diane and Beverly

Gloria married Willie Minter and had two children, Ronnie and Kathy.

Thomas married Ruth McGhee and had three children, Bill, Charlotte Carol and Libby

John C Goolrick married alice rock and they had one daughter, lisa cole

COMPLETE CAST OF CHARACTERS (ABRIDGED VERSION) AMERICAN CRIMINAL LIBERTIES UNION, PAUL AKERS, TEMPLE ALLEN, COACH GEORGE ALLEN, GEORGE ALLEN, LINDSAY ALMOND, AMERICAN NAZI PARTY, HUNTER B. ANDREWS, APOLLO X1, ARROW SHIRTS, ASHBY FAMILY, JAMES ASHBY, JAMES ASHBY JR. LOUISE ASHBY, O'CONOR GOOLRICK ASHBY, TURNER ASHBY, NANCY ASHBY MCNEIL, ATHENS HOTEL, AUSCHWITZ, FRANK ATKINSON , ED ALLISON, PETER BABALAS, BABE RUTH, ROBERT E.L. BAKER, COL. BALLARD, ALVIN BANDY, TIM, KRISTEN, EDEN, B.B. BAROODY, WARREN BARRY, HERBERT H. AND LAURA BATEMAN, LEWIS BALL, BERT BATEMAN, LEON BAZILE, CHESTER BAYLOR, BAYLOR'S BARBER SHOP, BURGESS BARBER SHOP, AMBROSE BAILEY, WELDON BAILEY, JUDGE BAZILE, BROOMHILLARY JOE BEAZLEY, BILL BECK, TOMMY BELL, BELMAN'S GROCERY, M.S. AND FERRIS BELMAN, JOHNNY BENCH, CARL BERNSTEIN, CHUCK BERRY, COTTON, RALPH AND SYDNOR BILLINGSLEY, TONY BLAIR, FRANK BOLING, LIZZIE BORDEN, NEWTON BOURNE, HAROLD AND LEROY BOUTCHYARD, TONY BRADLEY, BRECON WALES, JIGGS BRENNAN, JUDY BREVIK, TOM BRICKEN, ST. CLAIR BROOKS, JOEL BROYHILL, EARL BLEDSOE, BUCKNER'S SEAFOOD, BILL BULLOCK, PERRY BULLOCK, BURMA SHAVE, BUSY BEE RESTAURANT, DINO BRUGIONI, JOHN BUTZNER, HARRY BYRD SR. AND JR., TOM BYRNES, FRENCH CALDWELL, HAYSTACKS CALHOUN, CAPTAIN VIDEO, CARL'S FROZEN CUSTARD, MEL CARRICO, JOHN G. CASTLES, JIM AND MYRTIS CARVER, BOB CAVERLEE, SGT. CHICHESTER, UNCLE DAN CHICHESTER, DANIEL CHICHESTER, JOHN CHICHESTER, CARROLL CHILDERS, WINSTON CHURCHILL, ROY CLARK, JOHN AND BILLY COLE, DONALD CROWDER, MARK COLE, ANN COMPTON, EARLE COPP, FLOYD COOPER, COLONIAL THEATER, CONFEDERATE CEMETERY, CHRIS, JENNIFER AND REAGAN CONNELLY, CHILI COX, HUGH COSNER, BOBBY COWIE, DR. PHILIP COX, JO ANN AND CHUCK DAVIS, THE REV. LAWRENCE DAVIES, ANNA DEAN, SHERIFF DAVIS, JIMMY DEAN, GARRY DEBRUHL, HELEN DEWAR, V. EARL DICKINSON, VIVIAN DICKINSON, JOE DIMAGGIO, DOG MART, FATS DOMINO, FRANK DRAGER, LEFTY DRISELL, DUGAN'S, BUTCH DOWNEY, CATHY DYSON, DUKE SNIDER, WYATT DURRETTE, E.C. NINDE, WAYNE EASTRIDGE, EARL EASTRIDGE, EBBETTS FIELD, EDDIE MACK'S, JOHN W. EDWARDS, EARLE COPP, JOHN EHRLICHMAN, DWIGHT EISENHOWER, ELKINS FUNERAL HOME, ELKS, VERNON EDENFIELD, KEITH EPPS, DAN EPSTEIN, JAN ERKERT, LARRY EVANS, CHARLIE ESTES, EVERLY BROTHERS, F.W. WOOLWORTH, AL FAGAN, RICHARD FELDMAN, JOHN FENLON, NUNRA FERRARA, FERRARA'S, LEWIS FICKETT, WALTHER FIDLER, T. FRANK FINES, BILL FINNEY, WATSON FINNEY, H.F. FLEMING SR., HARRY FLEMING, FLIEGERHORST KASERNE, FMC CORPORATION, HANOI JANE FONDA, GERALD FORD, THE REV. DON FORRESTER, FT. KNOX, FREDERICKSBURG BAPTIST CHURCH,

Fredericksburg All-Stars, F. Freeman Funk, John Gallaher, Bill Garnett, Richard Garnett, T. Benton Gayle, Tommy Gayle, Geneva Summit, Wayne and Mary Frances George, Howard Gentry, Lloyd George, Phyllis George, George Nance, Billy Gibson, Gillette Blue Blades, Henry Gillis, Alvin Grey, Jim Gilmore, Ray and Patsy Glazebrook, Jim and Myrtis Carver, John Glenn, Mills Godwin, Paul Goldman, Ron Goldman, Judge John T. Goolrick Sr., John T. Goolrick Jr., Olive Elizabeth Goolrick, Charles Goolrick, Robert Goolrick, Robert Emmitt Mason Goolrick, Robert Mason Goolrick, Peter and Jane Tackett Goolrick, Kinloch Goolrick, Page Goolrick, Faye Goolrick, Rob Goolrick, Goolrick Family, Ray and Netta Glover, U.S. Grant, Goolrick's Pharmacy, Bill Greenup, Gulla's Restaurant, Gunnery Spring, Alexander Haig, Alex Hailey, Bob Haldeman, Bill Haley, John Wesley Hall, Charles Hall, Charles and Virginia Hart, Cotton, Ralph and Sydnor Billingsley, Bob and Bobbi Hamner, Earl Hamner Jr., Warren G. Harding, Albertis Harrison, Othello Jones Hayden, Ruby Hawkins, Devil Anse, William Randolph Hearst, H. Ryland Heflin, Tommy Heinrich, Patrick Henry, John and Kendrick Herndon, Tuffy Hicks, Benny Hinn, Rick Holcomb, Buddy Holly, Bill Hall, Duval and Peggy Haynes, Sherlock Holmes, Linwood Holton, Elvis Presley, Frank Sinatra, Chicago, Catherine Zeta-Jones, Jud and Ben Honaker, Lem Houston, Levin Houston, Chip and Susan Houston, Paul Howard, Moe Howard, Bill and Cessie Howell, Henry Howell, Peck Humphreys, JM Class of 1953, Sergeant Jacko, Frank and Jesse James, Robert James, Hotel Jefferson, Ruth Jessie, Johnny Mack Brown, Lynda Bird Johnson, Lyndon Johnson, Dick and Peggy Johnson, Hal and Raynor James, Johnson=s Grocery, Jimmy Jones, Charlie Jones, Ed Jones, Jones' Grocery, Jones Family, Jimmy Karns, Katzenjammer Kids, Keith and Eddie, Charlie Keller, George Kelly, Kenmore, John F. Kennedy, Bill Kilmer, James J. Kilpatrick, Florence King, Tilly King, David and Bev King, Kishpaugh's, Robert K. Krick, Jim Kutzle, Stewart Kohler, Ann Landers, Ed Lane, Phyllis Lane, Lash LaRue, Jim Latimer, Ace Lawson, Robert E. Lee, Bruce Leikett, Clarence 'Rats' Lewis, Lewis Drug Store, Fielding and Betty Washington Lewis, Hugh Mercer, J.J. Newberry, Jack Daniels, Bernard 'Deacon' Jackson, Jackson Family, Rev. Jesse Jackson, Dick and Lucille Limerick, Liberty Café, Tony Likins, Abraham Lincoln, Nick Lopomo, Lips and Louie, Little Big Horn, Lord Menzies, Goldie Lowry, Walter Lowry, Sonny Ludlam, Lum's Den, Madison Square Garden, James Madison, Dr.Lou Massad, Jim Mann, Paul Manns, E. Solon Marshall, Emmitt Marshall, Lisa Goolrick Martin, Corey and Cody Martin, Dino and Pebbles Martin, Maury Stadium, Mayflower Restaurant, Jake Maynard, Joe

Lockhart, John McCormack, Charles and Mary Wynn McDaniel, Elizabeth McDaniel, Charles McDaniel Jr., Arch McDonald, Mac McGhee, L.M. 'Dick' McGhee, George McGovern, Jim McKnight, Charles McLeod, Meadow Farm, Anne Gordon Mercer, Mickey Mantle, Clinton Miller, Andrew Miller, Nathan Miller, Leon Mills, Willie Mills, Frank Mines, Atty. Gen. John Mitchell, Tommy, Berkeley, John Mitchell, Nancy Moore, Tom and M.C. Moncure, Elza Monroe, James Monroe, Gorilla Monsoon, Bernard Law Montgomery, Hotsy Moore, Nancy Moore, H'race Morrison, Richard Nixon, Geoge Nance, Ollie North, Buster O'Brien, Billy O'Brien, Oak Hill Cemetery, Dabney Oakley, Aunt Othella, Bobby and Betsy Orrock, Ozzie Osborne, Satchel Paige, Landon and Alice Parvin, Passapatanxy International Airport, University of Passapatanzy, Passapatanzy Pete, John Patler, Joanne Holbrook Patton, John Pavlansky, Julia and Slickpot Payne, Tom, Mennis and Togie Payne, John Pearce, Julia Payne, Dudley Pendleton, Pepsi Cola, John F. Perry Jr., Sam Perry, Silas Perry, Pete Smith Specials, A.L. Philpott, Benjamin T. Pitts, Polo Grounds, Bill and Betty Poole, Jimmy Pates, Jim Pates, Shirley Povich, Tyrone Power, Chief Powers, Jim Powers, John Lee Pratt, Gail Presnell, Frank Pratt, Sumpter Priddy, Princess Anne Hotel, Proctor's Store, Dan Quayle, Sheila Quinn, Raleigh Hotel, Horace Morrison, Harry Berry, Morton's Drug Store, Thomas Moss, Paul Muse, Joe Namath, Warren Nash, Virginia and Ethel Nash, National Bohemian Beer, Rat Hole, Steve Ravinsky, George Rawlings Sr. and Jr., Billy and Chip Reamy, Alice Rabson, Melvin Davis Rees, REFORGER, Christian Renault, Horace Revercomb, Allie Reynolds, RF&P Railroad, Melvin Rhea, J. Sargent Reynolds, Bobby Richardson, Socks Richardson, Rick Richardson Rising Sun Tavern, Riva Ridge, Shelda Roach, Lori Roach, Charles Robb, Jim Roberts, Argentina Rocco, George Lincoln Rockwell, Charles Rowe, Joe and Anne Rowe, RPI, Bobby Rydell, Tootsie Rose, Joe Synan, Salem Church Dam, Sammy T's, Sandy, Sammy, Sandra, Samuel (Corgis), Foster Grant (Sheepdog), Calvin Sanford, Gail Sayers, Malone Schooler, Hugh D. Scott Jr., Chief Scorntiino, William Scott, Scott=s Hardware, John Scott, Judge Scott, Scott's Barber Shop, Sprow's Barbert Shop, Andrew Seay, Secretariat, Walter Jervis Sheffield, Gordon Shelton, Shibe Park, Carl Shires, Jay Shropshire, Erika Sifrit, Larry and Deborah Silver, Carl and Maxine Silver, Israel Silver, Joe, Karen and Madison Schumacher, Carol Shulenberg, Bill and Angela Welch, Silver Companies, Nicole Simpson, O.J. Simpson, Benny Skinner, D. French Slaughter Jr. Susan Spears, , Bill Spong, Jenny Stein, Pina Brooks Swift, Toby and Friday Swift, Al Smith, Arthur Smith, David

Smith, Howard W. Smith, Slyman's Grocery, Spotless, Malone Schooler, Ollie and Bobby Stephens, Bill Stern, Earl Sullivan, Jack Sullivan, Super Suds, Stratford Hotel, Sylvania Plant, Elizabeth Taylor, Bruno Techner, Temple University, Mary Sue Terry, Texas Wildcats, The Big Bopper, The Blue Mirror, The Mosque, The Palms Restaurant, The Three Stooges, Gwen Woolf, The Colonel, The Fashion Plate, The Golden Terror, Dr. Hunter Thompson, Wheeler T. Thompson Sr., Thrift Auto, Clarence Todd, Marion Timberlake, Paul Trible, Frank Trippett, Virgil Trucks, Trussell=s Jewelry, Penny Tweedy, Charles Unglebower, Dean Pinchbeck, Robert Van Valzah, John Van Hoy, George VanSant, VCU, Jimmy Ventura, Solly Ventura, Al Ventura, Paul Ventura, Victoria Theater, Victory Services Club, Virginia Charitable Gaming Commission, Virginia Press Association, Virginia Board of Historic Resources, Virginia Lottery, Virginia Protective Force, Virginia Military Advisory Council, Greta Van Susteren, Joe Vizzi, Dr. Robert Vranian, Wakefield Hotel, Walker-Grant, Wilbur Wallace, A. Nelson Waller, Mark Warner, John Warner, Bob Walker, Sandra Walker, Washington Woolen Mills, Washington Capitals, Mary Washington, George Washington, Dr. John Watson, Bill and Angela Welch, Western Union, Western Auto, Bill Withers, L. Douglas Wilder, Shelda and Lorrie Roach, Vance Wilkins, J.M.H. Willis Jr., Joe Wilson, Bob Wolf, Roy Wright, Yankee Stadium, Young Men's Shop, Young Motors, Duffi Young, Heather Young, JoAnn Young, Maty Young-The Beagle Lab, Phil Zako

Grandfather Judge Goolrick with President Warren Harding, October, 1921, Wilderness Battle reenactment. In Center is Marine legend Gen. Smedley T. Butler

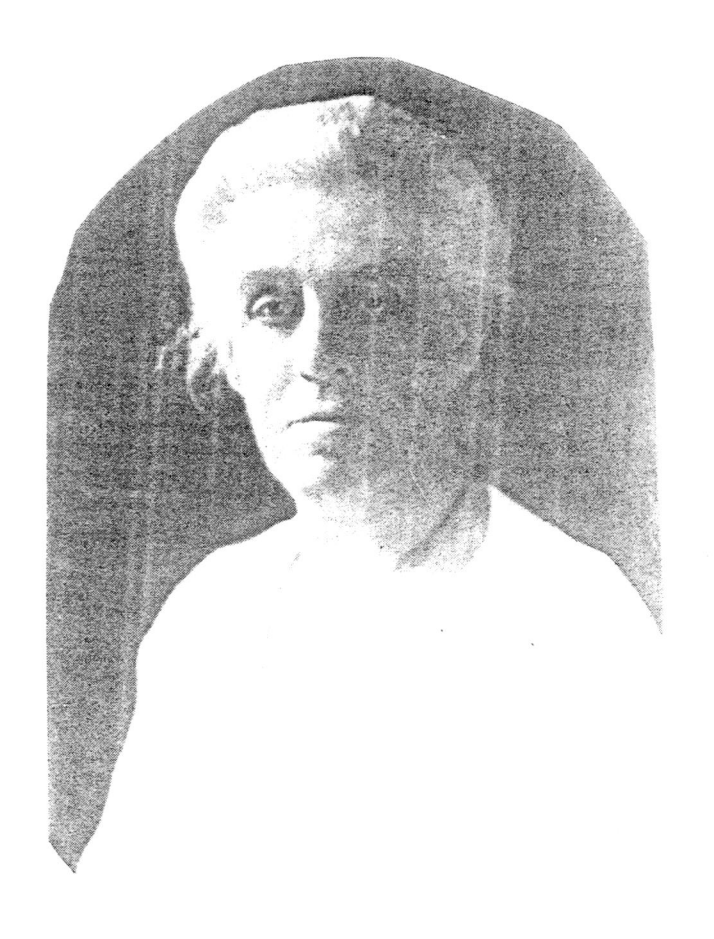

Grandmother Goolrick who wrote about her experiences as a child during the shelling of Fredericksburg.

Maternal grandparents Andrew and Elizabeth Jones

With brother Bob

John T. Goolrick Jr.
in center of photo

COVER PHOTO: MOTHER AND AUTHOR

Easter preparations with mother

Clockwide: Future wife, Alice; Grandsons, Corey, Cody, daughter Lisa and me in San Francisco; the author by Churchill statue across from House of Parliament

GRANDSONS, DAUGHTER WITH VIRGINIA GOV. GEORGE ALLEN AROUND 1995

**WAYNE AND JERRY NEWTON
KIWANIS CLUB SHOW 1950S**

**WHERE SILVER COMPANIES
STARTED: PRINCESS ANNE
STREET AROUND 1950**

Established 1947

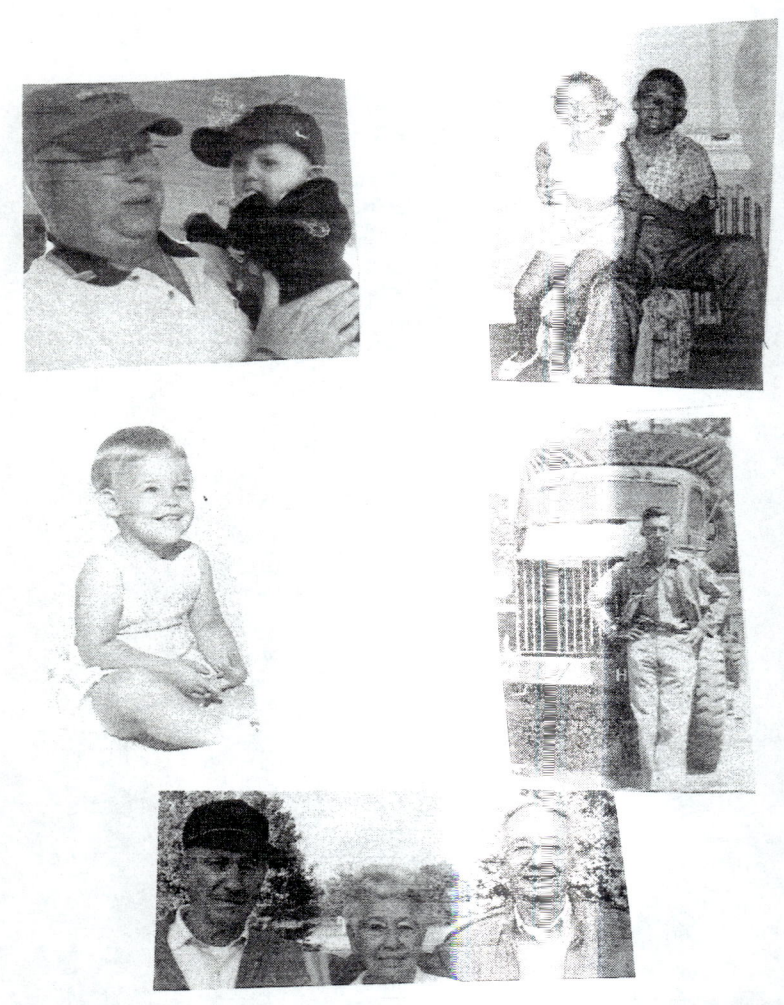

CLOCKWISE FROM LEFT; COUSIN WAYNE GEORGE WITH GRANDSON; COUSIN SHELDA AND AUTHOR; LISA GOOLRICK MARTIN; UNCLE BEN JONES ARMY DUTY 1943; UNCLES THOMAS AND BEN JONES, AUNT JUNE GEORGE.

MEADE GOOLRICK,
AUTHOR'S MOTHER,
CONNER GOOLRICK
COREY MARTIN
SANDI GOOLRICK

LISA GOOLRICK
MARTIN, FOSTER
GRANT

AUTHOR WITH
GRANDSONS

My cousin Shelda and daughter, Lori, 1997

Aunt Othella, who practically raised me, with daughter Shelda for birthday party

Author Jennifer Connely, Reagan Connell, March, 2003

Eden Baroody ready For Easter, 2003

With Heather You[...]
Eiffel Tower, Paris
February, 2003

50 YEAR REUNION JAMES MONROE HIGH SCHOOL CLASS OF 1953
From left, John Goolrick, Jerry Bird, Bill Hall, Tom Mann, Mary Faber Masloff, Majorie Garnett O'Kelly, Alma Rowe Jenkins, Garnett Payne Milstead, Anne Wilson Rowe, Nancy Haehl Badejo, Betty McGinnis Sullivan, Shirley Jenkins Wood, Majory Rothschild Gallahan, Peggy Garrett Hearn;
2nd Row, Dennis Morris, Tommy Higgins, Kenneth Parcell, David Limbrick, John Davenport (not Visible), Ronnie Aydlotte, Pete Tansill, Jack Apperson, Shirley Greene Hardisty, J. Whittaker Jones, Peggy Ward Perry, Frances Myers Martin, Beverly Graves King, Joel Brown, Elsie Brown Mastin, Nancy Hart Berry, Bill Wilkinson

SOUTHERN GRILL FREDERICKSBURG

1013 - 1017 PRINCESS ANNE ST., FREDERICKSBURG, VA.

THE KENMORE TAVERN   On the Highway   Fredericksburg, Virginia

HOTEL McGUIRE — FREDERICKSBURG, VIRGINIA — (U. S. ROUTE No. 1)

James Monroe High School, Fredericksburg, Va.

FROM BILL GARNETT'S FASCINATING AND EXTENSIVE POSTCARD COLLECTION

Free bridge — Fredericksburg, Va.

COMMERCE STREET FROM MAIN STREET, FREDERICKSBURG, VA.

HOUSE OF REPRESENTATIVES
WASHINGTON, D. C.

January 18, 1949.

Dear Mrs. Goolrick:

You and your two sons have my deepest sympathy in the sorrow which you have sustained.

Your husband will still live in the works which he has accomplished, and I pray that Divine Providence may help you to bear your loss.

Please call on me for any service I may render you at any time.

Yours very sincerely,

CCB.

Mrs. John T. Goolrick,
Fredericksburg,
Virginia.

From Rep. Howard Smith

HEADQUARTERS FIFTEENTH US ARMY
OFFICE OF THE COMMANDING GENERAL
APO 408

24 October, 1945

My dear Goolrick:

The Life of my great-grandfather by one of your ancestors just arrived and I cannot tell you how pleased I am to have it because, except for his statue at Fredricksburg and Princeton and a picture I have of him getting bayonetted, he is more or less an unknown character to me.

I trust that your wounds have healed and that you are in good shape again.

If you want to get even for any nastiness I did to you go in the churchyard of the Episcopal Church and you can step on the tombstones of a number of Pattons, Mercers, Thompsons, etc.

With warm personal regards and renewed thanks, I am,

Most sincerely,

G S Patton

G. S. PATTON, JR
General

Captain W. K. Goolrick, Jr.
502 Lewis Street
Fredericksburg, Virginia

also an ancestor

Lexington Va: 30 Nov 1868

My dear Sir

I have rec[eive]d the pair of blanke[t]s forwarded to me by the Washington Manuf[acturin]g Comp[an]y, Fredericksburg, & can only return to them my sincere thanks. They are the finest blankets I have ever seen, & their value is greatly enhance[d] from the fact of their being Virginia manufacture & made of Virginia wool. As a token of the kind remembrance of the Company, they will be greatly prized.

Very esp[eciall]y your ob[edien]t serv[an]t

RELee

Mr. Jno: E. Tackett
Pres: Wash[ingto]n Manuf[acturin]g Comp[an]y

AUTHOR'S FAVORITE POEM

[IF]

If you can keep your head when all about you
Are losing theirs and blaming it on you,
If you can trust yourself when all men doubt you
But make allowance for their doubting too,
If you can wait and not be tired by waiting,
Or being lied about, don't deal in lies,
Or being hated, don't give way to hating,
And yet don't look too good, nor talk too wise:

If you can dream--and not make dreams your master,
If you can think--and not make thoughts your aim;
If you can meet with Triumph and Disaster
And treat those two impostors just the same;
If you can bear to hear the truth you've spoken
Twisted by knaves to make a trap for fools,
Or watch the things you gave your life to, broken,
And stoop and build 'em up with worn-out tools:

If you can make one heap of all your winnings
And risk it all on one turn of pitch-and-toss,
And lose, and start again at your beginnings
And never breath a word about your loss;
If you can force your heart and nerve and sinew
To serve your turn long after they are gone,
And so hold on when there is nothing in you
Except the Will which says to them: "Hold on!"

If you can talk with crowds and keep your virtue,
Or walk with kings--nor lose the common touch,
If neither foes nor loving friends can hurt you;
If all men count with you, but none too much,
If you can fill the unforgiving minute
With sixty seconds' worth of distance run,
Yours is the Earth and everything that's in it,
And--which is more--you'll be a Man, my son!

--Rudyard Kipling

AUTHOR'S FAVORITE SONG

WHITE CLIFFS OF DOVER

There'll be bluebirds over
The white cliffs of Dover
Tomorrow, just you wait and see

There'll be love and laughter
And peace ever after
Tomorrow, when the world is free

The shepherd will tend his sheep
The valley will bloom again
And Jimmy will go to sleep
In his own little room again

There'll be bluebirds over
The white cliffs of Dover
Tomorrow, just you wait and see

The shepherd will tend his sheep
The valley will bloom again
And Jimmy will go to sleep
In his own little room again

There'll be bluebirds over
The white cliffs of Dover
Tomorrow, just you wait and see

ISBN 141200699-6